Kinabalu Escape

Kinabalu Escape

The Soldiers' Story

RICH MAYFIELD

with
Bob Mann and Martin Dunning

CONSTABLE · LONDON

First published in Great Britain 1997
by Constable and Company Ltd
3 The Lanchesters, 162 Fulham Palace Road
London W6 9ER

ISBN 0 09 476970 2
Reprinted 1997

Printed in Great Britain by
St Edmundsbury Press Ltd
Bury St Edmunds, Suffolk

A CIP catalogue record for this book
is available from the British Library

The Grand Old Duke of York, he had ten thousand men
He marched them up to the top of the hill
And he marched them down again.
And when they were up they were up
And when they were down they were down
And when they were only half-way up, they were neither up nor down.

(Trad.)

Contents

Illustrations

Photographs in this book were taken by
members of the expedition:
Hugh Brittan, Bob Mann and Rich Mayfield

Acknowledgements

This book could not have been completed (or, for that matter, even started) without the help and support of many people. Collective thanks are due to: Adrian Wardle and his staff, especially Iain Smith, for his diagrams; Peter Davey and the crew at LWT; Paul Birchell and his staff and coffee machine at Rock and Rapids, the specialist climbing shop in Plymouth.

Rich and Bob would like to thank: the expedition members, all the villagers of Kampong Melangkap Kappa, the staff and residents of the Travellers' Rest, Danny Chow, the staff at British Military Hospital Hong Kong, British Airways, the staffs of Royal Naval Hospital Plymouth and Derriford Hospital, Paul Hughes, Paul Edwards, families, friends and anyone else we might have inadvertently forgotten.

Bob would like to thank: 'my wife Sue for her love and understanding and for dealing with the press while I was in hospital; my son Robert for never tiring of hearing of Dad's adventures; and Mr Hanley, the consultant surgeon at Derriford, and his two physiotherapists, Bernie and Judy, for rebuilding my hand.'

Martin: 'family and friends for their support, encouragement, food parcels and pints of beer.'

We would also like to thank the *Guardian*, the *Evening Standard*, the *Daily Mail*, and the *Independent on Sunday* for their permission to print the headlines and quotes in chapter fourteen. Also *The Times* for quotes in chapter fourteen Times Newspapers Limited, 1994, and the British Mountaineering Council for their permission to reproduce the 'Advice to Climbers' in Appendix Two.

Authors' Note

On 6th April 1994, at Imphal Barracks in York, Lieutenant Colonel Robert Neill, Major Ron Foster and Corporal Hugh Brittan held a press conference concerning the events of Exercise 'Gully Heights', the Royal Logistics Corps expedition to Low's Gully on Mount Kinabalu in the Malaysian province of Sabah, Borneo.

Lt Col Neill accused the expedition's front group of disobeying orders and said that they proceeded down the gully without his authorisation. This was an unjustified attack on the front group, which the press and some expedition members' units took as true, along with its implications of desertion.

The subsequent Board of Enquiry concluded that Lt Col Neill's leadership and judgement during parts of the expedition had been 'flawed', and that he had been 'over-ambitious'. It also cleared the members of the front group of the allegations of disobeying orders, and concluded that the conduct and performance of Cpls Mayfield, Brittan, and Cheung were such as to deserve formal recognition; this took the form of GOC Eastern District commendations.

This book is a personal account of what happened and why the decisions that were made proved to be so controversial. It is intended to help fill in the holes that are left after Lt Col Neill's and Major Foster's book, to allow readers to look at all the facts and decide for themselves what really happened.

Expedition Personnel

Lieutenant Colonel Robert Neill
Expedition leader.
Relevant qualifications: TR&A, MLC.

Major Ron Foster
Expedition second in command.
Relevant qualification: TR&A.

Sergeant Bob Mann
Video recordist.

Corporal Hugh Brittan
Stills photographer.
Relevant qualification: TR&A.

Lance Corporal Kevin Cheung

Lance Corporal Richard Mayfield
Technical adviser.
Relevant qualification: JSRCI.

Lance Corporal Pete Shearer
Relevant qualifications: TR&A, JSMEL.

Lance Corporal Steve Page
Relevant qualification: TR&A.

Private Victor Lam

Private Chow

The Legend of Kinabalu

The language of the people of Sabah varies from village to village, but there seems to be a general consensus that 'Kina' and 'Balu' mean 'massive' and 'rock' respectively; this would appear to be the origin of the name. The words come from the old tribal languages, as do the legends surrounding the mountain in general and Low's Gully in particular.

Local people believe that the gully is the resting place of the souls of dead tribespeople, and it is said that, late at night, you can hear the tapping noises of the departed spirits crossing the many rickety bridges on their way to the final resting place. The many rock pools are said to be the most sacred resting places, as they enable the souls to wash away the dirt of their lives. At the head of the gully a dragon guards the spirits and a huge pearl.

To this day, the locals fear the mountain and its inhabitants, and local holy men still carry out the ritual sacrifice of seven white chickens, seven eggs and seven feathers as an offering to the dragon before setting foot on the mountain.

The legend says that a group of Chinese merchants climbed the mountain and, on discovering the pearl, attempted to steal it. The dragon slayed them and vowed that any Chinese who set foot on the mountain would perish.

All three attempts by Lt Col Neill and Major Foster to conquer the gully have included Chinese personnel, and all three have ended in failure, none more dramatically than the last. In Chinese the words 'Kina Balu' mean 'Chinese Widow', but this *is* only legend . . .

Prologue

I was sitting up in my hospital bed reading the latest edition of *High* magazine, and waiting for the next set of test tubes to be filled with my blood. The curtains around me were drawn, and as people brushed past on the other side they moved gently, giving them a disturbing 3-D effect. I carried on reading the article.

Out of the corner of my eye I see the greens and browns of the curtains swaying gently from side to side, and slowly the dirty colours creep out across the floor to touch the edge of my bed. I move closer to the middle of the bed, not daring to look up. A trolley goes past; *it sounds like rain and the vegetated floor takes on a wet look, with water dripping from the leaves and hanging vines. Thick branches and bastard trees bar any real progress. My map is wet, but even if it was dry and readable it would be of no use to us; it bears absolutely no resemblance to the surrounding terrain. I stare, trying to penetrate the foliage, but I can't see Bob. A voice, not Bob's though:* 'This is Richard . . .' *Maybe it's the others, the rear group, or even Britt. I turn my head towards the sound. Greens and browns moving violently: I'm falling! But without movement. Out of focus, the colours of the jungle flicker past. Get out. Move. Run! Go, now, before it's too late. I roll to the right, pushing the bushes and rotten debris out of the way to force a hole through the jungle.*

I found myself back in the corridor, sweating, shaking and shocked at the realisation I had been awake throughout the nightmare. My arm was still behind the curtain attached to the drip, the needle pulling my skin tight under the bandages. A disembodied voice came from behind the curtains.

'Where's he gone?' A friendly face appeared. 'Are you alright?'

'Open the curtains.'

'We only want a chat.'

'I don't care – open the curtains.' She opened the curtain and I returned shakily to the bed.

How did all this happen, anyway . . . ?

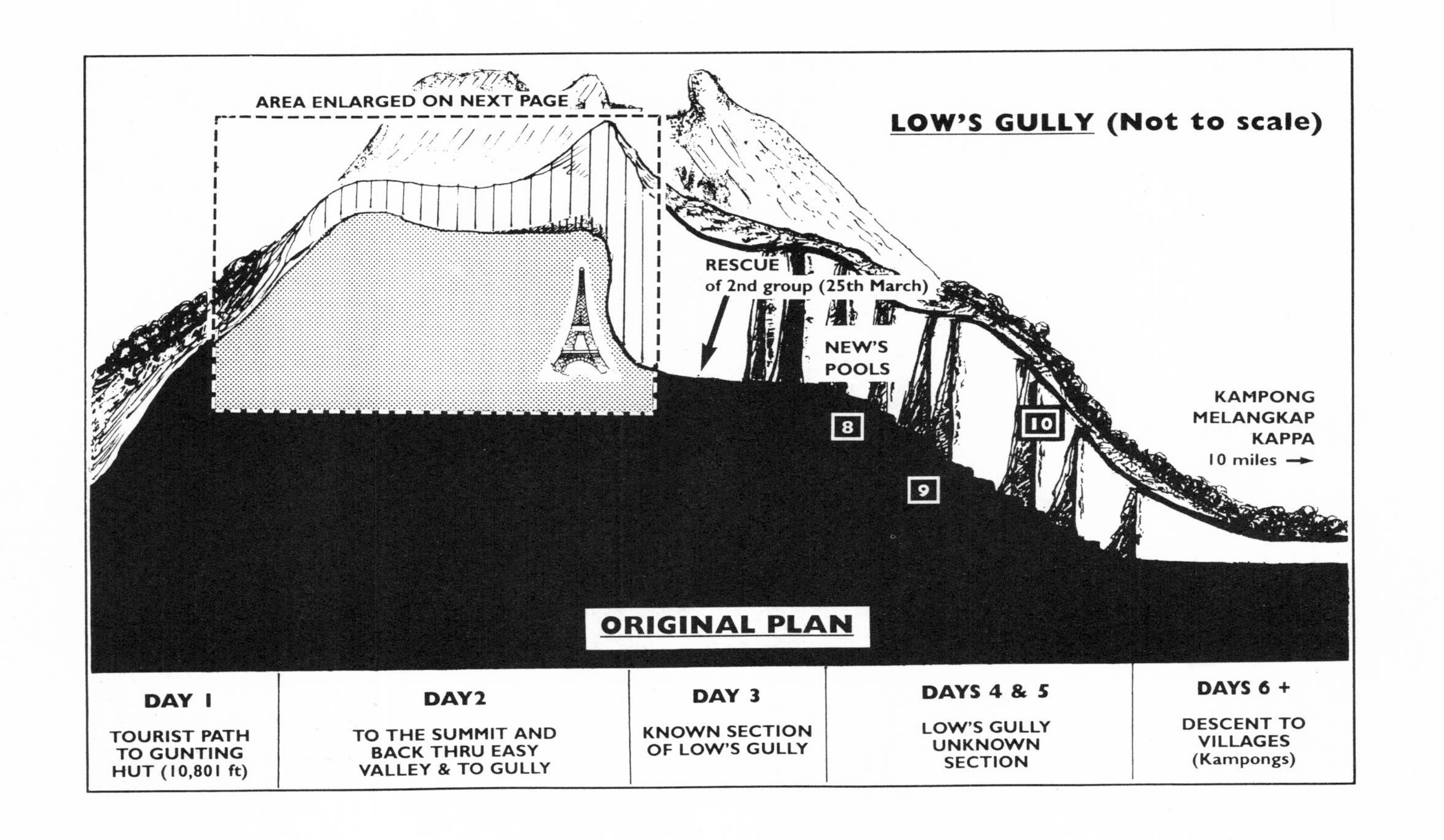
LOW'S GULLY (Not to scale)
AREA ENLARGED ON NEXT PAGE
RESCUE
of 2nd group (25th March)
NEW'S
POOLS
8
9
10
KAMPONG
MELANGKAP
KAPPA
10 miles →
ORIGINAL PLAN
DAY 1
TOURIST PATH
TO GUNTING
HUT (10,801 ft)
DAY2
TO THE SUMMIT AND
BACK THRU EASY
VALLEY & TO GULLY
DAY 3
KNOWN SECTION
OF LOW'S GULLY
DAYS 4 & 5
LOW'S GULLY
UNKNOWN
SECTION
DAYS 6 +
DESCENT TO
VILLAGES
(Kampongs)

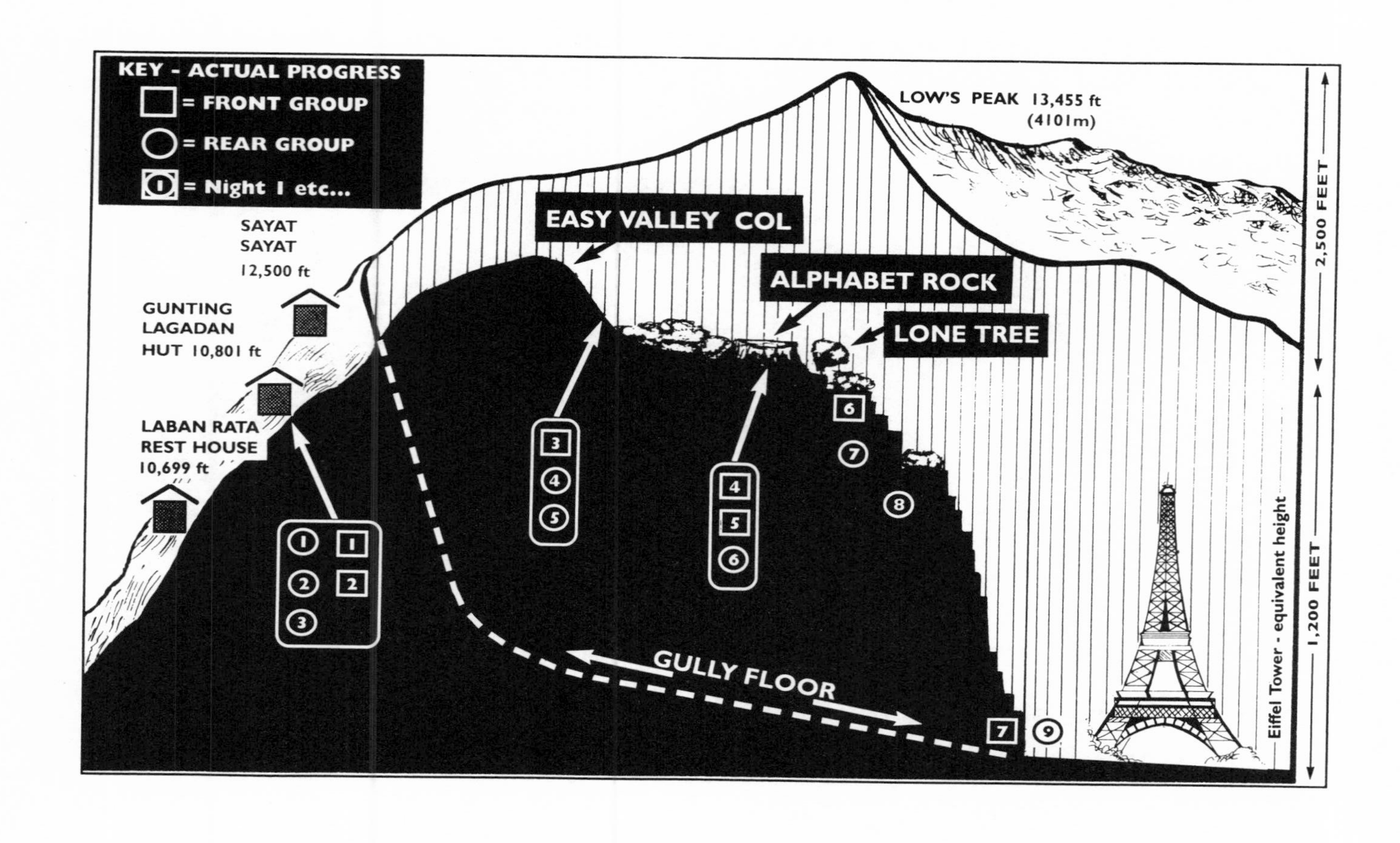
KEY - ACTUAL PROGRESS
= FRONT GROUP
= REAR GROUP
= Night 1 etc...
SAYAT SAYAT 12,500 ft
GUNTING LAGADAN HUT 10,801 ft
LABAN RATA REST HOUSE 10,699 ft
EASY VALLEY COL
ALPHABET ROCK
LONE TREE
LOW'S PEAK 13,455 ft (4101m)
GULLY FLOOR
Eiffel Tower - equivalent height
2,500 FEET
1,200 FEET

CHAPTER 1

'Because I was asked . . .'

Commando Logistic Regiment is a death posting for any self-respecting Royal Marine, and to end up in the only 'Pongo' squadron was the pits. The boss was away and had left me in charge of the Technical Quartermaster's store – not a big task, but one which carried a lot of responsibility. Noel and Andy were the two Royals left behind in the store and having an Army Lance Corporal in charge was the final insult.

We had all given a massive sigh of relief when Geordie left for his six-week-long Regimental Quartermaster's Stores course. Nobody ever seemed to see eye to eye with him; probably something to do with his height, but his attitude didn't help either. He was the type of senior NCO with whom you always knew where you stood, which was usually 'in the shit', but he was one of the characters that make a unit memorable. In his absence, I was trying my best to re-demand some stores which had been rejected from the RQMS, but being used to the army way of doing things, I was having some problems – in this unit (the Marines come under the Navy's umbrella) everything was in naval jargon. It might as well have been in Bulgarian, and I was scratching my head in perplexity when a welcome distraction arrived in the form of Major Ruff.

'Fancy a climbing trip to Malaya, Corporal Mayfield?' I stared foolishly at him. This was too good to be true – I had just become the head of my department (only in an acting capacity, true, but head none the less) and my OC was asking if I wanted to go climbing. When asked that question, I invariably answer in the affirmative. He knew that. It seemed like a bloody silly question really. Geordie had already said that I wouldn't be able to go to Spain climbing because of operational commitments, but he wasn't here and by the time he returned it would be too late to stop me. Telling him would be an altogether different matter and my stomach turned at the thought. However, Major Ruff's words were causing vistas of lofty, snowclad Himalayan giants to unfold in front of me. Had I heard him correctly?

'The Himalaya, sir?'

'Malaya. Malaysia if you want to be absolutely correct. Mount Kinabalu.' I think he expected me to instantly recognise the name and reel off the vital statistics of the mountain.

'Never heard of it, sir!' Embarrassing to admit, of course; most people in the squadron seemed to think I had some sort of obsessive personality disorder where climbing was concerned and it might disappoint them to discover that I was not a walking encyclopaedia of mountain statistics.

Major Ruff raised an eyebrow. Ever conscious of wind-ups – and this seemed like the ideal scenario – I wondered if I could trust my own OC. He had considerable virtues but that sort of humour wasn't one of them, so I decided to go along with it. I told him, with some enthusiasm, that I wanted to go, and asked when it was scheduled to happen.

'February to March,' he replied.

'Isn't that during winter deployment?'

'Yes, but if you would prefer to go to Scotland for two months . . .' He let it hang on the air.

'No, that's quite alright, sir, I'd much rather go to Malaya.' I gabbled it out as fast as I could, not wanting to appear anything less than keen; I didn't know anything about the mountains of Malaya, but chances like this weren't handed out on a plate every day. The thought of being able to tell Geordie that I was going was great. He was bound to at least try and stop me, and if he couldn't then he'd acquire a large 'sad on' and I was taking a childish pleasure at the thought of his discomfiture.

Noel wandered in from one of the jobs that he was trying to make last all day. He listened for a few seconds to my conversation with Major Ruff and grinned at me.

'How big is Mount Kinabalu?' I enquired, stumbling over the unfamiliar name. He obviously felt I should know this, but I'd never been anywhere near the Far East, and Malaya wasn't exactly one of the hallowed venues for climbers, anyway. A steaming jungle is not the sort of landscape that springs to mind as a suitable arena – most climbers tend to think of the Himalayan vistas that had flashed across my mind when Major Ruff first raised the subject.

'You should really speak to Sergeant Hughes, he's been out there and did a similar expedition a few years ago, or Staff Sergeant Burgess – his father-in-law has also done it.' He glanced at his watch. 'Give Sergeant Hughes a call up at 383 – I think a place has been offered to them as well. I'll put your name forward then, Corporal Mayfield?'

'Yes, sir, that's great.' I still couldn't quite believe this was happening.

'What qualifications have you got?' This was the big question.

'I'm a JSRCI, sir.' The Joint Services Rock Climbing Instructor course isn't too hard; it is the Joint Services' senior climbing qualification but is by no means exhaustive as regards advanced techniques. I'd been up to North Wales for the course a few years earlier and had an excellent instructor by the name of Mike Elesmore. I thought that possession of that piece of paper would almost certainly guarantee me a place – if it was an all Royal Logistics Corps expedition then there were only a handful of us who held the qualification.

'Talk to Sergeant Hughes, he'll put you right on the mountain.' With that he left and I knew I had more than a good chance of getting onto the expedition. My wife Sandy wasn't going to be impressed, but I'd have been away then anyway, up in Scotland; I'd rather have been doing something constructive than sat in a tent peeling spuds while it rained outside. What a proff! Noel was still grinning at me.

'Yes, what?' Anything to get that grin off his face.

'Not saying nothing.' But he couldn't resist having a quick gloat: 'Geordie's going to love you!' He was grinning like a Cheshire cat. 'Make sure I'm here when you tell him.' The stupid grin was infectious.

'I don't see what the problem is; if the OC's asking, and I'm the head of my own shed, there's no problem!'

'Just make sure I'm here when you tell him.'

Andy walked in. 'What did the OC want; haven't cocked up, have we?'

'Better ask Rich.'

'The OC's asked me if I want to go climbing in Malaya during the winter deployment.' Cheshire cats were in evidence on all our faces.

Andy chuckled: 'Geordie's going to kill you!'

CHAPTER 2

Preparation

I made the call to Sgt Hughes up at Derriford. 383 Independent Commando is the Territorial Army support unit for Commando Logistic, and although Paul Hughes was in the TA he worked full time; before this he had been the Technical Warrant Officer down at Commando Logs. I'd seen him about the squadron and had heard that he was a mine of useful information but we'd never really spoken. Over the phone he was more than helpful and invited me up to see him over lunch. With Geordie away and nothing important pending I decided to make the short trip across Plymouth to Derriford in my dinner hour.

383 Commando shared their camp with another TA unit and were also attached to Seaton Barracks so it was quite a large camp. I arrived at 12.30 to be confronted by an automated front gate with an intercom. Some bafflement ensued as, after eight years in the Army, I had become used to guards requesting identification rather than having to press buttons and communicate with disembodied voices. I eventually managed to announce who I was and that I'd got an appointment to see Sgt Hughes, and then stood back and waited for the gate to open. Nothing happened, and I was beginning to wonder if it might not be a good idea to invest in a copy of 'How to use everyday modern appliances without making yourself look a complete technological peabrain', when Paul appeared from a side door of the building and opened the gate. I drove in, the gate closed behind me and I parked my car. Paul, a stocky man in his mid forties, walked up the hill to greet me. We shook hands and entered his office – two rooms with so much computer equipment dotted about that it threatened to send my technophobia off the scale.

I decided to get right down to business before he asked me to do anything technical: 'So you're going back to Mount Kinabalu?'

'Well, I've been asked.'

We entered the second office and Paul made coffee while I surveyed the walls, which were covered with training programmes and other notices. He handed me a cup and sat down opposite me.

'Colonel Neill asked me to go,' he repeated, 'but I've got no head for heights, and I found it extremely hard going at that altitude last time.' My curiosity rose at the mention of altitude; was I at last to get the opportunity to tick a major peak?

'How high is it?'

'Big! It's thirteen and a half thousand feet.' Not so big in the great scheme of things, of course, but big enough; the highest I had been was just over 8,000 feet on Naranjo De Bulnes, in Spain.

Paul resumed: 'The main reason I turned the Colonel down was that I found the going very very hard last time. It would take me ten minutes to walk just a hundred yards, I could feel my heart pounding, trying to escape my chest and I'm too old for all that. Besides, I've had all the proffs – I'd rather let one of the younger guys in the unit go.'

I remarked that I hadn't realised there were any climbers in 383 Commando; climbers are always on the look-out for other climbers and I would have been surprised if I had missed out on a potential climbing partner so near by.

Paul must have guessed my line of thinking, for he grinned. 'No, we don't have any climbers, but I think Bob Mann put his name down – he's one of our sergeants.'

I'd seen several senior NCOs from 383, who all seemed to be eight feet tall and built like houses. The only other contact I'd had with them was seeing a few 'Stabs' (Stupid Territorial Army Bastards – the less than flattering regular army term for our part-time colleagues) on exercise, with their webbing up around their armpits and helmets all skew-whiff.

Paul interrupted my musing. 'I think this time it's starting at the top of Kinabalu and trying to go down Low's Gully.'

Still blissfully unaware of any of the background information that I would need to know, I asked: 'So how hard's the climbing on the way up?'

'It's a tourist path, the way up is easy – well, not that easy, it's a long hard slog up a path, but there's no climbing involved; kids and old grannies do it all the time, but when I spoke to Colonel Neill he said we'd be carrying lots of weight. That's the main thing that put me off – last time I found it hard enough carrying next to nothing!'

'Major Ruff asked me about my qualifications – I thought that they were after a JSRCI to do some climbing.'

'You'll need some sort of climbing qualification to do the gully. I've got some photos from the first time. I've been out there with Colonel Neill and Ron twice.' He rooted around in some cupboards and produced a photo album.

'Here they are.' He opened the cover and grinned; it obviously brought back memories. 'It's an incredible place!' He pointed to a photo of several people in a gorge roped together and fighting their way upstream against what appeared to be a powerful current.

'That was in 1982 – we were trying to follow the River Penataran up to Low's Gully that time.'

'So he's planning on coming down this – it's a gorge walk.' I was quite surprised. Although I'd done several gorge walks in North Wales where I grew up and first started climbing, this really wasn't my area of expertise; rope work in moving water is more the preserve of a caver.

'So what qualification has Colonel Neill got?'

'Oh, he's well qualified, he's an ML. At least I think he's an ML. This is his third attempt.'

'Has the gully been done before?' The gorges I did in North Wales were great fun, although I remember being very wet and a touch scared.

'No. It's been attempted a few times, but no one's actually done it.' He pointed to the set of photos on my knee: 'That was on the second trip. We went upstream for three days, but had to turn back because we came across this enormous boulder in the middle of the river and couldn't get around it.' He took the album from me and flicked through.

'There it is, the size of a large house. We were all very tired after moving upstream and only had six days' food with us, so we really had no choice but to turn back.'

'Looks interesting. How far upstream did you get?'

'There's a difficult section in the middle of the gorge, where that boulder is; we got as far as that, but as I said, we had to turn back or we would have run out of food. I think that's why the rucksacks will be so heavy this time; he's planning on taking ten days' food.' He flicked through the photos again.

'Here, this was taken on the second try – from the top down. A lot of those peaks haven't been climbed.' The phone warbled into life and Paul answered it. While he talked I studied the photos; this was my first glimpse of the mountain and I was impressed by the scale and the amount of rock – great grey walls and pinnacles of what looked like granite. If they hadn't been climbed before we might be able to do some first ascents. Paul hung up and started looking through his address book.

'I've got Colonel Neill's number here; why don't you give him a call? He'll be able to set you right on what's happening this time. Here. York. HQ Eastern District. Just dial straight out.' It was amazing how fast things seemed to be moving; the operator put me through, the phone rang and I was talking to Colonel Neill.

'Hi sir, I'm Corporal Mayfield.'

Before I could get any further, he interrupted. 'Oh, yes – I've been trying to get hold of you all afternoon.' I looked at my watch. It was half past three. I hadn't planned on staying out this late, and hoped Andy and Noel had covered for me.

Neill continued: 'Major Ruff said you've got the full ticket. What exactly do you have in the way of qualifications?'

'I'm a JSRCI, sir.'

'Great,' he exclaimed, 'that's one of the stumbling blocks out of the way – I didn't know anybody with their full ticket. I'll speak to your OC and confirm your place on the expedition today. I'll put the expedition outline in the post to you, so you know exactly what's going on.'

I was quite shocked that I'd been accepted on the expedition so readily and just on the strength of being an instructor, but then this was an opportunity not to be missed – travel, mountains, a whole new culture. . .

Neill continued: 'I'd like you and Sergeant Mann to organise a training day for the team down in Plymouth in December. Sergeant Hughes and your OC should be able to help with accommodation.' I asked how many personnel that would mean. He said that as well as myself and Sergeant Mann, there would be his deputy, Major Foster, and four others. I grabbed a pen off Paul's desk and started writing.

'What sort of thing do you want me to cover climbing-wise?'

'Has Sergeant Hughes told you much?'

'Yes, up the tourist path, down the gully, and then down the river to the kampongs.' I made it sound very simple, but all I knew was what I'd been told so far. I asked what he had in mind for the training day.

'Well, if we go to the Dewerstone we'll be able to do some abseiling off that. Put some thought into what equipment we'll need. We'll need some kind of ascender as well as descenders, but I want to keep the amount of hardware down as much as possible because of the weight.'

'OK sir, what about dates?'

'When do you finish for Christmas?'

'The 16th.' I looked at Paul for confirmation and he nodded.

'That will be the best weekend, everybody should be able to make it. If you get any problems or you need some clout behind any letters let me know.' We said goodbye. That was it.

I turned to Paul: 'Looks like I'll be going then. Have you got any climbing gear I could borrow for the training weekend?' I knew that one of their old seniors, 'Mac' Mackay, had been a very strong canoeist and climber and had acquired some equipment from somewhere.

'There's some there, certainly – if you've got time we'll go and have a look.'

I looked at my watch. It was four in the afternoon. What the hell, I couldn't get back to work by half past, not in rush hour traffic, and I'd have had to pass 383 on my way home anyway. As we walked over to the hangars Paul fondly reminisced about some of his exploits in the Far East – he seemed to have been a bit of a lad in his younger days. A place called 'Hot Lips' in Hong Kong was the place to be, he explained, as he opened the door to one of the hangars. We walked through a small room and into the main part of the hangar.

'I didn't know you had boats as well,' I said, referring to the Dancer canoes stacked in the corner, still in their protective polythene.

'All this is what's left from when Mac was down here – now that he's gone there's no one qualified to use it all.' He open a large grey cupboard and dragged out a cardboard box full of brand-new, shiny climbing gear, again still in its polythene bags. I had a quick look through. There were ten sets of everything. More than enough gear for the planned weekend. We placed the equipment back in the cupboard.

'Can you give me Sergeant Mann's phone number? I'll give him a ring tonight.'

'That's back in my office.' As we walked back Paul continued to tell vivid stories from 'Hot Lips.' We arrived at his office to find his wife waiting to give him a lift home, and after giving me Bob's number he offered to help in any way he could. I had a feeling that I'd be seeing more of Paul. Knowing my unit I would probably have to take him up on his offer when organising the training weekend.

I headed for home, hoping that my absence from work hadn't been noted, and that evening called Bob at his home in Plymouth; my first impression was that he had a broad janner accent. We made provisional plans to go climbing, but he said that he would be at the TA centre in a few days' time and we could meet up then. We thought it would be best if we partnered up on the expedition, as we only lived a few miles apart and would therefore have a good chance to get to know each other beforehand.

The next day at work, I discovered that Andy and Noel had covered for me well when the OC had come looking for me to tell me that I had a place on the expedition. Royals may have their faults but the unwritten rules dictate that you cover for your mates and anyway, the more dirt they could get on the army lance corporal who was in charge the better they could manipulate him. As a result I had to let everyone leave early that day.

Paul Edwards phoned a few days later to discuss our planned project to build an international standard indoor climbing wall in Plymouth. There seemed to be an unofficial competition between us as to who could get the best proff from an expedition, and I thought that I would win at least for the time being, but Paul's much more of a mountaineer than I am and couldn't understand why anybody would want to go abseiling down a mountain. Admittedly, it did sound uninspiring if you put it like that, but this wasn't just a 'rather large abseil,' as he put it. This was the gorge walk to end all gorge walks, judging by what I'd seen in the photographs. It was bound to be an experience. The gorge walks I'd done in North Wales had an air of seriousness and commitment about them and were very inescapable. It occurred to me for the first time that this trip would probably be just a bit on the scary side, and most definitely committing, but then we would have the reassuring presence of an ML with us and, what's more, one who knew the mountain.

I went up to 383 to see Paul Hughes again and was fascinated to find out that he had been Geordie's boss when he was a private. He was intrigued to find out how the man had turned out from my point of view as a junior rank under him, and wasn't surprised to find out that the junior ranks had a less than flattering opinion of him. Paul told me that Bob was due in to discuss their training programme, and while we were waiting he continued to reminisce about the Far East. He was a great story teller with a good memory for the sort of absurd detail that makes a story really funny and the time passed quickly until a short, slight man entered the office, his uniform sporting sergeant's stripes, Para wings and the Commando dagger. He was in his early thirties, with watchful eyes and dark, cropped hair, but his most striking feature was his voice. That Janner accent again – I was still not accustomed to it, and listening to him talking brought a slight smile to my face.

'Bob, this is Rich Mayfield, he's going on the expedition with you.' Paul motioned in my direction by way of an introduction. We shook hands. I wondered if he was just a 'Stab' or whether he had seen some real service. He did have some acclaimed badges, however, and things like that didn't get handed out free with breakfast cereal.

Time was pushing on and, determined not to give Noel any more ammunition to use against me, I quickly arranged with Bob to go to Haytor on Dartmoor in order to do some climbing and get to know each other. I made my excuses and left to get back to work in time.

Driving back down the steep hill into Forder Valley, I mulled over the first meeting with my partner for the expedition. I'd assumed that Bob would be six feet tall, built like the proverbial outhouse, and that he'd be an accomplished mountaineer with vast experience. He was none of these, but past experience told me that initial appearances could be very deceptive. As the car came to a halt at the lights at the bottom of the hill, my mind wandered back to the Army Mountain Training Centre at Silberhütte in northern Germany, and Major Hawker, a short man of considerable years, telling us all that if he beat any of us on the Basic Fitness Test, then all those he'd beaten would have extra duties. Nobody took him seriously until he had gained a hundred-yard lead on the main group, when the thought occurred to me that he was serious, and that if I was the only one to beat him I'd not have any duties for weeks. I started to speed up, overtaking the slower members of the group, but didn't seem to be gaining, so I accelerated again to near my maximum and slowly started to reduce the distance between us. I was almost within striking distance, but my breathing was becoming laboured and he heard me; I was shocked to discover he still had some legs left as he pulled away again. I stayed on his shoulder but wasn't sure if I could maintain that sort of speed for the next half-mile. I could hear his breathing becoming as laboured as mine, but my calves were tightening and there was a sharp pain in my side. I formed a strategy; I would leave it until the last hundred yards and hope that youth would win out over old age and guile. He slowed slightly, giving me time to recover, and I made my break. To my horror he stayed with me, but I managed to get my nose in front and crossed the finishing line with legs like overcooked spaghetti, followed a split second later by Major Hawker. Between gulps for air we congratulated each other on an unexpected race well run.

My reverie was rudely interrupted by the sound of an impatient car horn behind me – the lights had changed. I pulled away, the memory of Major Hawker bringing a smile to my face. Appearances can indeed be deceptive.

The following day I drove the four miles to Bob's house at Honicknowle, keeping an eye on the weather which seemed a bit threatening. Using the A-Z, I eventually found Bob's cul-de-sac, pulled up outside the house and walked down the steps to the front door. A petite women answered the door and, in a thick janner accent just the same as Bob's, invited me in.

'I'm Sue, you must be Richard?'

Before I could reply Bob came haring down the stairs, wide-eyed and keen to go: 'All set? Have you decided where we're going?'

'Haytor. There's a climb on Low Man I've been wanting to do for ages. It's called Aviation. I put all the extra gear for you in the car.'

As we left, the weather was looking even more ominous and drops of rain landed intermittently on the windscreen. I put a tape on and asked Bob how much climbing he had done. He admitted that his only experience was the adventure training that had been run by Mac over the last two years. I couldn't help but poke fun at Bob's accent. It reminded me of the television advertisement for Ovaltine Light:

> My family got the energy of three
> Don't need a mum need a keeper with a gun
> Have you got a light boy?
> Ovaltine Light?

Bob remembered the advert and laughed. It was good to know that we shared a sense of humour; if we were to be partners on this expedition, then shared humour would make the difficult times bearable. More common ground emerged when the conversation moved to our families – Bob's son was twelve months older than mine.

We turned off the A38 onto the narrow lanes that lead through the oak woodlands on the edge of Dartmoor, and as we gained height, clearing the wooded valleys and reaching the open moorland, the weather really started to deteriorate. The pregnant black clouds burst open just as we pulled into a deserted Haytor car-park, where even the resident ice-cream van had moved on to sunnier climes. I'm not generally a devotee of climbing in the rain; moves that would usually present no problem take on a whole new character and I particularly hate the way that the water invariably runs down into your sleeves. I reminded myself that the climbing wasn't the sole reason for being there – it was important that Bob and I formed a good relationship, and climbing in these conditions would probably lay strong foundations, but whatever the implications for male bonding, I was still feeling a little wimpish.

'Do we really want to go out there?'

'Well, we're here now.' Bob was keen, so we braved the weather and went to the boot of the car. I put my rucksack on and gave Bob one of the ropes to carry. The grass squelched underfoot and the winter wind bit hard. Haytor on a summer's evening can be an idyllic spot; it lies at fifteen hundred feet on a hilltop overlooking one of the most beautiful parts of the moor, but this very exposed position means that in anything other than perfect conditions it becomes positively hostile. As we reached the bottom of the crag, water was running down the face and spilling over the overhangs to explode on impact with the granite boulders beneath. I looked up at Aviation; it was certainly no wetter than the rest of the crag, but then again it probably wasn't any drier, either. When first climbed in the sixties, it was given the then top grade of 'Extremely Severe.' Standards have moved on since then and the grading system has been extended; its current grade of E1 is one of the middle grades, but in these conditions . . .

'Fancy it, then?' I enquired, hoping that he'd want to back down.

Bob had no understanding of grades, so E1 meant nothing to him, and he was obviously adopting the philosophy that, if I was happy to lead it, he was happy to follow: 'We might as well go for it now that we're here!'

I realised that Paul Hughes had been talking up my abilities and that Bob had complete faith in me. After much prevarication, I finally gave Bob a crash course in climbing technique and launched myself up the first steep, dripping crack; the holds were big but the water ran down my fleece sleeves and the wind, howling down from the north-west over the open moor, threatened to detach me from the rock. Climbing timidly I reached the point where you have to traverse right to reach a large flake where it is possible to take a belay.

'Bloody hell,' I muttered under my breath; I hadn't realised just how far away the flake was, and how sparse the holds were. *Bob's going to have problems on this! He can't come to any harm, but it might test his composure.* I placed a runner to protect myself and tiptoed rightwards on small quartz crystals. As I neared the flake, with my protection now some distance away, the holds thinned out and I teetered for a few seconds before again launching right, my fingers finally (and thankfully) sinking behind the flake. The belays were bombproof, which was a relief, as I had a slight suspicion that they might be called upon to take the weight of the entire party.

Bob was still full of enthusiasm. He threw himself at the first crack and was soon looking at me from the wrong side of the traverse, realising that he was about to find out what it was like at the sharp end.

He took out the last protection, timidly extended one arm, and moved. Trainers aren't terribly effective as climbing footwear in perfect conditions, and in the wet they are next to useless. Hanging off the same small crystals I'd used, feet slipping, Bob gave a creditable impression of someone riding an imaginary bicycle until, soaking wet and with eyes like dinner plates, he made a final despairing lunge and grabbed the flake with his right hand. I attached him to the belay and readied myself for the next pitch. It looked unnerving, a shallow groove which would have to be climbed on rounded, frictiony holds, and friction was something in short supply at that moment in the presence of all that water. My appetite for adventure in general, and this route in particular, was fast evaporating. I spied a likely escape route off to the right and the decision was made. Another protectionless traverse but at a much lower level of difficulty, and ten minutes later Bob joined me on the wet, cold southerly slabs. We threw all the equipment into my sack, ran down the slopes to warm up and made a beeline for the sanctuary of my car and a hot cup of coffee from the flask. We drove back through the rain with the heater on full blast to try and dry us out, steamy-windowed and stopping only once for some chocolate from a garage. I returned Bob in one piece to Sue, who was blissfully unaware of the near epic of Bob's first proper climb.

Over the next few weeks Bob and I received the expedition's outline plans and the joining orders. Paul helped us with the accommodation for the planned training weekend, and with Christmas approaching the time flew by.

Geordie returned from his course: 'So what's been cocked up then?' He readily acquired the predicted 'sad on' when I told him (in front of Noel and Andy, as promised) that I would be on the expedition over the winter deployment and ticked me off for going behind his back.

Neill called me a few days before the training weekend and asked me to acquire the full range of twenty-four-hour ration packs. He specifically wanted to see the new 'Boil in the Bag' and 'Arctic' rations; I took it from this that the last time he'd been out in the field he'd used tins, and quite understandably he didn't want to take them this time because of their weight. Acquiring rations in the Squadron was no problem as Combat Supplies usually had sufficient to supply small quantities for expeditions such as ours.

On the 15th of December we had the usual pep talk from the CO, who stated the obvious about drinking and driving, fighting, and misbehaviour in general over the leave period. This was followed by general misbehaviour at the traditional junior ranks' Christmas lunch, served to the boys by the seniors, and the equally traditional food fight. The following day, my car loaded with an assortment of rations, I drove the short distance from my home to the TA base at Derriford, where Bob introduced me to Colonel Neill, a tall, slender man with dark hair of a length that only senior officers are allowed to sport, and who spoke with a distinct plum in his mouth. He welcomed me to the expedition and said that the others should be there shortly.

Half an hour later, a brand new Rover with two occupants inside pulled up outside the main gate. The guards let it in, and as Neill watched it park he announced, with evident satisfaction, that it was Lance Corporal Page. Bob brought them up to the training room and Neill made the introductions. Steve Page was a touch on the wide side and ginger – the thought crossed my mind that he would burn easily – with several large tattoos, a packet of fags and (we'd later discover) a taste for beer: your typical squaddie. Steve in turn introduced his travelling companion, Corporal Hugh Brittan. Britt, wearing a Royal Corps of Transport Para T-shirt, looked strong and fit; with an air of self- confidence he took over his own introduction, announcing that he'd like a place on the expedition. Neill explained that the expedition was now fully subscribed, but that since he was here he might as well take part in the training, and assured him that if the opportunity arose he'd be put on the list as first reserve. Britt was quite happy with this; he seemed to have gained the confidence of the expedition leader in just a few seconds,and was quietly confident he'd now be offered a place sooner or later.

Major Foster, who arrived next, was built along the same lines as Steve Page for width, but was a few inches taller and shades darker. I'd heard that he'd worked his way up through the ranks, and so I was expecting a down-to-earth and very knowledgeable officer who would be able to relate to the juniors as well as he could to the Colonel.

He introduced himself: 'Hi everyone, I'm Major Foster, but you can all call me Ron.' Neill vigorously shook the hand of a long-standing friend, and the two officers engaged in a short re-acquaint-ance, enquiring after wives, families, dogs, horses and goldfish. Formalities over, the conversation turned enthusiastically to the subject of the expedition and Ron produced the slides we'd all been waiting to see: our first view of the mountain, apart from Paul's snaps, and first impressions of what was to come.

As the two officers talked their way through the slides, with constant reference to their previous two expeditions, their excitement about the project spread round the room. They outlined the plan for this attempt and detailed tasks to the individual members: Bob and Ron were to be the official video recordists, Pete the diarist and I the technical adviser. The slide show finished and Neill suggested that we carry on at a more leisurely pace in one of the local pubs. This met with universal approval and we all piled into the minibus that Paul Hughes had hired for the occasion, heading for the Glenholt night spot. Several beers oiled the social processes and by the time we headed back to the Barracks we had all started getting to know one another. Neill had confirmed that he was an ML, Bob and I seemed to have the beginnings of a successful partnership and, as I struggled into my sleeping bag on the floor of the TA centre, I felt that all was going well.

The next day was overcast, threatening rain at any second, and as I made my preparations I wondered if we were in for another Haytor. My first task was to talk about the advantages and drawbacks of the various ration types, mainly for the benefit of the officers, who appeared not to have used either variety before. I felt that I was stating the obvious to the rest of the team; these feelings were confirmed as Britt interspersed my talk with the odd knowing comment, and I felt the start of a rapport building between Bob, Britt and myself. Although Neill was Commando trained he seemed to have lost the sense of humour that's common throughout the forces, and typical of the more specialist units. I had noticed this at the pub the night before and put it down to a natural reserve, but now, on sober reflection, felt that it might be a sign of a narrow but unbridgeable gulf between Neill and the junior ranks.

I finished my talk and we boarded the minibus. The weather was deteriorating still further as Bob drove us the short distance to Plymbridge Woods, a few miles downstream from the Dewerstone. Neill had said he wanted a large abseil so that if anybody had a problem with heights it would be apparent before we got out to the Far East, and I had chosen the old railway viaduct. It was actually only eighty feet high but abseiling from the apex of one of its arches would mean that the abseiler was hanging free in space for at least seventy feet; it would enhance the experience and certainly highlight any qualms. As a climber, the whole concept of abseiling as an end in itself seemed a little absurd – normally I'd only abseil to gain access to the bottom of a sea cliff, or in an emergency.

After the short walk from the road to the bridge, I set up the main abseil using the rusted, cemented-in handrails as anchors. Everyone had a grumble about how unsafe they looked, but I pointed out that most of the climbing fraternity in Plymouth had probably swung from those rails and survived, which served only to reinforce their feelings that the rails must by now be very weak. I pointed out that the Victorians really knew how to build things, but for some reason this seemed only to heighten their fears.

Paul had supplied us with 'Pat Littlejohn' climbing harnesses, with which no one was familiar; even for experienced climbers a new design of harness can prove perplexing, and for relative novices the problem was even greater. Steve, however, having just completed his Top Roping and Abseiling course, figured it out quickly and helped the others. The two officers seemed rather confused at having fully adjustable harnesses and asked me for assistance, but after fifteen minutes we finally had everybody ready. I sensed that no one wanted to be first over the edge, so without further ado I attached myself to the rope, leapt over the rails and descended quickly to the valley floor. I unclipped myself, ran back up the path to the top of the viaduct and was surprised to find everyone standing there, unmoving.

'Who's next, then?'

Neill stepped forward: 'Can you just check my figure of eight, Corporal Mayfield?' I peered at him, not quite sure whether to take him seriously, but assumed that it was for the benefit of the less experienced members of the group. He offered his equipment; I took a quick glance and informed him that it was fine.

'What about a safety rope?' He emphasised the word 'safety' as if I should have used one myself. I assumed again that this was for the benefit of the beginners in the group and demonstrated how to use a safety rope on an abseil. As Neill climbed onto the parapet and disappeared over the edge, I pondered over the meaning of that brief exchange of words; he had seemed rather unsure of himself, and (again) it could have been merely a tactic to relax the others, but . . . it left me with a vague feeling of unease. The attention of everyone else had focused on the rack of climbing gear on my bandolier, and a hundred questions ensued about 'Friends', 'Rocks', and other shiny bits of gear. I answered them in a slightly distracted manner, still worried about Neill's apparent lack of confidence, but put it to the back of my mind and started seeing them down the rope. Once everyone had done it twice I told them to wait at the bottom. Neill had told me that the whole team needed to be competent not only in abseiling, but also prussiking, so I started to demonstrate how to climb up a fixed rope using prussik loops. I showed them how to turn the climb into an abseil, protect themselves on that abseil, turn the abseil into a climb and back to an abseil. I lowered myself to the ground to looks of total bewilderment – even our ML, Neill, looked unsure.

I tried to put them at ease: 'Don't worry. It's not as complicated as it looks – I'll talk you all through it.'

Everyone had a go and soon found there is a definite knack to climbing fixed ropes. Britt decided, as a matter of principle, that he would go to the top, which also made him appear keen and competent in the eyes of Neill, but found that prussiking on loops could be very tiring and had a minor epic transferring to an abseil to get back down. Nobody had any serious problems, but I suggested that we should take shunts (a mechanical prussiking device) because of their versatility: not only could they be used for ascending single or double ropes, but they could also protect abseils and would be unlikely to damage the ropes. I seemed to lose everyone in the details, but my mind was made up – having been tasked to supply the technical equipment for the expedition, I decided that the way forward must be with shunts.

With the dry run completed, and the rain in full flow, we trudged back to the minibus and headed for the Dewerstone, which rises from the steep wooded hillside above the River Plym. The wooded valleys that fringe Dartmoor are even more beautiful than the moors themselves and the Plym valley is no exception. We parked at the confluence of the Plym and the Meavy at Shaugh Bridge; both rivers were in spate, and it was obvious from the number of cars with roof racks that the canoeing clubs were planning a fun day out.

We left the relative warmth and comfort of the minibus and walked along the well-worn path up towards Devil's Rock, the highest part of the Dewerstone – 165 feet from the summit blocks to the river bank. I kept a wary eye on the river, unsure whether or not the base of the cliff would be flooded; there was certainly more than enough water to give the canoeists something to think about. I had been canoeing a bit but never on any serious moving water – surfing and the odd unintentional pop out when the front of the canoe hit the sand was just about my limit. Glancing at the river through the rain, I saw the first of the boats plummeting past. It looked thoroughly gripping and I was glad to be on (relatively) dry land.

To my relief the river was still some way from the base of the cliff. I made my way up to the summit, fixed some belays and dropped the end of the 250-foot black Marlow rope to the awaiting team; now that they knew the basics of prussiking on a free-hanging rope, they could attempt the same exercise on near vertical rock, which would be considerably more difficult. By now we were all fairly wet, but Neill declared that the conditions were 'perfect,' although he admitted that Low's Gully would be slightly warmer. Only one person could climb the rope at a time, and as I stood at the bottom giving pointers on technique, I heard Britt asking the Colonel about the difficulty of the river in the gully and the problems that we'd face; ever the positive thinker, Britt had now started saying 'We', as though his place was already secure.

Oranges, yellows and reds. Shouts of excitement from twenty feet away, as more boats shot down the river, their plastic hulls making painful thumping sounds as they bounced off the rounded granite boulders in the river bed.

Neill watched thoughtfully as the last of the boats disappeared down the rapids and round the next bend, and explained to Britt: 'Low's Gully is no harder than this river; in fact, we might be able to walk down. If we'd been able to find a way around that large boulder we needn't have had to turn back.' He paused for a few seconds to survey his surroundings and said: 'It's just like the Dewerstone!' I was to remember that comment; we were later to find out that the expedition that had attempted to climb up the River Penataran to Low's Gully, and that Neill had made reference to, had, in reality, been several miles from the gully and on a relatively easy stretch of the river.

Canoeists filed past, boats on shoulders, heading upstream to a launch site for a second run; Ron had a hard time trying to turn the abseil into a fixed rope climb when one of his prussik loops (as they tend to) became jammed. A small volume of shouted instructions and a short solo up 'Climbers Club' (one of the easier climbs on Devil's Rock) freed Ron, who glowered at his prussik loops and declared with some feeling: 'Having used your shunt, I think I'll buy one!'

'Prussik loops are only a back-up. Life is far easier and quicker with jumars or shunts,' I explained.

He lowered himself to the ground and I followed, carefully downclimbing; as I joined him back on the horizontal, more excited shouts came from the river. I looked round in time to see a canoeist with only half his paddle, but still going strong. A second canoeist was walking down the path carrying his boat minus its front end (which was probably somewhere upstream wedged under a boulder). He looked decidedly glum; apart from the fact that canoes don't come cheap, the River Plym doesn't often have enough water in it to become passable, and despite the current monsoon he might have to wait some time before he could make another attempt. I watched him trudge disconsolately down the path, canoe on shoulder. I knew from experience just how robust the newer plastic canoes were, and to see one so damaged was a sobering reminder of the forces we might have to face.

Everyone had completed the task on the rock, so we packed up the gear and, by now extremely soggy, made our way back to the bus. With the team on board, a debate started about where to go to dry out and discuss the tactics of the expedition. We decided on the Unicorn in Plympton and, to the accompaniment of derogatory comments about Bob's driving, set off down the narrow, high-hedged lanes. We arrived at the pub without incident and, slightly warmer, but still soaking wet, we traipsed through to the Lounge and ordered some drinks. Despite our wetting, confidence was high after the introduction to the more technical side of the business, and discussion turned to equipment. Neill produced the 'Cotswold Camping' catalogue and questions ensued as to which harnesses were best, which ascenders should be taken (although in my mind that question was already settled in favour of shunts) and a host of other matters. As the appointed technical adviser and the only real climber on the expedition, Neill pushed me to make the decisions as to exactly what gear was to be taken. I was still unsure about exactly what we'd face, but attempted to advise on the strength of my experience and in the knowledge of the previous night's slide show. I felt that the Colonel and Ron should know the conditions best, having been on the mountain before, but the catalogue showed an enormous selection of modern outdoor equipment and they seemed unwilling to commit themselves; the only thing they were insistent upon, and which Britt and I couldn't quite see the point of, was that we would be taking tents.

Neill had sent everyone a copy of an article taken from *The Times* in 1990, covering an attempt to descend the gully by two British climbers, Rob New and Steve Pinfield. They seemed to have had a very hard time, and had to fight their way out of the jungle as the gully became too serious for them. This article was the only independent information that our expedition members had to ponder on. The officers had decided that the expedition would have to carry ten days' food; Pinfield and New had taken six days to reach safety, so ten days should give us the necessary margin.

We ran through areas of responsibility again; as senior officer Colonel Neill would be the expedition leader, Ron his deputy and I the technical adviser. I was pleased to have been given that role as, having been involved in other expeditions and exercises in a lesser capacity, I'd seen things go wrong but not been in a position to advise or make a positive contribution to the proceedings. Now, although one of the junior ranks, I'd been given a responsible and important job. Bob, although a 'mountain-trained soldier', had no experience of mountaineering or climbing, and had volunteered to take care of the video side of things along with Ron; the two of them became immersed in videospeak.

With perfect timing, Britt let slip that not only was he a keen photographer but also jungle trained. I was surprised that Neill and Ron had not considered taking any jungle-trained personnel since any incident would mean that a subsequent escape bid would have to cross several miles of uncharted and potentially hostile terrain. Neill, responding to Britt's statement, repeated that he would put Britt down as first reserve; Britt (as usual) played it cool, but was still openly pleased at being a step nearer to gaining a foot on the plane. The conversation moved back to equipment and I was tasked to investigate suitable rucksacks; a decision was also made to ask Central Ordnance depot at Thatcham to buy some shunts, as they had already told the Colonel that they would to able to purchase certain bits of essential equipment for the expedition.

Neill turned to the tent section in the catalogue and announced the type of tent that we would be taking. Britt and I looked at each other for support and queried the decision; we both raised the point that we were all taking Bivvy bags anyway, and therefore tents would be surplus to requirements, extra weight and would probably prove difficult to pitch in the jungle. Our queries were quashed by Neill, who stated that they had found them invaluable on the previous expeditions.

I suggested as a descendeur the double nine-millimetre Sticht plate as this was a fraction of the size and weight of the figure of eight, which is more often used in military circles, but the general feeling was that the figure of eight should be taken as it was familiar to everyone – a good point, but one that reinforced my feeling that not only was I the only climber, but also the only person with any real mountain experience. In comparison with many mountaineers, however, I realised that my experience was limited; I had very little in the way of winter mountaineering skills, and indeed the only ice climb I'd done was when Dave Body and I soloed one of the Trinity Gullies on Snowdon, in marginal weather conditions and with only one axe each – a great day out, but not really an introduction to advanced mountaineering. This realisation caused me some doubts, but they were largely allayed by the fact that Kinabalu, being only six degrees north of the equator, was unlikely to ever see snow, let alone spring a glacier on me. Large-scale abseiling of the sort we were to undertake is more often the preserve of cavers; my only caving and potholing exploits had been a few weeks in the Harz Mountains in Germany, but despite Paul Edwards's dismissal of our expedition as a 'rather large abseil' I was confident of my ability. Climbers acquire a fairly comprehensive experience of abseiling in the course of a career; it's just rather unusual to contemplate an expedition where more abseiling than climbing is called for.

I attempted to dismiss any negative thoughts about the expedition and decided to concentrate on the positive aspects: after all, both Neill and Ron had been out there several times before, the Colonel was an ML (a very rusty one, it appeared, but still an ML) and a lot of these expeditions are less demanding than they appear to inexperienced eyes. In fact the army vetted this sort of thing very thoroughly, and wouldn't let a group overreach itself; it had always been drummed into me, while on courses, that safety was paramount, a sentiment with which I wholeheartedly concurred. I put my thoughts to one side and turned my attention to drying out and enjoying the beer. Conversation continued about the general shape of the expedition and Neill's stories of the previous attempts, until the thought of the long journey back to York prompted him to become the party pooper. Still a touch damp around the edges, everyone climbed into the minibus and Bob drove back flawlessly despite the odd jibe from his passengers. On our arrival back at 383, I handed in all the gear to Bob, after which we again ran through the team's respective jobs – mainly research into various bits and bobs – and the weekend ended on a positive note. Anyone else who had any distance to travel stayed and refreshed themselves at the TA centre before starting their journeys, but I left almost straight away to get home, and change into something warm and dry.

I saw Bob only a few times in the following month. We talked generally about the expedition and one thing he said (which was also vaguely mentioned by Paul Hughes) stuck in my mind.

'These are two officers on their last great hurrah. The expedition is something that they are determined to complete.' I was later to find out that Bob was a much better judge of character than I; even without the benefit of my technical knowledge, he too had some misgivings.

Our final training weekend was to be from the 28th to the 30th of January at Ripon, in Yorkshire. As most of my unit had moved up to Scotland for the annual winter deployment, the barracks was a ghost town and I was able to devote myself without distraction to the task of supplying all the rations and equipment for the expedition. Time passed quickly, and on the morning of the 28th I drove up to the TA depot to meet Bob again. With my unit unable or unwilling to supply transport, 383 had provided Bob and me with a minibus, and we set off up the M5 towards our first stop at Bicester where we were to pick up one of the expedition members we hadn't met, Warrant Officer Martin Meighan. After several trips to the Central Ordnance Depot at Thatcham, I had most of the climbing gear ordered and delivered. It was stored at Bicester, and the plan was to pick up WO Meighan with the gear and carry on to Ripon. Taking turns at driving, and after several wrong turnings, we eventually found Bicester Barracks, only to discover that WO Meighan had had some personal problems and was unable to come on the expedition. This meant that Britt was now guaranteed a place, but would he be able to turn up at such short notice? Our knowledge of Britt suggested that he would find a way. We loaded the gear and set off again in high winds and driving rain.

Rumours had been rampant back at the Squadron about a move up to the old RAF base at Chivenor in North Devon, and as we neared Ripon I spied a very appropriate sign – 'Logs for Sale.' Sign collecting is one of the major hobbies in the squadron and the temptation was too much. Bob jumped on the brakes and as the bus slid to a soggy halt I dived out, grabbed the sign and was back in the bus within seconds. Throughout the whole episode, barely a word had passed between us, yet we had had exactly the same idea and acted together, almost by instinct – a good sign for the future. As we drove off we wondered if we'd been seen and how to explain the presence of a large green 'Logs for Sale' sign in the bus, so we decided to leave it behind one of the seats and pretend we didn't have it.

We arrived in Ripon without further adventure and promptly became lost in the Bermuda Triangle that is the one-way system, but finally found a parking space and went in search of the pub that had been designated our RV; Neill and Ron were already there, as was the ever hopeful Britt and a new face, Lance Corporal Pete Shearer. Neill introduced us and then carried on with the story that had been interrupted by our arrival.

He and Ron had recently been on a Top Roping and Abseiling course at Ilkley; Ron was abseiling and the Colonel was operating an additional safety rope. Because he was not sitting in line with the belay, he was pulled several feet to the edge of the cliff before the belay came tight when Ron (abseiling faster than he should have been) jumped over the edge. The story worried me. In the first place, why would someone as qualified as an ML go on the very basic TR&A course? Secondly, the type of error he had described was not one that a man of his experience should have made.

I thought back to the previous training weekend, becoming distracted from the line of the conversation, and wondered if I should confront the Colonel with my concerns. I thought briefly of withdrawing myself from the expedition – how could I approach a very senior officer and question his ability? However, they would probably not be able to find a replacement in time, the expedition would fold and my unit would think I just wanted to dodge the winter deployment. On top of that I would be putting a very senior nose out of joint, and I was unsure of the implications and whether he knew anyone in the Squadron. Backing down isn't exactly in my nature, or a quality with which 3 Commando Brigade would sympathise, so I dismissed thoughts of withdrawing and rationalised the problem thus: there were only two abseils to get into the gully and then an easy walk to the part that hadn't been done before, which, from the aerial photos I'd seen, appeared to be not too steep, so I decided to ask Neill to leave ropes behind on the two large abseils in case we needed to get out quickly. I rejoined the conversation and voiced my opinion. Everyone seemed happy with the thought that I was attempting to cover every eventuality. My main concern was still the level of competence and experience within the group, but with only two abseils I could lower a whole unit in less than a day, so ten people shouldn't really present a problem.

Neill said that although it hadn't been done before he thought it possible to walk up from Low's Gully into Easy Valley, the subsidiary valley that runs parallel to the gully and would provide our access to the gully from the summit plateau. He went on to explain that on the last expedition he'd laid out with stones the letters RAOC (the old corps initials) in Low's Gully. He'd seen the mountain and been into the gully before. He'd know what to expect. By far the easiest option for me was to place my trust in him.

The Colonel bought the last round, the conversation moved away from the expedition, and with last orders being called we braved the still adverse weather to head for the sanctuary of Ripon Barracks, one of the few remaining Joint Services Mountain Training Centres. These camps are usually extremely basic – cold, damp and very draughty – and Ripon was no exception. Our Nissen hut was grey and uninviting, but with only sleep on our minds it made little difference.

It had been planned that the following day we would sort out the rations ready for shipping and then go to Malham Cove for some abseiling practice. I had secretly brought my climbing gear and boots, and if time and weather permitted I was hoping to tick off a few climbs. As we worked and talked I discovered that Pete Shearer held the Joint Services Mountain Expedition Leader qualification, which rekindled a few doubts – why would an ML want to take a JSMEL? If any more qualified personnel were required, we could have done with a caver or another JSRCI – someone experienced in technical rope work.

We sorted out our individual rations and those for the three Hong Kong lads who were to join us in Hong Kong, completing the team and bringing our strength up to ten. Next on the list was the climbing gear. I was concerned about having to take most of my personal climbing gear, plus extra karabiners, slings and ascenders – someone was bound to drop something sooner or later, and the chances of finding it in the jungle would be slim.

Time passed quickly and with the weather still unsettled, the decision to cancel the trip to Malham met with unqualified approval. The only person who had not been shown how to prussik was Pete, and as Ripon had its own free-standing outdoor climbing wall, I decided that this would have to do for his introduction. I had talked to the girls at Thatcham about buying in shunts for the expedition, but Neill had decided that tents were more important and that we would make do with 'Crolls'. They were less versatile than shunts and presented a minor problem in that individuals abseiling would now have to use prussik loops to protect themselves and someone was bound to get stuck, but as we would only be doing a couple of one-hundred-and-fifty-foot pitches it shouldn't be too much of a problem.

We finished packing all the kit ready for shipping and I took Pete outside to the climbing wall; I explained the methods of prussiking, abseiling and changing from one to another, using the Crolls instead of shunts.

With jobs finished, dates for flights planned and a myriad of other details checked, we departed for our respective journeys home with an air of expectancy; the next time we all met up would be on the day of departure.

CHAPTER 3

Getting there

The phone call from Neill came at work.

'There's a very good chance that free flights out to Hong Kong will be available on the 15th or 16th of February.'

It was arranged that we would meet in the main entrance of Heathrow airport at 2p.m. on the 15th. In Hong Kong we would meet the rest of the party for the first time, and then fly on to Brunei, from where a couple of ferry trips would carry us the 110 miles to Kota Kinabalu, the capital of Malaysia's Sabah province and only a short distance from Mount Kinabalu itself.

Responsibility for organising transport again fell to 383, and Paul Hughes offered to drive us to the airport. Bob and I met Paul on the morning of the 15th; Paul wisely asked if we had our passports, money, travellers' cheques and medical documents with us. Sheepishly I en-quired if we could make the short trip back to my house.

We arrived at Heathrow on time and surprisingly, given the size of the terminal, had no trouble finding the other members of the party. Neill had some bad news – a mix-up over the shipping of the rations and climbing gear meant that they would not reach Hong Kong in time for our planned flight out to Brunei. After some frantic calling, the rations were on their way to the airport by car, and we would have to pay for the excess baggage on the flight out, but he had now confirmed that we would be able to fly free, taking advantage of the Concessionary Non Fare Paying scheme available to service personnel on authorised exercises. Ron had flown out the previous day to meet with the Hong Kong lads, and also to find rations and clothing if we were unable to take our equipment as excess on our flight. By various means he managed, in the space of twenty-four hours, to assemble a complete duplicate set of kit, a herculean effort which turned out to be superfluous as our original kit arrived at Heathrow and was accepted as excess baggage.

We managed to lose the heavy bags, boxes of rations and climbing gear as we passed through Customs and booking in, but placed our trust in the efficiency of Heathrow Baggage Handling and decided to head for the nearest bar. It was plastered with an advertising campaign that had as its logo 'How LOW Can You Go?' which seemed particularly appropriate in the circumstances; we toyed with the idea of stealing one of the signs but the Colonel (not surprisingly) was opposed to the idea. An alternative strategy was called for and so, by asking the barman, we acquired one legally – a new and interesting experience for us, but lacking the sparkle of our more usual means of acquisition.

We moved to the departure lounge to observe the time-honoured ritual of sitting around and waiting for hours, as practised by generations of travellers in departure lounges all over the world, until eventually our boarding call came. I was not looking forward to spending fourteen hours cooped up in the cheap seats, but as a veteran of many long flights I had discovered that by far the easiest way to fly is asleep, waking only occasionally to eat. Half a day later I awoke to the nerve-racking experience of landing at Kai Tak airport in the centre of Hong Kong; the plane, which avoided several large buildings by what appeared to be only inches, landed without a bump. As we left the plane it was starting to get dark, and after a snowy Devon the heat was intense and seemed slightly unreal. The main terminal was air-conditioned and it was a relief to feel the cool air circulating around us; Kinabalu, 1,100 miles further south, promised to be even hotter, and I wondered how we'd cope. Collection of the luggage was easy, our large blue Karrimor rucksacks and the odd ten-man ration box standing out from the more conventional suitcases. The boxes were the subject of raised eyebrows from other British servicemen travelling incognito; normally we would have tried to hide the fact that we were servicemen travelling, but with no time to repack the boxes they stuck out like a sore thumb.

Neill went off to find Ron, and forty-five minutes later reappeared, saying that there was a real chance that further free flights would become available for Brunei. Several hours and interminable games of 'I Spy' later, we decided on a change of scenery and moved to the departure lounge, where we continued to wait. Ron appeared with the three Hong Kong soldiers but with only a few minutes left to board the flight to Brunei there was no time for introductions.

Boarding the second aircraft was a culture shock – this was definitely not British Airways. Although the aircraft might have belonged to BA twenty years before it was now operated by another country. Glorious and flawless Malaysian women in long saris patrolled the gangway offering hot flannels and strange food. Drink was of the non-alcoholic variety as Brunei is an Islamic country and we were flying on the state airline, Royal Brunei Air.

This was the first chance we had to talk to the three Hong Kong lads. Along with Ron, they had to sit several rows behind us, and as soon as the seat-belt sign went out we made our way to their seats. First to break the ice was Kevin, who introduced us to his companions Lam and Chow, and surprised us by saying that they had only been told of the expedition two weeks earlier. He said that he'd spoken to some friends of his who had walked up the mountain a few years before and that he was looking forward to the climb. I mentioned the planned descent into Low's Gully, and found them completely unaware of any details as to the main aims of the expedition. Ron, Bob and I discussed the plan in some detail with them and, although they had no experience at all, they seemed happy to be in on the best proff of the year. I returned to my seat, inserted a tape into my Walkman and assumed my usual flying position for the next three hours.

Bandar Seri Begawan (the capital of Brunei) was, as we had expected, intensely hot, despite the fact that we landed in the middle of the night. Kevin and company, being of Hong Kong/British nationality, had problems entering through Customs; they had all their bags searched, and we were handed a leaflet with 'Drug traffickers will be executed' printed all over it. It reminded me of the signs in shop windows back in the UK – 'Shoplifters will be prosecuted,' and I was quietly grateful that I had not brought any climbing chalk with me – if I had been searched it might have been a little difficult explaining the fact that I was carrying two ounces of white powder in a plastic bag. We eventually cleared customs and found ourselves standing in a covered area at the front of the airport, where we spied the familiar uniform of a British soldier, looking for his personnel arriving back from leave in the UK. Neill, ever keen to rope in as many people as possible, accosted him and secured a lift to the Royal Brunei Hotel. By this time, jet-lagged and woozy, I would have been willing to crash out on the nearest park bench, but Ron came into his element as a bartering expert; we all stood around for two hours while he haggled over a few pounds' worth of discount, and with most of the night gone we collapsed into the luxury of our air- conditioned rooms, waking the next day to brilliant sunshine and the uncertainty of the breakfast table.

'Great, I'll have some of that stuff, please!' I pointed to the longest looking word on the menu.

'What are we having, Rich?' Bob thought he was going to get a sensible answer.

'I'll tell you when it gets here.' I tried to sound knowing but, when it arrived, my credibility was sorely stretched by the discovery that I'd ordered shark's fin soup. We took full advantage of the free coffee on offer, and formulated an off-the-cuff plan to pair off and find cheaper accommodation and some film for our cameras.

Vacating the rooms in which we had spent only a few hours, Bob and I found ourselves sitting on an enormous pile of bags and equipment in the heat of the street until Britt and Steve returned saying that they had found a hostel that charged next to nothing. Ron went to pay the hotel bills and, to his horror, found that they were asking the full price, so another hour of haggling ensued and the price was dropped to business rates, thereby saving the expedition all of twenty pounds. The hostel was only 400 yards down the road, so we picked up the bags and started walking as Ron continued to haggle. It was a large square building made primarily of concrete and the main entrance, for some reason, was on the first floor. Our rooms were very basic, consisting of two bunk beds, a noisy air-conditioning unit in the wall and ablutions shared with the rest of the floor. We made ourselves comfortable, locked the rooms and as we left to look around the market, Ron arrived. He had hired a taxi to carry his equipment plus the ration boxes the short distance from the hotel to the hostel, and everyone thought this very amusing until he requisitioned us to carry it all from the taxi. We left him happily settling into his room and headed for the open market next to the canal. Having been to several Middle Eastern countries I thought I was well prepared for the sights and smells of such places, but time had mellowed and sanitised the memories, and the impact was every bit as great as the first market I'd experienced in the Middle East. Each stall had an individual standing behind it pushing his wares under the noses of anyone (particularly tourists) who walked within eyeshot. Unfortunately, we currently appeared to be the only tourists in the vicinity and therefore experienced a formidable onslaught of this oriental sales technique. Such was their persistence that given time we might have bought all manner of things, but by keeping moving we managed to avoid any transactions.

The canal was being used by some fairly mean-looking power boats which, in the absence of tourists, seemed to be providing some kind of taxi service for the locals and we watched one of them narrowly missing a bridge stanchion at full speed. It disappeared down the canal at a furious pace and the driver of one of the remaining boats shouted to us in broken English: 'Good price, take you round harbour!'

There was another near miss as one of the boats neglected to give way at the appropriate time, so we decided not to place our lives in the hands of these floating lunatics and turned our attention back to the market, where we found a stall with some of the largest chilli peppers I'd ever seen. Unsure as to what part they could possibly play in the expedition's catering apart from taking away the taste of army food, we bought a healthy bagful and wandered along the canal bank back to the hostel. Ron had disappeared back to the airport to collect the extra equipment he'd acquired in Hong Kong and I was feeling far too hot. The air-conditioned room was blissful and I was soon in the land of Nod.

Neill woke me: 'I want you and two others to go through the Hong Kong lads' equipment, especially their food.' Dragging my jet-lagged body from the bunk, stretching and yawning, I put on a T-shirt and headed for their room, where Pete had already made a start. I felt that having an uneven number of Hong Kong and British personnel might present some problems because of the difference in cultures, but food, I reasoned, was a pretty universal subject, and this might be a good chance to start breaking down some of the cultural barriers. Pete had been given the task of partnering up with Chow, and Bob with Kevin, which left me with Lam. I explained to him that we'd need at least ten days' food, and that Bob and I would be taking an extra two days'.

Lam seemed unsure as to why we needed to carry so much: 'One day to the huts, next morning to the summit and back down on that day.' In his limited English he described the tourist path well, having spoken to some friends who had done it before, and said he didn't need ten days' food. I was surprised that, at this stage of the expedition, he was still unaware of what was happening and again explained the expedition outline, showing him as I went what would be needed to sustain himself on a hard mountain day's walk. One thing that nobody had realised was that chocolate is not a part of Chinese cuisine; Kevin, Lam and Chow didn't eat it and would therefore be denied the steady flow of calories (so essential on a hard walk) that constant snacking on bars of chocolate can provide. Neill had worked with Hong Kong soldiers before and should, I felt, have used his previous knowledge to instruct Lam and his colleagues on what food they should take. The silver lining to this, of course, was that it meant extra bars were available to us chocolate-hungry Europeans when Ron opened the extra ration boxes.

We stayed one more night in Bandar before making the long walk with all our bags to the ferry that would take us to the island of Labuan, and then on to Kota Kinabalu. Not wanting to lose face by taking another taxi, Ron had reconnoitred the route a day earlier and discovered he could rest his rucksack on the railings that ran the whole length of the main road to the ferry port. Pete, who had brought with him the world's largest suitcase, carried it all the way and in the process it rubbed his legs until they bled; later, while rummaging through his bag for his first aid kit, he discovered that the suitcase had wheels.

Still giggling at Pete (service humour is not known for extending sympathy to its victims), we boarded the boat. It was more of a fast launch than a ferry and for a moment the memory of the crazed power boat drivers we had seen on the canal popped into my mind, but this skipper seemed to be a model of restraint. We settled down to watch an English film dubbed into Malaysian. It didn't do much to help pass the time, but in due course we arrived at Labuan Island and the first beer for three days – Labuan, although part of Malaysia, enjoys special rights. We spent some time at one of the local banks changing sterling into Malay dollars, and discovered that one of the Malaysian pet hates is writing on bank notes. It appeared that if you were caught doing this you were liable to be flogged, so we had to check through all our sterling for unauthorised graffiti; considering just how desperate some countries are for foreign currency, it all seemed a bit self-defeating and I couldn't help wondering if flogging tourists for minor currency offences was doing the industry any good. With financial affairs now in order and a few hours to kill,

Bob and I wandered around the port, absorbing the sights and sounds. Bob thought we'd found paradise when we came upon a shop selling Cornish Pasties, but discovered that the filling was curried fish.

The boat for Kota Kinabalu was slightly larger than the last one, but equally fast. I sat with Ron, who talked about the flora and fauna of Kinabalu. It was quite interesting for the first twenty minutes, but after a couple of hours of it I became a little desperate. Britt sat across the aisle smiling sweetly at me – he had sat next to Ron on the last ferry and was taking evident pleasure from my predicament. The only relief came as we neared Kota Kinabalu, when Ron announced that he could see the mountain on the horizon; we gazed hard in the direction he indicated, but as we were still a fair distance away decided that Ron's mountain was, in fact, a cloud.

An hour or so later we arrived at Kota Kinabalu, only sixty miles from our destination, and started to disembark. Chaos ensued as the crew wrestled with the heavy expedition rucksacks, and I noticed that some of the straps had broken. Several people passed comments as to who would have to jump into the less than clean water if the crew dropped a bag, but eventually the expedition kit was piled on the jetty, although mayhem continued and sharp elbows came in handy. Ron attempted to find his bearings, and the direction of the Travellers' Rest, the hostel he'd used on a previous visit with his wife. He left us standing in the blistering heat being pestered by small children who wanted to carry our bags, and disappeared in search of the hostel. On his return, we decided to make use of the the children who, without further questions, lifted some bags and told us to follow them. I offered my expedition rucksack to what appeared to be a five-year-old and he climbed inside the straps and stood up, but the rucksack was so big that he was able to stand inside the straps without the rucksack leaving the ground. Undeterred, he attempted to lift the rucksack with both arms, but unwilling to be responsible for the first casualty on the expedition I gave him my smaller rucksack. The children seemed to know exactly where to go, and in due course we arrived at the entrance of the building that housed the hostel. We climbed the stairs past some offices on the first floor and a doctor's surgery on the second before, wilting in the heat under the burden of the extra bags, we entered the clean but basic hostel, which seemed to be peopled almost exclusively by Australians. Two teenage girls showed us to a dormitory and, after unpacking at top speed, we all raced to be first to the sanctuary of the showers.

Refreshed, and with various tasks handed out by Neill, we departed for a look around town, where Bob and I were to find some webbing to make minor repairs to the broken rucksack straps. The streets seemed to have cafés or bars on every corner; small children, perhaps providing their family's sole income, stood behind cardboard boxes selling tobacco, lighters and key-rings. Several walks around the city centre failed (not surprisingly) to uncover a climbing shop but revealed several Burger Kings and Kentucky Fried Chickens and a Pizza Hut – the true eastern experience. We returned to the hostel and repaired the rucksacks using zinc oxide tape and what little spare webbing everyone had brought with them.

Tasks completed, thoughts turned to a relaxing nightcap and we arranged to meet at one of the local street bars. There was a natural three-way split in the team, the two officers tending to stick together, and the British NCOs and the Hong Kong lads doing likewise in their respective peer groups. No one seemed concerned at this stage that we were failing to bond as an expedition and I mulled over the situation; everyone seemed happy (if rather hot), we'd all bonded well within our groups and I assumed that, once on the mountain, everything would come together. Our group (as usual) was the first to the bar. We commandeered two tables and some chairs ready for the others' arrival, and a waitress with a skirt far too short for her age took our simple order: 'Five beers please.'

The rest of the expedition soon joined us and we settled down. The air was humid, the cold beer slipped down easily and the officers, presumably feeling the age gap and deciding that discretion was the better part of valour, left after only one beer, shortly followed by Kevin and his colleagues.

As Europeans we stuck out like sore thumbs and attracted some interest from the locals, a table full of whom called us over and offered to escort us around town. Initially we were suspicious of their motives, but without an inkling of where to go we decided we had little choice but to place ourselves in their hands, and two more beers later we departed, believing that we were heading for the best night spot in town. We descended a hideous stairwell and ended up in a club of sorts, which was so badly lit it was impossible to see from one end of the room to the other, and where the clientele consisted of six men sitting at strategic points around the darkened room. Everyone drew their own conclusions from the men's body language and the general ambience and we instinctively closed ranks. The only female in the group that had taken us there grabbed my arm and attempted to pull me into a corner so dark that I wondered for an instant if I'd gone blind. Fighting hard not to panic I returned to the group, gently pushed Britt in the direction of the girl – greater love hath no man than that he should lay down his sex life for his friend – and he was dragged off into what I could now discern through the gloom was just a toilet. Our anxiety was rising rapidly; we stood with backs against the wall, one hand in a fist and the other on our wallets as Britt fought to pull the door open and escape the monster in the loo. Seeing muggers, murders, rapists, zombies and deranged lavatorial hookers at every turn we made a rapid exit, pursued by the dreaded female and two of her many brothers. Out on the street, we regained our composure and tried to decide what to do next. We'd heard that a club called Rocky's was the place to be, but were unsure where it was. Not wanting to lose us to a taxi, our hosts volunteered to walk us there with promises that it wasn't far and we guardedly agreed. After walking for half an hour we arrived at yet another stairwell, narrower and longer than the last. Summoning our courage we entered, encountering a large person on the door who charged us the equivalent of five pounds. The beer was also expensive, but someone bought a round and we started to relax, feeling far more at home in an establishment that had a fairly even mix of the sexes. Finding a table wasn't hard, more beer was downed and just as the conversation started to descend to the ridiculous depths that only beer can induce, someone noticed that Pete was missing.

Bob and I looked outside but in the throng we became separated. I lost my bearings and, unable to find the stairwell that led back to Rocky's, decided to go back to the Travellers' Rest. Feeling increasingly dizzy and sick I headed down the nearest alley to lighten my load and then set off in what I thought was the right direction. The large concrete buildings of the city petered out, to be replaced by wooden ghetto shacks and trees, which in turn transformed into what looked suspiciously like jungle. My impaired faculties came the conclusion that I was lost and it occurred to me that getting lost in the surroundings of a reasonably westernised city didn't augur well for one who was shortly to set off into a largely uncharted wilderness.

I leant against a convenient wall which seemed to be moving all by itself and observed, hanging on a house across the street, a large white banner covered with oriental writing. I made a mental note to return later and acquire it for the Squadron, tried hard but unsuccessfully to focus on my watch and decided that the best thing to do was to get some sleep. My eyes closed. I made an abrupt return to my muddled senses as the hard floor acted as a crude alarm clock.

'Get a grip!' I said to myself, a little too loudly, and then, 'Travellers Rest, Travellers Rest,' as if the mere action of saying it would cause my bed to appear. It didn't. It seemed that the only course open to me was navigation.

'Right. Kota Kinabalu is behind me, the jungle is on my left and so the sea must be on my right.' I surveyed my surroundings and wondered where the other large white banner had come from; in fact, local elections were only a few days away, hence the banners, and the city was in a state of upheaval, but politics were the last thing on my mind.

'Turn right, hit the beach, turn right again, market and then the Travellers Rest sooner or later.' I tried running but my legs didn't want to co-operate and I slowed to a walk. The beach appeared on cue, and a few hundred yards away I saw a large concrete building – Centre Point – the main westernised shopping complex, from where, to my relief, it was only another quarter of a mile to the hostel. Staying on the beach, I peered into the market, where each stall had its occupants asleep under tables and small children the same age as my daughter ran around, playing in the litter and squalor. Faces dirty and clothes in rags, but happy (like children the world over) in their world of make believe, they stopped to return my stare solemnly as if I was from a different planet; the gulf between us was too enormous to be crossed. I turned to leave, disconcerted by the encounter, and sought reassurance in the comfortingly western digital figures of my watch face.

Half past four. Did I really want to wake the whole hostel this early? Slowly sobering up and in no hurry, now knowing where I was, I continued down the beach towards another large building and a jetty. The smell hit my stomach as hard as it hit my nostrils and, trying not to heave, I decided to give the fish market a wide berth, heading instead back towards the sea, where the waterfront was now a concrete jetty with shabby-looking house boats and a further abundance of small children playing unattended.

I came across a bench and rested my aching legs. It was 5.30 a.m. and the sky was changing from its earlier indigo, through purple, to reds and oranges, heralding the sunrise. I sat on the bench and watched, falling prey to the usual philosophical state of mind that the dawn inspires. A warm feeling of well-being engulfed me. Two hours passed in the blink of an eye.

Considerably more stable on my feet and fully aware of my direction of travel I headed for the hostel. The bars and cafés where last night's adventure had started were still busy serving, and I wondered if they stayed open all night. I found the entrance to the hostel blocked by a half-hidden, shin-biting shopping trolley which, I discovered later, had been used by the others to bring the unconscious Pete back to the hostel. I slowly plodded up the stairs, the exertion and the rapidly increasing heat causing my head to throb painfully. To my relief the door was ajar; tired and aching but mellowed by my experience on the beach, I pushed it open and walked in, trying to make as little noise as possible. I sat on the large settee and mellowed some more, until I was dragged back to awareness by a hearty voice: 'Glad to see you up early, Richard. Everyone else had too much to drink last night.' If only he knew.

'Morning, Ron.' Not the height of wit, but all I could muster.

'I'm going to have a light breakfast and then go off to do some sightseeing. Coming?'

'Maybe later.' I stood up and tottered over to the dorm, where the free-standing fan was going flat out in a vain attempt to cool the room. I was asleep before my head hit my makeshift pillow. Almost instantly I was prodded in the back.

'What happened to you last night? Shit, look at your back!' Steve was standing by the bed. I looked at my watch; it was mid afternoon.

'What?'

'Your back's covered in bites.' He paused to poke at them and I rolled over. 'And your front, you're covered in them. Do you feel OK? Where did you sleep last night?'

'Yeah I'm fine, just hung-over.' I swung my legs out of the bed. They were also covered in bites and Steve took great delight in calling everyone in to take a look. Feeling like the Elephant Man in some sort of freak show, I grabbed a towel and headed for the showers. I emerged refreshed but just as spotty, and still dripping from the shower in an attempt to stay cool. I put a boil in the bag on the stove just as Britt appeared and asked me where I had got to last night.

'Looked for Pete and got lost.' What more could I say?

'We found him in the toilets and looked for you, but you were long gone. Does that hurt?' He pointed at my legs.

'No.' I pulled my breakfast out of the boiling water and Neill entered.

'Can the same people who worked with the Hong Kong lads in Brunei take them through what to take on the mountain?' That meant Pete, Bob and myself. My eyes met Britt's; he shrugged his shoulders and smiling, thankful not to have been given a job, disappeared back to bed.

I found Lam and we emptied his sack out onto the floor. As we sorted through the gear it became very obvious that they had little experience of living and working in the field. Their food had not been altered since we left Brunei and they appeared only to have enough for two or three days at the most. I stressed again that we would need at least ten days' food and Lam nodded in acknowledgement, but I felt that they were all embarrassed at having to have their kit examined by us. Another concern was that they had no fleeces or warm clothing, although they did have green Gore-Tex suits from the extra kit Ron had brought with him. Neill floated impatiently between the three groups of two, making us all uncomfortable, and tasked Lam, Chow and Kevin with organising the transport to Kinabalu National Park Headquarters. The officers discussed the meeting they were to have that night with Rob New. I asked if they would like me to attend, but was told that I wouldn't be required; Bob, who was present while we had the conversation, later said that he thought it was an officers' thing and they didn't want the rank and file there drinking all the gin and tonic.

Ron had acquired the use of a small room to store the expedition members' personal kit while we were away on the mountain, so with the expedition bags packed ready to go and the excess left in the spare room, we headed off for what might be the last beer before the mountain.

We met at the same bar as we had done the night before. I was unwilling to drink too much, given the daunting prospect of a sixty-mile trip on local roads in a dusty old minibus during the heat of the day, but we visited several pubs and street bars, steering clear of the dodgy hangers-on of the previous night, and managed not to lose anyone.

I had rather unfairly doubted Kevin's ability to organise the transport to Park HQ but my misgivings were unfounded and the minibus turned up bang on time the following morning. I sat next to Bob as the heavily laden little blue bus pulled away and the rush of air as we picked up speed was better than any air-conditioning. We watched the city change as we drove through it; tall office buildings and hotels became factories and warehouses, which in turn became shacks. The amount of greenery in between the buildings increased until the city petered out and we left it to its uninterrupted routine. A large metallic monument in the middle of a roundabout brought with it a shout from the Colonel.

'There it is, look!' We came to a halt alongside some small shops and ramshackle huts. In the distance Mount Kinabalu loomed. It looked very big – steep, forested ridges and valleys rising up to a layer of cloud that, we were to discover, wreathed the mountain almost continually. The summit itself was hidden in the cloud, but we studied the mountain for some time before Neill broke the silence.

'Right. Ron and I will see if we can buy some parangs from these shops.' The parang was the local equivalent of the machete and there had been some discussion as to whether we would need them; Neill had voiced the opinion that they were more trouble than they were worth (a sentiment with which Bob would later agree heartily), but now appeared to have changed his mind. Closely followed by the rest of us, he and Ron entered a hardware store that could have doubled as a Samurai armoury, stacked to the rafters with enormous knives. The Colonel opted for two of the smallest, with blades a mere two feet long and leather sheaths. We concealed them well, as parangs were not allowed in Kinabalu National Park; this policy was presumably to prevent tourists denuding the more popular areas of the park, but we felt that in our case their use was excusable as we would be well off the beaten track.

We had a quick photo session with the mountain behind us, then legged it back to the bus and the relief of the flow of cool air. The mountain grew larger as we rounded each bend and the sparse jungle increased in density to such a degree that it seemed almost impenetrable. The road gained height, in places washed away by the monsoon rains, leaving great holes and huge unprotected drops ready to claim any driver who wasn't concentrating. We did nothing that might distract our driver's attention.

As we drove up the hill the lower, jungle-covered slopes of the mountain towered above us to the right and I mulled over the possibility of escape through such dense vegetation. The sides seemed ridiculously steep to be covered in such jungle and the prospect of climbing near vertical vegetation was not an attractive one. From what I recalled of Ron's discourse aboard the Kota Kinabalu ferry, the lower forests, below 3,500 feet, were the densest. What I hadn't picked up was the fact that above that height the forest, although less dense in terms of trees, had much more undergrowth and that as altitude was gained, this undergrowth, in the form of tree ferns, climbing bamboos and rhododendrons, became increasingly thick, particularly between 6,000 feet and the treeline at 10,000 feet.

At the next photo stop we could see for the first time the great bare whaleback of the summit plateau above the clouds, and persuaded the bus driver to take a group photo with everyone's cameras – no simple assignment as we all had at least one camera. The bus pulled away again, protesting at the double strain of altitude and overloading, and the road continued to wind uphill, never going in a straight line for longer than a few seconds at a time. I started to feel a little green. Too late to banish my queasiness entirely, the bus came to a stop at one of the many roadside stalls erected for the benefit of tourists en route to Park HQ and selling ordinary goods at tourist prices. Neill bought what he thought was a melon; there was much speculation as to exactly what it was, and a lot of high-spirited laughing and joking ensued as we set off again. I joined in rather half-heartedly; concentrating on my travel sickness had turned my thoughts inward, and some old doubts had returned, brought more sharply into focus now I'd seen the steepness of the jungle on the lower slopes.

Does anyone else know any kind of rescue techniques? Did the Colonel really need me to check his figure of eight that day on the viaduct? Did they really have a near accident on a Top Roping and Abseiling course, and what was Neill doing on a TR&A course if he's an ML? Is he an ML? This is all self-motivated, of course – if something happens to me, will the team to able to climb out and drag a casualty with them? Time for a decision. Britt seems the most likely and able candidate for a crash course in mountain rescue, with hoists being top of the list, just in case the unthinkable happens to me and I can't climb or operate any rope systems. First chance I get, I'll talk to Britt.

The bus stopped just inside the park gates and, with the increased altitude, we all noticed the drop in temperature. Park HQ is at nearly 5,000 feet and with a lapse rate of between two and three degrees Celsius for every thousand feet gained, the air was at least ten or fifteen degrees cooler. Everyone piled out of the bus and Neill went off into an official-looking building to find out where we'd be spending the night. In his absence we unloaded the kit, only to have him reappear and tell us to re-load the bags as the hut we were to stay at was some way off. It turned out to be a large, two-storey, brick and wood structure, perched on the side of the hill. The coolness and damp in the air made a refreshing change, and as we unloaded the bus for the last time and made our way to the rooms, we barely broke into a sweat. Glancing up at the mountain, I noticed that the cloud that had been on the northern side had slowly crept around to the south side to form a halo around the summit. In all our briefings the weather, other than the monsoon rains, had never been mentioned, yet clearly the mountain did have its own weather systems – all mountains of any size do and Kinabalu, at 13,455 feet, was no exception. Exactly how this would manifest itself and what effect it would have on our expedition was a question I was pondering when Neill entered the room and told me to give the Hong Kong lads a quick session of rope work. Still somewhat distracted I walked out onto the balcony and looked down; it was twenty-five feet to the ground and there were some railings on which to belay – a ready-made classroom without even having to leave the comfort of the hut. As I prepared the climbing equipment I told everyone to meet me under the balcony in ten minutes for an introduction to crag rescue and a spot of revision for anyone who wanted it.

Using one rope, I made four fixed lines hanging off the stairs and balcony. Kevin, Chow and Lam arrived, eager for their first lesson. I hadn't realised that this was to be their first ever lesson and failed to hide my frown of disapproval, but they made good pupils, with Kevin in particular showing a natural aptitude for rope work. After a ten-minute session on how to wear a harness we progressed to abseiling.

Kinabalu is not normally a destination for climbing parties and as a result a small crowd gathered at the top of the stairs to watch in fascination as we lowered ourselves to the ground and then promptly ascended the ropes down which we had come, like some kind of formation caving team. The other members of the group arrived to join the fun and Pete, who despite his TR&A seemed to know little about matters technical and wasn't about to ask any questions, attempted to use his Crolls but mistakenly clipped his main karabiner to the release handle of the device. He made good progress considering that his full weight was on the release mechanism, but after gaining several feet the inevitable happened and he landed upside down, narrowly missing a concrete drain. I pushed my way past everyone to see if he was hurt, but there appeared to be no damage. Neill had witnessed the incident and enquired sharply as to what had gone wrong; I looked at the Croll which was lying beside Pete on the ground, picked it up and turned to the rest of the group.

'Can anyone see what's wrong with this?' There was no answer,and I was about to explain when an unfamiliar voice interrupted.

'He's clipped the release mechanism.' A new face had materialised in the audience.

'That's right, who are you?' I questioned the clean-shaven, well-spoken Englishman who appeared to know more about climbing than all the other expedition members put together.

'I'm David Powell.' He offered a hand, we shook; he had a strong grip.

'Rich Mayfield. You a climber?'

'Yes.' My attention returned to the group, who had recovered from the excitement and were carrying on with their practice. Their concentration seemed to have sharpened up and I turned back to David.

'Staying in the hut?' I enquired.

'Yes, I've got a group from the UK with me – we're walking up the mountain tomorrow.'

'So are we. Look, I'll meet up with you later, after I've sorted this lot out.' He left and I returned to the group. After a further hour the enthusiasm was wearing thin and most of the party disappeared, but I asked Britt and Neill to stay and run through rescue techniques with me, hoping that the Colonel would finally spark and rekindle my fast evaporating confidence in him. It was Britt, however, who really sparked; even without the benefit of being a climber, he quickly grasped the principles behind hoists, while Neill appeared thoroughly bored. It started to rain lightly, so I quickly packed everything away and headed off to the bar on the bottom floor of the hut in search of David Powell; I was interested to hear his thoughts on Kinabalu and its weather system. David was sitting at the head of a large table full of English-speaking tourists. As I entered the room he excused himself and left the table to speak to me. We shook hands again.

'Are you really going to try Low's Gully?'

'Yes,' I answered, taken aback by such an abrupt question. 'Why?'

'Have you seen it?'

'No.' I was starting to regret looking for the man now. 'Why?'

'I watched the group this afternoon – they're just not up to it.'

'Well, there are only two abseils from Easy Valley to the floor of the gully. We'll leave ropes behind to cover any retreat.'

'Who told you that?' he exclaimed, obviously puzzled.

'Colonel Neill did.'

'I spoke to him this afternoon, he hasn't got a clue.' David's analysis was disturbingly frank and not a little unsettling – he seemed to have come to the same conclusions in one afternoon that I had been slowly moving towards over the last two months, but I decided on a temporary change of subject and asked him about the weather system.

'There's usually permanent cloud on the north side to around 9,000 feet. When it gets that high it then creeps around from the east to cover the south side. Did you see it today?'

'Yes, I did.'

'It came all the way round and joined up with itself. I don't think the rains have finished yet.' This was worrying. I hadn't experienced true tropical rain, but knew that it could be up to twelve feet annually, possibly more at altitude. I tried to imagine all that water sluicing down off the bare summit plateau of Kinabalu; it was not a pleasant prospect. David, meanwhile, gestured towards the table he had left.

'My clients. I run an adventure holiday centre from England, specialising in walking on Mount Kinabalu and in the state of Sabah.'

'How often do you climb the mountain with that many people?'

'I try not to do it more than once a week.' All I knew of his climbing experience was that he knew the right way to clip into a

Croll, so I pressed him on the subject of climbing to see if his was an informed opinion. It turned out that he was a climber and mountaineer in his own right, and a successful one at that; the doubts he had expressed earlier arose from his experience and an extensive knowledge of the mountain and its conditions. He mentioned that he had done some climbing with Steve Pinfield (Rob New's partner on the last, abortive attempt to descend Low's Gully) when he was over here. I asked if he had ever been into Low's Gully.

'No, but I've seen it from several vantage points and I've been into Easy Valley.' I had started to warm to him but he had to return to his clients, and I asked him if there was a telephone around so that I could take my last chance to call Sandy before leaving for the mountain.

'Over in the corner, but you'll be lucky to get a line to the UK from here.'

I smiled. 'I better had – I haven't phoned home since I left Heathrow and Sandy's going to kill me if I don't phone soon.' He was right about the inadequacies of the local telephone system, however, and after half an hour of trying to get through I gave up and resigned myself to the consequences. I returned upstairs and found an English couple settling down in the shared room. I wriggled into my sleeping bag and, as I slowly drifted off, wondered what the locals made of mad westerners who came all this way to climb their mountain. Mad or misguided . . ?

CHAPTER 4

Differences of opinion

David Powell's comments were still troubling me the following morning, but I was unsure what to do about my worries and whether I should discuss the matter with anyone. The business of final preparation put my doubts to the back of my mind as we packed and talked of what was to come, and one thing that soon became apparent was that no one seemed to be looking forward to the walk up the tourist path – it was going to be a long, tedious slog with heavy loads. Boil in the bag for breakfast (oats with apple flakes), and we were all ready to move by 7.30 a.m., but our departure was delayed as Neill had to meet with the park warden Eric Wong in order to obtain permission to climb the mountain unguided. Tottering under the unaccustomed weight of our ninety-pound rucksacks, and with the forbidding bulk of the mountain to our backs, we walked up to the park offices. Neill disappeared inside and we waited, time passing slowly as the temperature steadily rose. Eventually the Colonel emerged and announced that we would have to wait until 9.30 for the park warden to come to work. We settled down to wait and watched the park awaken as staff and tourists milled around doing their early morning routine, until David Powell drove around the corner and asked if we were having problems. We explained the situation. He confirmed that Eric Wong wouldn't be in until gone nine and his gaze fell on the rucksacks.

'Where's the Colonel?' We pointed to the officers, some distance off; David went to join them and they disappeared again into the offices.

Several Cokes later, Neill returned with the long-awaited permission to climb the mountain without a guide; during his absence we had discussed the matter and everyone had expressed some concern that permission had not been obtained before we left home.

I was unsure anyway how useful a guide would be – the officers knew the mountain already and it seemed unlikely that a local guide would have the skills necessary for descending the gully.

Before leaving we had to go to the office to have copies of our passports taken and sign indemnity forms, which made it perfectly clear that the park would take no responsibility whatsoever, a situation that was reiterated strongly and rather unnervingly by the park warden's deputy in his broken English. By the time everyone had gone through the red tape and was finally ready for the long day's walk it was 10 a.m. David's group of tourists had already started, but thankfully he'd waited behind and offered to give us a lift from Park HQ to the power station, a distance of around three miles on a metalled road with no shade. We accepted his offer gratefully, loaded his small van with half the expedition and set off up the steep, winding road, the engine working hard under the weight. Once at the power station the van turned around for the return trip and we waited, anxious to get under way without any more unscheduled delays. Forty-five minutes later the van struggled into view and, with the expedition reunited, Neill ran through the plan again.

It was to be every man for himself up to the Gunting Lagadan Hut, a tactic that would allow members to go at their own pace and therefore ease acclimatisation – it had proved successful before and he saw no reason to adopt any other plan. Ron informed us that water would not be a problem on the walk up due to the presence of a water pipe with taps every few hundred yards, but I opted for the belt and braces approach and took a couple of two-litre bottles – running out of water in this heat could prove painful, even dangerous.

At last we were under way. To everyone's disgust, the path started off downhill. What goes down must go back up again, and we would only have to regain the lost height. We arrived at the official entrance to the tourist path, stopping for the obvious photo opportunity, and then carried on down the hill, the party beginning to split up. Britt, Steve, Kevin and company were well ahead and I walked with Bob, who appeared to be finding the going hard; we reached the point where the path declared its intention of going uphill in a big way and Bob decided he was going to wait for the officers to catch up. Sitting on my rucksack I scanned my surroundings. The path was wide and very well worn from the thousands of feet that trod it every year. The jungle on either side was dense and uninviting, and the odd strange noise emanating from it added to my sense of unease; my mind wandered to what might lie ahead on the other side of the mountain.

Fifteen minutes later Ron came into sight carrying his video in his hand, closely followed by Neill. Reaching us, dripping with sweat and out of breath, they rested on the high steps that formed this part of the path. I was ready to go after my rest, but Bob wanted a few more minutes. I asked Ron why he was carrying his video in his hand and he replied that there was no room in his rucksack.

Everyone had decided to take the detachable side pockets and if necessary use them as a lightweight day sack. Bearing in mind the extra width of the pockets and the instability they might cause on abseils and whilst climbing, I'd not brought mine, but had instead made a makeshift frame out of a Karrimat and added my small day sack to my load. Most of us were carrying extra kit: Bob had the big yellow box that housed his video, Britt his camera and accessories, and I was carrying a full rack of climbing equipment and extra hardware. Neill carried no extra kit so I expected him to be faster. My thoughts drifted back to Major Hawker in Silberhütte – looks could be deceptive but in this case I feared that what you saw was what you got.

We set off again, very slowly. Tourists passed, giving us funny looks. Two or three minutes on another stop, this time for twenty minutes, and I began to get impatient; I estimated that we might not be able to make the hut before dark. This was no great problem as I had insisted on head torches and if the path stayed like this we couldn't get lost, but I didn't feel like hanging around getting cold when I could be with the others up in the huts. Ron was finding that carrying a video camera in his hand as well as a heavy rucksack was extremely hard going and I suggested, forgetting his earlier comment, that he put it in his rucksack.

'I haven't got enough room,' came the grumpy answer. 'Could you carry it?' I was a little taken aback by his nerve in asking me to carry his own kit in front of the Colonel, but the temptation of being able to use the camera proved too great and it would also give an excuse to push on. Ron gave me a crash course in how to use the video and I packed it away. As I watched them putting their sacks on I couldn't help thinking how ill fitting they were, and as a result unstable and difficult to carry; if they weren't carrying any extra gear and had no room even with the side pockets, then what on earth *did* they have in their sacks? Feeling bad about leaving my partner Bob with the two officers I pushed on.

The path was well defined, but in places the polished rock demanded care. On the steeper sections there were steps, made either from tree roots or planks; some of them, thigh high, necessitated the use of hands and with the extra weight in my sack I started to feel the strain. I formulated a plan to walk for ten minutes and rest for two, taking on water and nibbling some chocolate. Despite passing the odd tourist and nodding hello, I started to feel a bit lonely, but thirty minutes on I caught up with Lam and then Chow. My slow, methodical pace continued and I soon left them behind. Next to come into view was Steve, sitting at one of the shelters, so I took my rest a couple of minutes early and drank from the tap as we chatted. On each of the shelters I'd noticed a sign and took time at this stop to read one. I was amused to find that each shelter had its own name, and the sign told me the distance, the height difference, and the time it should take to get to the shelters both up and downhill. This shelter was of an open construction with a steep roof and pillars in each corner supporting some benches, and although sheltered by the surrounding jungle, in adverse weather the lack of walls would make it of questionable value.

I left Steve and soon caught up with Pete. We walked together to the next shelter, where we found Britt having a drink. I told him about Ron's video and my feelings that the others wouldn't make it to the hut before dark. He summed up my feelings in one word – 'Hats.' We chuckled, picked up the rucksacks and continued, leaving Pete to wait for Steve. Walking behind Britt proved to be a smelly and uncomfortable experience as the curry he had eaten the night before escaped with monotonous regularity until, unable to stand it any longer, I pushed past him and started to force the pace. Not wanting to lose face to a Commando, he matched me step for step; not wanting to lose face to a Para, I upped the pace again and this petty but good-natured inter-service rivalry continued for the next ten minutes until I stopped. Britt looked questioningly at me, issuing a silent challenge, and I explained my strategy of ten minutes' walking followed by two minutes' rest, which he seemed more than happy with; we both felt that we were very evenly matched and any competition would drive us both into the ground. He produced a cloth water bottle, offered me a drink and we set off again, making good progress and feeling that we would make the huts by two in the afternoon. Stopping at one of the shelters we discovered that we were keeping up with the time scale suggested on the signs, and we even overtook some of the less fit tourists. The path was hard going – the steps seemed to get higher and the use of hands to pull on anything within reach became more frequent. The uninspiring view of thick jungle on either side did little to help pass the time, and to relieve the tedium we tried to recall Ron's lecture aboard the ferry and identify the local flora and fauna; as far as either of us could remember, or ascertain from the surrounding vegetation, we should be well into the third vegetation zone – the mossy forest which started at about 5,500 feet and contained such species as tree ferns, climbing bamboos and rhododendrons. With the notable exception of a spectacular pitcher plant, however, we signally failed to identify anything.

Britt suggested that we should wait for some of the others to catch up, and we decided to wait an hour and see if anyone materialised; we estimated that we could actually wait for three or four hours and still reach the hut just before dark, but were unwilling to leave it that long as, with the increase in altitude, the temperature had dropped and our bodies, soaked in sweat, would cool down rapidly. Another sign of the altitude was that the vegetation had become noticeably less dense and the cloudbase, hitherto a comfortable distance above us, seemed threateningly close; I checked my altimeter, which read 9,000 feet and attempted, rather inaccurately, the conversion from imperial to metric. The scenery from our shelter included tantalising glimpses of deep valleys and towering, vegetated walls, views that were soon obscured by rain and a fine mist. The temperature had fallen considerably; we both felt cold and after the hard exercise I feared the onset of cramp, so in an attempt to decrease the effects we put on our fleeces and ate more food. In due course Pete arrived at our little waiting place, intent on a rest, but Britt and I were very keen to get going and warm up again.

The green and brown weave of the jungle was becoming monotonous, the trodden soil (where it existed) damper and darker, and the polished rock more slippery. I brushed against a branch and in return it relieved its water-laden leaves onto my head, to the delight of Britt. The air was thinning; our rest breaks became slightly longer, and at one of our stops, Ron's video came out of my rucksack. I commenced a David Attenborough style documentary with the aid of the very accommodating Kinabalu rats who seemed to have almost no fear – due, no doubt, to the vast amount of food the average tourist carried.

Pete reappeared and shortly afterwards I was surprised to see the ungainly form of Steve toiling up the path towards us. He dropped his sack on the damp floor, flopped onto the bench and exclaimed to no one in particular but with a great deal of feeling: 'Sod this for a game of soldiers.' To counteract the thinning air he decided the only thing to do was have a fag and was joined by Britt. I asked after the others: Steve said he'd seen Kevin and Lam at the last stop, and that they had been OK. Reassured that most of the rest of the party were in no trouble, Britt and I got ourselves going and, with protesting calves, pushed on slowly towards the next hut, grumbling about the weather. As if on cue, there were glimpses of blue sky, a light breeze dispersed the cloud and we were treated to one of those sudden revelations that only the mountains can give: the summit spires came sharply into focus against the sky, the surrounding jungle took on a new vibrancy and our dulled senses were jolted into action by an almost overwhelming wave of sensations. The warmth of the sun on my face cheered me and I felt distinctly overdressed in my fleece. We stopped to remove our warm clothing, glad to be above the clouds, and the walk took on a less serious atmosphere.

Feeling more confident and comfortable we decided to wait for at least three or four of the others to catch up and then walk together to the hut. Quietly sunning ourselves we were soon graced with the presence of Pete and then Steve who, despite being of large build, was coping well. Kevin and then Lam appeared, and we asked if they knew who was behind them, but they had not seen anyone for an hour or so. We assumed that the other four had formed a group, and Britt and I pushed on, pleased that the first day's walk was coming to an end. The final stretch of the path was very open after the close proximity of jungle on the lower section, and the sun hung low on the horizon, sinking slowly in the west and blissfully unaware that it was a cliché.

With massive relief we reached the lower hut and rested, thighs burning with exertion and calves screaming under our loads. Only another 400 yards to our hut. One last push. I hit a psychological barrier and my rucksack seemed suddenly to be incredibly heavy. My mind went back to Mountain Training in Scotland last year where the done thing was to try and sneak a large boulder into your mate's rucksack, the best part of the gag being to watch as he discovered he'd been carrying half the mountain with him. I reasoned that no one had the energy for such a joke, but forgot about the four litres of water, still untouched, that I'd been carrying all day.

To my horror the entrance to the Gunting Lagadan hut was up several steps, and for the first time my rucksack started to feel unstable due to my weakened legs. I dropped it heavily on the wooden floor, flopped onto a chair, and checked my feet for blisters and hot spots. They were fine – tired, but still intact. I picked up my rucksack and tottered along the narrow corridor into which Britt had disappeared, pleased to have made the hut with an hour of light left. I entered the dormitory, bagged the left-hand bunks for Bob and me and, resisting the all too powerful temptation to lie down and sleep, went in search of the kitchen. The first priority was to have some food. I dragged out two days' rations and started to cook, double quantity so that Bob could eat as soon as he arrived. It was just gone six; Pete came in and I asked him how far behind he thought the others were. He thought they shouldn't be too far back, given the time we had spent waiting on the path, but agreed when I remarked upon their slow progress. Kevin, Steve and Lam arrived, tired out and unsure how far back the rest were.

I started my mountain of hot food and moved to the balcony overlooking the path, joining Britt, who was wolfing down an equally enormous plateful.

'No sign of the others yet?' I asked him.

'No, not yet.' He spoke with his mouth full so as not to waste any eating time. We kept a watchful eye on the path and after tea I dug out my camera for some happy snaps of the sun setting; there was still no sign of the others. We all felt tired and I wondered about the fitness of the officers and my partner Bob, who had all seemed to be moving far too slowly.

Pete joined us on the balcony after he'd finished eating: 'Any sign of the others yet?'

We replied in unison, and in the negative.

'OK. Who's coming down for a beer?' For a moment I thought he was suggesting that we go back down to Park HQ, but then remembered that the lower hut had a restaurant and more importantly a bar. The thought of a beer was enticing and David Powell, who had started off behind us, might well have arrived at the lower hut and be able to give us some news. I nodded my agreement to Pete and asked Britt if he was coming.

'You must be mad if you think I'm walking back down there!' His comment lightened the atmosphere; I scuttled off to find my head torch and met Pete at the hut door. Descending the steps, the realisation of stiffening legs came home to me and at the bottom I stopped, pretending to examine a small lamp post that wouldn't have looked out of place on a London street corner. We pondered on how it had got there: visions of a small Malaysian man carrying the twenty-foot pole up the mountain path amused us both as we headed downhill with the single light fading into the distance. Walking downhill was a strange feeling and the sensation of no weight was bliss. My head torch gave enough light for us both to see by and as we neared the lower hut I heard someone coming in the opposite direction. Was it the others? I looked at Pete and the approaching figure revealed itself to be David Powell, who said he was coming up to see us. I asked him why, unsure that I wanted to hear the answer.

'I passed Colonel Neill at three this afternoon. At the speed they're going and in their condition I don't think they're going to make it in one piece.'

'How far down was that?'

'Three quarters of the way up, but they were on their last legs then.' My concern was primarily for my partner Bob, who (I assumed) was still carrying all his kit, whereas the two officers had no extra kit – I'd carried that for them – and Chow had seemed fitter than the other three.

'Did you see how Bob was?'

'They're all on their last legs, I think we should go down and help.' Coming from an outsider to the expedition, his willingness to help was greatly appreciated, but before I could take him up on his kind offer two more figures appeared, out of breath and exhausted.

Neill was supporting an unsteady Chow, who was minus his rucksack. He stood in the pool of light thrown by my head torch, glared at us, and before we could say anything, barked out venomously: 'Where the bloody hell have you two been?'

I was shocked by his tone of voice and puzzled at his anger. We in the first group had all been carrying some form of extra equipment; with the exception of Bob and his video, the others had carried only their own equipment. We'd waited in total for over three hours on the path, keeping one half of the expedition together, despite Neill saying we could move at our own pace, and now we had come back down looking for them only to be faced with this outburst. It seemed unfair at the very least; worse, even allowing for Neill's obvious exhaustion, was his loss of control. Chow was very unsteady on his feet and looked completely bewildered; I wasn't sure that he was fully aware of his surroundings, let alone the confrontation that was in progress. Neill pointed a shaking finger at us, barely able to suppress his anger.

'I want you two and Corporal Brittan to go down, get Sergeant Mann, who's carrying Chow's rucksack, and come back up to the hut. You of all people should know better!'

He pushed Chow forward and started to climb towards the hut. There was a bemused silence until Pete spoke; being without his head torch, he decided to go back to get it and if possible warn Britt that the Colonel was on the warpath.

I was left standing on the path, wondering what David's feelings were regarding the little scene that had just been enacted, but before I could speak he echoed my thoughts: 'How many times have you seen behaviour like that from the leader of a group in the mountains?' As I waited for Pete and Britt to appear we discussed again the ability within the group; if we were having these problems on the tourist path then what chance did we have on the other side?

David pointed out the obvious: 'There's no tourist path on the other side of the mountain and no water on tap.' He paused to let the importance sink in: 'I hope you realise there are no rescue services in Sabah?'

'Yes, I know.' All my previous negative thoughts came flooding back with a vengeance.

David continued: 'There are only four people in the state who can even get into Low's Gully safely, let alone mount a rescue operation.' I was looking directly into his eyes and had to adjust my head torch so as not to blind him. More than suspicious we might need outside help, I asked who the four people were.

'You.' He paused for effect. 'Me, but I won't be able to do anything as I've got twenty clients to look after. And two divers out on some island, but they don't climb any more and have no gear!' I knew he was concerned for our safety but it was still hard to take; to have my own doubts confirmed so candidly, to actually hear the words articulated, was a shock. What could I do? Confronting a senior officer would be difficult at the best of times, but one in this mood?

'Don't do it, Rich – don't go. You've seen the state of that Chinese lad, and the Colonel.'

There were heavy footsteps and loud breathing as Ron arrived, white-faced and struggling under the weight of his rucksack. He'd said before the start of the walk that he'd spent the last two months instructing skiing in the Alps and felt very strong; now he looked ill, near to exhaustion. David took his rucksack and helped him towards the hut, leaving me alone on the dark path, my head torch flickering.

'Shit, that's all I need.' I turned it off and waited for the others to come back down from the hut.

The first I heard of their approach was Britt: 'What would happen if the number two on the gun team couldn't carry the spare rounds? They have a contact with the enemy, the gun runs out of ammo. What does the number two do – "Oh sorry mate, couldn't carry it, ditched it three miles down the road." They came into view and, grumbling about the apparent inadequacies of our superiors, we set off down the path past the lower hut, its lights comforting in the darkness.

'Does anyone know how far down they are?' I asked, but Britt was too busy winding himself up to take any notice.

He turned to me and stopped: 'Did you feel the weight of Neill's rucksack? It wasn't even a third of ours!' This concerned me. Had they thrown stuff away? I decided for the moment to make light of it, just to ease the atmosphere, but Britt was having none of it: 'I'm telling you there was no weight in their bags. They must have ditched things.' We resumed walking, the night air cold on my legs, and my head torch died.

'Fucking great.'

Relying on the light from the others' torches, we continued down the path and came across an abandoned sack. Britt picked it up and passed it to me one-handed: 'Shit, you can't tell me that everything they're going to need is in here. I think it's full of pillows.' Pete offered to take it back up, leaving Britt and me to look for more debris, and a few hundred yards further down we were confronted with the strange sight of Bob apparently asleep on his rucksack.

I prodded him. 'Bob, you alright?'

He lifted his head. 'Am I glad to see you !'

'What are you doing?'

Britt butted in: 'Hat! Can't carry your own gear.'

I glared at him, and Bob replied: 'I'm finding it very difficult to breathe properly. The Colonel told us to leave half our food and all the climbing equipment further down the path, to speed everyone up.' He stopped for a breath. 'I've got two rucksacks, I thought I could carry them both as they're lighter now.'

'Ten out of ten for effort, Bob.'

'I was fine for the first hundred yards, then it just hit me. I had difficulty with my breathing.' This was potentially serious – the night air wasn't far off freezing and without a sleeping bag hypothermia could have taken hold in less than an hour. Britt took one sack, I the other and unwillingly, under protest that he could carry his own kit, Bob set off up the hill with us. Even with nothing to carry he was slow, and I wondered if my partner was up to this expedition.

'So where's the kit you've dumped?' Britt asked Bob.

'Quite a way down the path.'

Simultaneously, Britt and I answered: 'The rats will get the food!'

'No. We put it all into the dive sacks. Nothing will get in there.'

We argued briefly about retrieving the food, but Britt settled matters in a characteristically blunt way: 'Bollocks. I'm not walking any further than I have to.' We made slow progress but eventually the whole expedition was in the hut, and I heated Bob's food as he sorted out his feet and rucksack. Watching Bob eat made me feel hungry again and I shared his meal.

There was an atmosphere in the hut; everyone was spread out, talking in soft voices and sticking to their partners for company. Bob and I discussed the expedition. He felt that he wasn't up to it and I could tell that it hurt to admit it – it was a long way to come to fail on the first day. I admired his honesty and had to agree.

'What happened to Chow?' I was eager to find out how we had sustained a casualty on the tourist path.

'I don't know. We came across him spreadeagled on the path in a bad way. Colonel Neill exploded – you should have seen him.'

'Do you think I should go and have a word with them to see if they're OK? Where are they, anyway? I haven't seen them come out of their room.' I left Bob in peace to finish his meal and went in search of Kevin and company, only to find them all tucked up in their sleeping bags. Chow was still pale and very subdued. I crouched down next to Kevin's bunk and asked how they were.

'We not happy,' came the reply. 'The Colonel push us too hard, we not ready for this. Chow not want to carry on, he too ill. You tell the Colonel.' He paused, obviously waiting for an answer, but I was unsure how to respond, and he continued: 'It's OK for you, you mountain troops. You all have special skills, we have none.'

None of us were actually 'mountain troops,' as he put it, but he did have a point. There were several people on the expedition who shouldn't have been there. Chow, although fitter than the officers, had not been eating enough on the walk up, which had led to his collapse; it wasn't his fault that he had no experience of either living in the field or climbing, he should not have been selected in the first place. I was going to have to approach the officers and hope that they listened.

'OK, I'll talk to Neill and get Chow off the expedition. How do you two feel about what we're doing?'

Kevin was acting as spokesman for them all: 'We not happy.' He held my gaze and gave no further comment, but there was no misunderstanding there.

Before I spoke to Neill, I needed to know how the others felt. I had a suspicion that I was in for a bumpy ride and wanted to be sure I had some moral support. I decided to do the easy ones first. Bob reiterated what he had said earlier – that he didn't feel up to it. I could tell that having to admit this choked him, and I admired his courage and honesty; there weren't a lot of soldiers who could be so clear-headed. There was one question left for me to ask, but I was hesitant. How would he take it?

'Bob, if I pull out will you still go on?' His face dropped in astonishment.

'No!' Pleased that I had my partner's support, I moved on to the next most important member – Britt. The atmosphere in the hut was becoming brittle and the other tourists that we'd met were avoiding any eye contact with us.

I finally managed to get Britt, Pete and Steve to one side, and put my question to them quietly, but directly: 'If I pull out will you continue?'

Britt smiled, unsure if I was joking, but the penny soon dropped. 'No.' There was a certainty in his voice.

I turned to Pete for his response: 'I don't know why everyone's so uptight, there's no great problem.' Of all the people on whom I thought I could rely, Pete was one – he had mountain experience and was qualified as a JSMEL. Surely he could see what was going on.

'If you don't go there's no problem because Neill's an ML.' He was noticeably angry at my line of questioning, but instantly came under a barrage of abuse from Britt. I didn't try to change Pete's mind, reasoning that I might inflame an already volatile situation.

Steve's turn: 'I'm sticking with Britt. No. You're the only one that knows what's happening here.' Two out of three would have to do. Next and most difficult was Ron. He was sharing a room with Neill, but I wanted to speak to him alone as I had a suspicion that if I asked him in front of Neill, he would naturally take the senior officer's side. Neill went off to start cooking again and I nipped into the officers' room, nervous but determined to see it through.

'Can I have a word, Ron?'

'Yes of course you can, Richard, what about?' Very accommodating. So far.

'I've spoken to Chow and the others. I don't think he should carry on and he's asked me to excuse him from the expedition.'

'You'll have to speak to Colonel Neill about that. I can't really comment.'

'Do you think he should be told to carry on?' I wanted an opinion of some sort.

'You'll have to speak to Colonel Neill.'

I tried a different tack: 'How do you feel about what happened today?' Surely he had an opinion on that.

'Today went fine, slight hitch, but everything's fine now.' How could he say that? You could cut the air with a knife.

'I don't think it went fine.' Ron shifted on his bed uncomfortably and started to stare at the floor. I felt like a headmaster trying to exact the truth from one of the pupils and was about to try again when I became aware of someone standing behind me. I turned and saw Neill.

He made chit-chat about what he had just prepared to eat, while Ron avoided eye contact with us both. I got the feeling he'd heard every word, but his comments about the weather, the mountain and how well the team members did on the walk up gave nothing away. I wondered for how long he could talk about nothing. Who would break the ice first?

'Ron and I are having a private conversation.' I hoped this might encourage him to leave; I was unwilling to tackle both officers at once. Ron and I could have been discussing anything, but Neill's reaction confirmed my suspicions of eavesdropping.

'I know exactly what you're doing.' His newly released anger surpassed that of earlier and his voice rose to a bellow. 'You're to stop it RIGHT NOW!'

I couldn't believe it. I was doing my job, the job *he* had given me. How could I advise if I didn't speak to people to find out how they felt and in turn would perform? I didn't see him talking to the men. At this rate we didn't stand a snowball's chance in hell of doing the gully, although we'd probably get far enough in to get stuck, or worse, sustain a casualty. If that happened, and we could only rely on half the team being able to carry their own rucksacks, how could we expect to get a casualty out? This was the second time he'd had an unjustified go at me. Surely he realised that the expedition couldn't carry on? He didn't even have all his food or any climbing equipment. I felt the urge to punch his pompous face but resisted; it would have been one way of getting the expedition off the mountain but I didn't want to descend to that level. I stood up, eyes locked onto his. Walked towards him, and paused, inches from his nose, before pushing him to one side and walking on. There was no point me staying; I couldn't reach him and, if I didn't get out of the situation, I'd do something I'd regret later.

'Corporal Mayfield. If you're going down to the lower hut, see if they're still serving in the café.' An enormous and expectant silence had descended on the hut. You could have heard a pin drop at fifty paces. What made him say that I have no idea. Everyone in the hut knew what was happening.

I didn't look at anyone on my way out, but knew I was being watched; I walked quickly down the steps half expecting to hear footsteps behind me, but none came. I took a few deep breaths of the cold night air, tried to relax, and by the time I reached the lower hut I was on a more even keel, but still quietly simmering. Inside I found a large hall with people sat around in relaxed groups, blissfully unaware of the recent drama in the higher hut, and I attracted no undue interest. The return to relative normality helped me to relax further. I ordered a beer and without thinking asked if they were still serving food – eight years of army life and the power of the hierarchy made me automatically carry out Neill's order despite the masterly irrelevance of it.

I found an unoccupied corner and sat down, trying to mellow. Sat at a nearby table was the familiar figure of David Powell with his tourists and we glanced briefly at each other, but I looked away, not really wanting to talk to anyone.

Steve came in and approached my table: 'Hi Rich, you alright?' He sounded almost apologetic and I answered him monosyllabically, unwilling to be drawn into a conversation.

'The Colonel wants to speak to you.' I could feel him holding his breath.

'If he wants to speaks to me he'll have to come down here.' Steve pressed no further, and as he left with my message I wondered about the wisdom of my attitude and how Neill would react. One letter from him to my CO could well serve to end my career. I rethought my stance, weighing up the rights and wrongs and trying to give a fair hearing to my self-doubts. I drew strength from the fact that most of the expedition were firmly of the same opinion as I and, after a long hard think, still reached the conclusion that the expedition couldn't continue in its present form. How to get myself out of the hole I'd dug was a different matter entirely; merely thinking about it sent my stress levels soaring, so I stopped thinking and stared morosely into my beer.

David left his table, obviously concerned: 'Alright? What happened ?'

'Fucking idiot. He's still fully committed to doing it and he's not taking a blind bit of notice of me.'

'Rich, you do realise you can't do this.' He sipped from his bottle. 'If you take them into the gully, people will die.' I didn't need to be told that and sat in silence, brooding.

Britt arrived and pulled up a seat: 'Hi Rich. Everybody heard that you know.' He grinned at me, and I couldn't help but smile back.

'Yes, I thought as much.' David turned to Britt and reaffirmed what he'd just told me; Britt nodded, in harmony with the sentiment, and transferred his attention to me.

'Watch yourself with him, Rich. He wants you to come back and talk to him.'

'If he wants to talk to me, he'll have to come down here!' Like Steve, he didn't push it. I could tell just by his presence that Neill had told him to come and get me, Britt being a full Corporal and therefore senior to me. In normal circumstances I'd be looking at being charged with insubordination and put on CO's orders, which could only mean one thing: being busted to Private. I was now a stage beyond that and, if I was still unwilling to co-operate, the offence might well incur a short stay at Colchester military prison. The prospect was not a pleasant one, and again I asked myself if I was right. If I was, then my behaviour could be justified, but if I was wrong . . . ? A slight doubt entered my mind – Neill was the one with previous knowledge of the mountain – but I dismissed it, knowing I had the support of most of the expedition.

'There's going to be an O group at 2100.' Britt watched for my reaction. This was obviously a direct result of my confrontation with Neill. A formal Orders Group held the potential for a further heated argument; would the others back me in front of the Colonel? They too had careers to think of.

'I'll be there.' I was surprised and somewhat unnerved to see Neill enter the hut and walk straight over to the table – Steve had obviously briefed him well. As he approached he noticed David Powell and scowled at him, now openly hostile to the outsider. David took the hint and returned to his table. It was quite obvious that we were the talk of the higher hut and fast becoming the talk of this one; conversation had died and sly glances were making us all feel uneasy. There was a distinct whiff of High Noon about the proceedings. Which one of us was Gary Cooper? The Colonel gave me a flinty stare.

'O group at nine. I'm going to have a quick shower. Be there.'

'I'll be there.' I tried to appear calm, but my mouth was dry and I felt sick. Neill went off to the showers and David returned to our table.

'I was expecting sparks.'

'So was I.' I felt suddenly deflated.

Britt left for the upper hut, and David resumed: 'I've been thinking, Rich. Why don't you suggest to the Colonel a split in the expedition. You and the stronger, more able members go and do the gully, and the others can go around to the bottom and work their way up to meet you. That way if something does happen then at least they'll be able to resupply you with food.' It seemed a good idea, and we discussed the pros and cons as I finished my beer. I didn't require a lot of convincing and agreed to suggest it at the O group. David also offered to act as 'cut-off' for us; that is, to be the person who would raise the alarm if we became overdue. It was another kind offer, and one which I was later to regret turning down, but Neill had already said that he'd arranged a cut-off and I didn't want to aggravate him further.

Not wishing to walk back up with Neill, I departed before he came out of the showers. Taking my time up the path, I concentrated on the night's events, trying to find the right angle so that we could resolve the issue without anyone feeling aggrieved at having to climb down; if in the process I could save my career, so much the better.

I decided to talk to Bob first, but he beat me to it: 'Rich, I've got something to say.' He took my elbow and led me off to our room. 'Sit down and listen. You don't talk to a Colonel like that. You're a regular, and you've got your career to think about.' I made to speak, but Bob carried on: 'Let me finish. I know I'm TA, but I'm still a senior. If you have anything to say, say it through me. Firstly, because I'm a bit more diplomatic than you, and secondly, I don't have a regular army career to think about. I'm not disagreeing with what you're saying, it's the way you're going about it, and I feel that what I'm going to say to the Colonel will help sort it out. I know I'm not qualified, but listen to what I've got to say.' I looked him straight in the eye; he'd obviously been thinking about this a lot, and rightly so.

'If we split the expedition into two, you can lead the front group into and through the gully, and I can go back down with the officers and the Hong Kong lads and come up the river to meet you with extra food.' He explained the detail of what he'd spent the previous hour planning. I was amazed. He'd just quoted the bones of David Powell's suggestion, and without any prompting. Despite Bob's relative inexperience in the mountains, his innate common sense had come up with a sensible solution.

'I've just had a similar conversation with David.' Bob looked puzzled. 'That's what I'm going to bring up at the O group.'

'No, Rich. Leave that to me.' I was touched by his willingness to make that sacrifice and relieved that I wouldn't have to be the prime mover in the impending confrontation with the Colonel.

'Thanks, Bob. I'll back you up and make it clear that I fully support this plan.'

As 2100 hours approached, I woke Kevin and his pals; Chow still looked pale and was unsteady on his feet. We started to congregate around a large wooden table in the main communal area and the other tourists, either tired by the walk up or (more probably) sensing the atmosphere, disappeared into their respective dorms. There was an air of expectancy around the table as Neill and Ron sat down. We sat in silence. I avoided eye contact with Neill and pretended to study my altimeter.

Neill started the ball rolling with masterly understatement: 'Corporal Mayfield and I have had a disagreement. I'm sure that Corporal Mayfield thinks the responsibility for the safety of expedition members is his. It is not. I am the expedition leader. I organised the expedition. I am running the expedition. It is *my* responsibility to ensure the safety of the expedition members, *not* Corporal Mayfield's.'

I breathed a sigh of relief. He was correct in saying this, of course, but he had effectively just absolved me of any responsibility for safety matters and in front of all the other members as well. If this thing screwed up and people started asking questions, at least I had tried to stop him.

He continued: 'Now in turn I'm going to ask each one of you how you feel about today's events.' I made a mental note of the fact that he made no reference to future events.

Bob stood up: 'Colonel Neill, I'd like to go first.'

'Sit down, Sergeant Mann!' Bob looked at the rest of us, belittled and bewildered by the four words, and plonked his arse back on the chair. Astonishment had appeared on everyone's faces; it was almost unheard of for a senior officer to address a senior NCO like that in front of junior ranks. If this was to be his attitude then I had no chance. Apparently oblivious to the atmosphere, Neill pointed to the other end of the table and hesitantly Lam spoke up.

'I think today was a very hard walk, we should have porters.' During his short statement he looked at no one and kept his eyes lowered.

Neill worked his way round the table; everyone in turn made an almost identical statement to Lam's, and Chow asked to be excused from the expedition. Nobody made any reference to the future of the expedition as it appeared he didn't want opinions on that, the inference being that it was his show and his alone. At last he pointed at me and I rose nervously to speak.

'After seeing the performance of the expedition up the tourist path and talking to the locals I feel the expedition should be reorganised. Chow has asked to be excused from the expedition. He's not strong or technically competent enough to carry on and I think he should be excused, but obviously that's Colonel Neill's decision.' We made eye contact for the first time and held it for a few seconds.

'Sergeant Mann has come up with a plan that, as technical adviser, I feel we should adopt.' I looked at Neill again; he was quietly smouldering. If looks could kill . . . Holding his gaze, I sat down and Bob took the stand.

'I've given this a lot of thought.' He paused to take a deep breath. 'I thought I was stronger than I am, the walk up today was bloody hard. It chokes me to say it but I know I'm not strong enough to carry on.' I studied his face as he spoke, seeing the disappointment written all over it.

'I feel that there are several people, myself included, who shouldn't go.' He took another deep breath, trying to soften the blow to come. 'Chow has already said he doesn't want to carry on.' He was looking round the table, engaging with as many people as possible. I really felt for him.

'Based on the last expedition, if half of us come up river with extra food while the other half attempt to descend the gully then we can resupply them, and if there's a casualty or any other problem, the fresh ones will be more able to help.' The wisdom behind what he was saying seemed obvious and very well founded; he carried on, nearing the crux of the matter.

'I think the people who should be in the river party are: myself' (he kept emphasising, bravely, that he included himself in the weaker group) 'Chow – he doesn't want to go anyway – Kevin and Lam – they're not very good on ropes. Major Foster – not really fit enough-,' Bob looked straight at Ron and gave him his best puppy-dog eyes '- and Colonel Neill.'

Shit! He'd said it. If we'd been tortoises, we'd have been rapidly retracting heads and legs into our shells to avoid the fall-out from a Colonel exploding nearby. But none came. Instead there was a flat reply: 'No.' Bob sat down, unsure what to expect. 'We've tried that before and were defeated by the strength of the current.'

Bob replied: 'But, boss, that was in November and December, at the height of the rainy season.' I could see what Bob was getting at; it was now February and there hadn't been any rain for six weeks.

Neill dismissed Bob's suggestion again and resumed: 'The reason why we didn't hire porters was that time was pressing and I didn't think that we could afford to lose any more time.' Having to explain himself to NCOs seemed to be very uncomfortable for him and he spoke quietly.

'At the time, I thought the lift that Mr Powell gave us more than made up for the lack of them, but in the light of today's events, I was wrong.' He moved on to a different subject. 'Corporal Mayfield's role on the expedition is only in case of an emergency. If there is a need to climb out, then he is king on the rock, but I am as qualified as he is in any other matters.' This was almost true if he was an ML, but with his attitude and the way he was handling things I was now sure he was not an ML. What should I do? I couldn't stand up and actually accuse him of lying; that would ensure a one-way trip to Colchester military nick, although at this rate I'd be lucky to get off this hill, let alone see England's green and pleasant land again. The irony brought a smile to my face – I was worried about the consequences of my actions, but if I was right then it wouldn't matter what I said or how I said it.

He continued: 'If I'm not happy with his belays then I'll change them, and if I'm not happy with his abseiling line I'll change that too.' All this from a man who one month ago was unsure of how to use a figure of eight, let alone set up complicated and marginal belays for abseils and Tyrolean traverses. The thought that if it came to the crunch then I had the support of the expedition members was of great comfort.

'Sir, do you expect me to climb out solo, trailing ropes and dragging eight non-climbers and a casualty behind me?' I regretted calling him a non-climber, thinking it might cause more friction, but he just nodded in agreement.

'Yes!' His face was expressionless but his eyes were fuming. 'That is your role on the expedition.' Apparently my role had changed.

'I haven't got the equipment for that and we won't have time unless, of course, there *are* only two abseils into the gully and we leave ropes behind, *if* we can get back that far.' I remembered David Powell laughing when I said there were only two pitches of abseiling.

'Corporal Mayfield, I don't see how you can pass comment when you have not even seen Easy Valley, or Low's Gully, or the River Penataran. I've been into Easy Valley and on the last expedition I even marked the level of achievement by leaving RAOC in stones. I've also been up the River Penataran. I feel that this expedition is capable of achieving what we set out to do.' If he was right I'd be in for it when we got back. Maybe it had all just been exaggerated, partly by the officers, partly by Steve Pinfield and Rob New, and partly by David Powell. There seemed little point in arguing further; I'd find out tomorrow when we went in.

He continued: 'As you all know, Chow is unwell so tomorrow will be a rest day.' He paused for a reaction; there was none. 'The four who left kit on the path will go down and collect it.' Could this be the real reason for the extra day's rest? 'As for everyone else you can do what you like.'

I detected a hint of despondency in his voice and tried to make a positive contribution: 'I'll go into Easy Valley to have a look.'

'I don't care what you all do, but I advise you to rest.' With that, he brought the O group to an end. Despite my misgivings and the fact that I felt Neill hadn't been willing to listen to or consider the ideas put forward by team members, I decided to try to smooth things over for the good of the expedition. We would have to work closely together over the next few days and it would be beneficial at least to attempt to clear the air between us. I bit my lip and looked at him.

'I'm sure everyone heard the disagreement that Colonel Neill and I had earlier, and I'd like to try and put that behind us.' He gave an audible sigh of relief, as if he had been expecting another challenge, but his reply seemed to indicate an unwillingness to accept that I was trying to mend some fences.

'I hope it doesn't happen again.' I felt that my small olive branch had done nothing to relieve the tension, but merely reaffirmed that he wasn't going to listen to anyone on the subject of how the expedition was going to run. He stood up and, closely followed by Ron, walked off to his dorm as I mused over the contribution (or lack of it) that Ron, as second in command of the expedition, had made to the O group. Kevin took his not so merry gang back off to bed, leaving a group of silent and disheartened NCOs sitting at the table.

'Britt, want to take a look into Easy Valley tomorrow?'

'OK. What time are you thinking of starting?' We'd all had a hard day, some more than others, and needed a good rest. I looked at my watch: 2230.

'Start about 7.30?'

'No, I'm not getting up that early.' We discussed what to do; I wanted to move fast, get as far into Easy Valley as possible and be back out on the tourist path by two at the latest as that was when the weather had closed in on the last couple of days. Britt had a headache and really didn't relish the thought of an early start, followed by another and possibly harder day's walking or running, and decided instead to join Steve and Pete, who were going to take a relaxed walk up to the summit and have a look around. This left me in a difficult situation – I really needed to see Easy Valley for myself, mainly because that was the only excuse that Neill had left. I hadn't seen it, but needed to do so before we committed ourselves to the descent. With Britt unwilling to come and none of the others fit or fast enough to cover the distance required, it looked as if I would have to do it alone, something that went against my better judgement and the received wisdom of generations of better mountaineers than me, but it seemed that I had no choice; to know what was on the other side of the mountain was essential. I made a mental commitment not to climb anything too hard and to move as quickly as possible between any climbing sections; I'd aim to be back at the Easy Valley Col by 1.30 p.m., which would give me an hour at most to get back to the tourist path. I would take my day sack containing a bivvy bag, thirty-six hours' food (leaving a generous margin in case of any problems), cooker, my four litres of water (still fresh from the taps at Park HQ), fleece, altimeter and map. I'd wear trainers, shorts, T-shirt and hat, and take plenty of sunblock; I don't burn easily, but the thinner atmosphere at altitude allows through far more ultra violet and the last thing I wanted was a serious dose of sunburn.

No sooner had my head hit the pillow than my watch alarm sounded. Seven in the morning seemed to have sneaked up on me; I dragged my aching legs from my sleeping bag and yawned my way through a healthy but by now boring breakfast of oats and apple flakes before packing my gear and preparing to leave. The only other person awake was Ron, and I couldn't help feeling that Neill had sent him to make sure I wasn't going alone.

'I'm off now, Ron – I've got enough food to last thirty-six hours. If I'm not back tonight, don't worry; I've got my bivvy and plenty of water. I'll see you tomorrow morning. If I'm not back by first thing come looking.' I wondered if he was going to challenge me about the wisdom of my solo trip, but he seemed happy to see me go.

'OK, Richard, see you tonight and, if not, tomorrow morning.' He smiled and made no further comment.

The morning sun was already well past the horizon and doing its best to warm the cool air. I set off at a slow but steady jog, and after only a hundred yards of open path found myself in dense and steep jungle, but the path was still very well defined, with the customary steps made from wood or the roots of trees. My heart rate increased as the path became steeper and I slowed to a walk with my thighs protesting from the exertions of the day before, grateful for the handrail that appeared from time to time. In places the green patchwork of the jungle parted to reveal magnificent views of broken cloud lower down and, beyond that, low-lying hills covered in thick jungle. Half an hour after entering the jungle I reached the treeline at the bottom of the Panar Laban rockface and rested briefly next to a grotesquely twisted and stunted hardwood tree, which wouldn't have looked out of place in Hansel and Gretel's forest.

I followed a thick white rope up the bare rock of the well-worn, polished path; the general steepness had not increased but the lack of steps and the openness after the confines of the jungle path was slightly unnerving. The view more than compensated for any unease, however, and I began to enjoy the continuous upward movement and sense of achievement as I saw the height I was gaining. I started to find my rhythm, my legs now loosening up nicely after the steep jungle section, and after a further twenty minutes I arrived at the Sayat Sayat huts, made from aluminium and reflecting the sunlight violently in all directions; I tried to imagine the storm of protest that would follow if such huts were erected on Snowdon. The vegetation at this altitude had changed to the odd dense thorn bush, twisted by age and its harsh environment. I stopped to admire the view and watch some tourists I'd passed on my way up. I looked up at the summit area, impressed by the skyline and the amount of unclimbed rock in the form of pinnacles and peaks of varying severity and size. To my left were the Donkey's Ears, a pair of fine granite spires which had already been climbed, but by far the most impressive was the peak between Cauldron Gap and the Easy Valley Col, an enormous rhino horn that dwarfed everything.

The path was busy with tourist traffic heading downwards, each party with a local guide: I watched one of these guides pass me wearing an old and worn-out pair of plimsolls and carrying the Malaysian equivalent of a Tesco's carrier bag, and I couldn't help but wonder about their qualifications, or whether they were the result of some local job creation exercise.

I decided to have a look into the head of the gully proper at Cauldron Gap and at the same time view the as yet unclimbed rhino horn peak. I drank some water, and set off at a right angle to the path up clean, slabby and unworn rock, passing small clumps of thorn bushes making the most of the sparse soil that accumulated in the more sheltered hollows. To my left I could see the tourist path heading off towards the summit area, and to the right the access into Easy Valley; ahead of me was Cauldron Gap, through which I would shortly have my first sight of the other side of the mountain. As I neared the gap I felt a breeze blowing over the top and, stopping a few paces short, I took off my rucksack and slowly edged towards the drop. To my right the rhino horn overhung at an alarming rate for several hundred feet, and I marvelled at the huge potential for possible climbs, while on the left towered the Donkey's Ears. Reaching the edge on all fours, I peered timidly into the gloom; there was instant exposure, and dizziness. The ground dropped away in only a few feet to oblivion, and so narrow was the gully that even on a bright sunny day it was impossible to penetrate the darkness of the gully floor 4,000 feet below. I rolled over onto my back to try and regain some perspective, my eyes struggling to focus on the huge leaning walls above, but light wispy clouds gave the impression that these colossal walls were moving, even falling, and I had to close my eyes to restore equilibrium. I tried to imagine what it would feel like to step out onto the uncharted immensity of that leaning wall, but ran out of adjectives. I have a friend who would have described it as 'scrotum tightening', but even that evocative phrase didn't do justice to the scene in front of me. I spent a good half-hour just looking at this awe-inspiring sight, sipping water and nibbling chocolate as I contemplated my position on the mountain. Looking at the map I saw that the rhino horn (at least 800 feet high) was marked only as a boulder; the local equivalent of the Ordnance Survey, it appeared, had its limitations, and I wondered how accurate the rest of the map was – after all, the rhino horn was easily visible from the path and an omission of that magnitude was akin to leaving the pyramids off a map of Cairo.

Although the sun was high in the sky, I was in the shade and starting to feel cold, and after a last spine-tingling look down into the gully, I set off for the col at the entrance to Easy Valley. Descending a few hundred yards from the gap I started to traverse along the bottom of the massive tower over steep rock, having to use my hands in several places, but soon spied some cairns not too far below me and dropped downhill in search of a path and an easier passage. Following the path was easy – the cairns were frequent, the rock in places was slightly worn and I wondered how long it would be before it became as polished as the more frequented summit path. Half an hour after leaving the gap I found myself at the col. Easy Valley stretched out in front of me, flanked on each side by high granite cliffs and dotted lower down with patches of dense, dark jungle. The col itself was very sharply defined, the ground on either side dropping away steeply at first and then flattening out, while at each side of the col the land rose into the peaks and ridges that formed the skyline. I admired the surroundings for a short time and tried to fix some landmarks in my head before setting off down the valley.

Initially the ground was steep and demanded care and good judgement, but as it flattened out I increased my pace, keen to make as much progress into the valley as possible. Looking at my watch, I decided to allow myself forty-five minutes down the valley, leaving me with an hour and a half to get back to the path. I increased my pace further to a slow jog, hopping and jumping from one boulder to another, periodically stopping to look up at the massive walls that marked the borders of the valley: huge corners soared thousands of feet, and massive overhangs, thirty or forty feet across, were dwarfed by the enormity of the walls on which they perched. The sun beat down on my neck and I moved my hat backwards for more protection. Making good time I passed large boulders, the clumps of vegetation increased in size as the altitude decreased, and I checked my altimeter for any indication of a change in the weather and to see how far I'd gone.

Encountering the first patch of jungle, the ground dropped away sharply into the uninviting vegetation; with only another ten minutes left I decided not to proceed further but instead found a good vantage point for my first look into Low's Gully. The ground didn't look too difficult, but I was at least a mile away, and looking down into the shadow it was not easy to assess what it was really like. I broke out Bob's binoculars and studied the ground in detail; the bits that I could see didn't look impassable, but I couldn't see the steep section below me which was the crucial link between Easy Valley and the gully floor, or the hard section around the corner at the end of the gully. Although still very unhappy with the expedition proceeding as it stood I felt more comfortable knowing that at least the section that I had seen looked passable.

I made a mental note of the height loss: 1,500 feet from the col. Taking a large swig of water, I turned and headed back up the valley, to be confronted by a large RAOC written in stones. Even though they had only had a day to explore Easy Valley, I was surprised that Neill's previous expedition had not gone further in; I had expected it to be a lot further down, but perhaps he had written it twice and I hadn't gone far enough to see the second one.

I had a race against time on my hands as in the short time I had spent in the valley the cloud level had visibly moved and at some speed; out of breath, working hard, and sometimes using my hands for balance on the final steeper slopes, I reached the col in only forty-five minutes with the cloud at my heels. As I looked down to the tourist path the cloud was attempting to outflank me by coming in from the east, following the pattern I had observed on the last three days. Wasting no time, I set off down towards the path, following the cairns over the steep ground until I reached the huts of Sayat Sayat and the relative safety of the well-defined tourist path, where I stopped to take on more food and water before setting off at a more leisurely pace. To my surprise I met Kevin at the top of the roped section of the Panar Laban face and stopped for a chat; I didn't really want to spend much time at our hut and neither, it seemed, did he. We admired the view together, watching as the cloud engulfed us, and after sweating so much earlier I soon felt cold as the sun was blocked out by the shifting clouds. Kevin said he'd wait for the others to come down from their summit trip as I set off on the last leg of my day, jumping from step to step on the way down to arrive at the hut in no time at all.

I entered the hut at 1.30, and lay on my bunk musing over my finding of the RAOC in stones; I came to the conclusion that there had to be two. By 2p.m. the weather had completely closed in and I felt pleased that the decision to get back by 1.30 had paid off. If I'd been on the other side in those conditions I would have had to spend an uncomfortable night out.

The group who had left equipment on the tourist path had set off at ten and arrived back shortly after two, hot and sticky from the climb and the moistening air, and closely followed by Britt and his summit party with Kevin in tow. I was quietly relaxing when Neill walked into our room.

'I want the same people who checked the Hong Kong soldiers' kit to go through it again. Make sure that they have enough food for the ten days.' I couldn't believe that he was treating them like raw recruits, but pulled my now stiffening body off the bunk and headed to the main communal area, which was almost empty as all the other guests had now either gone down off the mountain or were sleeping. Britt had grabbed one Hong Kong lad and so had Bob, so I took a rather sheepish Chow; before I could say anything, he expressed his opinion again: 'Tell Colonel Neill I don't think I should go.'

'Look mate, if you want out you're going to have to speak to him yourself – you know he won't take a blind bit of notice of anything I say.' I doubted very much that he'd take any notice of Chow either, but at least I would be able to avoid another argument. We emptied his rucksack onto the floor, and I separated his personal climbing gear and his clothes.

'OK. Go and get the rest of your food.'

He looked even more sheepish: 'That's it,' was all he could muster.

'That's all the food you have?' I was sure that he'd mislaid the food he'd left on the path on the way up.

'Yes, that's it. Please tell the Colonel I shouldn't really be going.'

I was fast running out of patience. 'I don't believe that's all the food you have!' I didn't want Neill to overhear us; sparks would fly, luckily not in my direction, but providing yet another nail in the coffin for the expedition. I collected all his food and bagged it up, one day's rations to a bag; I was only able to fill two and a half bags, and needing someone to talk to I decided to see how Bob and Britt were getting on with their lads. Seeing the amount of food on the floor I knew Britt was in the same predicament as I. As usual, he wasn't beating around the bush.

'Fucking arseholes. They've only got enough for two, three days at the very most.'

'Mine's the same.'

Bob, seeing us talking, came over with a big grin on his face: 'How much has yours got?'

I looked over to Kevin's pile of food. 'About as much as yours, Bob.'

'Look on the bright side – this means that two of them can't go, even if they want to.'

Neill, who had been floating around in his usual style, came over to see why we were all standing around and Britt leapt in with both feet: 'They've not got enough food. Look.' Neill went from one to another in turn and I could tell from his mannerisms that he was slowly winding himself up; the question on all our minds was whether they had thrown the missing food away on the way up to save weight. I was dreading his reaction, but there was nothing we could do to forestall it, not at this stage.

'I told you three to make sure they had enough food. They've only got three bars of chocolate each and barely enough food to last three days.'

Bob was first on the defensive: 'We showed them exactly what to take, and how much to take – you were there when we we were doing it.'

'So where is it *now*?' Here we go again, I thought, and all three of us argued the toss for ten minutes – a pointless thing to do, but one which made us feel better. I thought about suggesting that they didn't want to go anyway and that this was probably their way of saying it, but then thought better of it. Why annoy him further, for no reason?

Kevin was standing with his friends, talking quietly in Cantonese; Neill turned on them and demanded to know where the rest of their food had gone. No sensible answer was forthcoming, and the discussion continued until Neill came up with a blinding suggestion: 'I want all of you to give two days' food to them, we'll collect it all and split it down as far as we can to make it last as long as possible.'

A good idea, but not one guaranteed to enhance his already fragile popularity, and as we disappeared off to our rooms Britt summed up all our feelings: 'I'm pissed off with this! We carry all the extra kit! Then we carry *their* kit!' His voice rose, but at this stage he didn't care if Neill heard him or not. 'And *now* we have to give them our food. Our food that we carried up. Bollocks! I'm not giving them any of my food.'

Bob and I went through our own rations as Britt lay on his bed smouldering. We had taken it upon ourselves to take twelve days' food instead of ten, which could make the situation easier, but it still didn't seem right. We discussed it at great length, opening and then closing bags.

'Britt's right, this is way out of order.' Bob nodded in agreement. 'Let's go and tell the Colonel we can't spare anything without going short ourselves.'

This was the best thing I'd heard all evening, but Neill had absolutely no sympathy.

'Even if you have to go down to eight days yourselves then do it.'

As he said this I sensed everyone's resolve stiffening; this was not on. Just about the only thing in the forces that is sacrosanct is a man's food. Abuse his family, abuse his sleeping bag, abuse your position and you might get away with it, but take his food and you will be in trouble. It occurred to me that if we just gave two days each, we should be able to supplement the loss by buying noodles and chocolate at the shop in the lower hut. One thing they wouldn't ever get from us was our chocolate. We went back to our room to find Britt still lying on his bed.

'You haven't changed your minds, have you?'

'We haven't really got any choice in the matter.' Stony-faced, Bob and I sorted out our most unusable foodstuffs and put them in a bag; Britt, keeping an ultra-low profile, actually managed not to have to give up any food at all. As we handed over our offering we discovered that Neill had given Kevin and Co. a couple of hundred dollars and a large list of food and sent them down to buy the extra from the shop's limited stock; I realised what would happen.

'Shit! They're going to buy out the whole shop!' I turned on my heels and ran at full speed into the dorm to find my trainers. Seconds later I was flying down the steps, much to the amazement of Neill, who didn't have a clue what all the fuss was about. My head torch was almost useless and I ran as fast as I dared down the steep path in near darkness, to my relief passing Kevin who hadn't cottoned on either. I was first into the shop, closely followed by Bob, and we embarked on a spending spree, ignoring the bemused faces of tourists and staff who, unaware of the latest friction in the other hut, had only seen the 'Mad Englishmen' running through their hut to get to the shop – they probably thought we had spent too long in the midday sun. Between us we probably bought as much food as we had given away, including half a box each of precious chocolate.

Kevin arrived, the penny having dropped: 'I hope you've left some for us?'

'Yes, there's loads left.' We were in fact unsure whether we had cleared the shop out, but the comical race had at least lifted our spirits. Bob and I laughed our way back, thankful that we had made it to the shop first – callous, perhaps, but that is the nature of squaddie humour. After Bob had cooked our evening meal we retired early, in a better state of mind.

Neill walked in. 'O group at 2100 hours.'

He walked out again to a general chorus of disapproval. We climbed out of our pits and headed back to the large wooden table in the communal area. Bob and I sat together. We'd all bonded well, but with our respective partners and most definitely not as an expedition. There was a strong feeling of every pair for themselves. The O group started as before, but this time Neill brought his guns to bear on the Hong Kong lads over their lack of food. He was still very angry, threatening to write a strong letter to their CO back in Hong Kong complaining about his soldiers' conduct. I felt that this was not the time or the place for such comments, which would serve only to strengthen the divide. The O group was following the same format as the previous day; Neill laying down the law, followed again by the 'How did we feel we did today?' statements. Again, everyone made some statement of no relevance to the future of the expedition, which seemed to please him – as far as I could tell, his attitude seemed to be the fewer people with a brain the better. This time all three Hong Kong lads asked to be excused from the expedition and I could understand their feelings; they were no longer volunteers but pressed men, but Neill was deaf to their request.

As usual, Bob and I were left until last, and when it was my turn I explained where I'd been. As I was about to reinforce Neill's view that at least the first section of the Gully was passable I noticed a look of total boredom on his face and stopped in mid sentence, thinking how arrogant he could be sometimes. I didn't have the guts to say it but everyone knew what I was thinking. I sat down. It was his loss; I had been going to try and support him, but he obviously felt he knew it all. He continued, making no reference to anything that anyone had said, as if nothing had happened, and dictated the routine for the following morning; reveille would be at 0300 hours, Kevin was to be responsible for it, and we would move at 0400.

'I haven't got an alarm clock.' I didn't think that was one of Kevin's smartest moves.

'I don't care if you have to stay up all night. You will wake everyone at 0300 hours, is that understood?' An aggressive look came over both their faces, and for a moment I wondered if Kevin was going to challenge him, but the Hong Kong soldier broke off eye contact, unwilling to be drawn into a slanging match.

Neill continued: 'We will carry half of our kit up to Sayat Sayat.' Britt shifted uncomfortably in his chair. 'We will then go to the summit for sunrise, and do the touristy thing. Corporal Mayfield, you will set up an exposed abseil in the Sayat Sayat area for the benefit of the Hong Kong soldiers.' He paused to see my reaction, but I made none. 'We will then come back down to the hut and spend a last night here.' Britt's face stiffened at that statement; he had been complaining about a headache again, blaming it on the thinner air, and was understandably keen not to spend another night at this height. Whatever we might encounter in the gully, at least we would be losing altitude.

The O group ended abruptly as the two officers vanished into their room, leaving us to chat in peace. Britt voiced all our feelings in his usual subtle style: 'I don't see why we *all* have to carry half loads just because those two can't carry their own kit.' He did have a valid point, with which everyone sympathised.

'Bollocks to this.' He stood up and walked off in the general direction of the rooms. Bob and I discussed the situation we were about to enter. With his small frame I didn't envy him carrying his rucksack or doing these planned shuttles back and forth. Britt appeared with a glint in his eye: 'I'm taking all my kit up tomorrow. Who's coming with me?'

Steve, who had until this point stuck to Britt like glue, saw no reason to change: 'I'm in.'

'Have you okayed this with Neill?' I asked, keen to avoid another confrontation.

'Yes, we'll take all our kit up to Sayat Sayat, leave it there, and go to the summit. I don't really want to go back up there, I've already been once.' A look of despondency; the expedition had lost all of its appeal and everyone just wanted to get it over and done with. 'Then back down to do Richie's thing, and into Easy Valley. We'll wait there for the others to catch up the next day.'

I looked at Bob. 'I'm in. What about you?'

'I don't know, Rich. I think I'll have to stay with the slower group for now.' His usual keenness seemed to have deserted him and an understandable caution had taken over. We talked about it and decided to split up for that night. Pete, although nominally partnered up with Lam, volunteered regardless; of all the people on the expedition he must have been finding it the hardest, for although not a loner, he hadn't managed to form a relationship with anyone and in the absence of a confidante was having to make decisions without the reassurance and support of a partner.

It was settled: Britt, Steve, Pete and I would wait in Easy Valley for the others. We would need to be in Easy Valley by two at the latest, and by far the best place to bivvy and rendezvous would be a prominent boulder I'd seen during my trip into the valley. Pleased that we now had some sort of plan, but worried that we were twenty-four hours behind schedule, we returned to our rooms for what was to be our last night in a bed for some time.

CHAPTER 5

Up (and down)

I was woken at half past three by the sound of bleeping from my wrist. Kevin obviously hadn't woken on time and I thought I'd better go and see if they were all asleep before Neill realised, but I was too late; he had already kicked them into action verbally. I was glad I hadn't been in their shoes – they had only been given the task in the first place because they'd screwed up and had now compounded the original transgression. I wondered how it had affected Neill's mood.

Bob and I had our usual tedious breakfast of oats and apple flakes and were raring to go. I was looking forward to the summit and the knowledge that there would be no more uphill involved. I'd fixed my head torch and was hanging around impatiently when Pete asked me to help look for one of his chest straps that had gone AWOL. We searched unsuccessfully as the rest trooped slowly out of the hut, and stayed on for ten minutes but still didn't find it. Pete resigned himself to doing without it and we set off to catch up with the others at as fast a pace as we could muster under the weight of our rucksacks and the oppressive darkness, dodging in and out of the lines of tourists struggling up to the summit for sunrise. After only five minutes of walking we bumped into the back of our party and, once within talking distance, asked Bob how it was going.

'OK, but we're moving ridiculously slowly.' The three of us sat on one of the large steps and waited for the others to gain some distance on us, turning our torches out to save on the batteries. Darkness engulfed us, and we sat for ten minutes in an eerie silence, interrupted only by the odd panting tourist and their guides.

We set off again. Even with a half load Bob was still struggling to keep up with us, but a few minutes later we had stopped again behind the rest of the group and Bob decided to carry on with the main party. Pete and I, frustrated by all the stopping and starting, were keen to push on at our own pace and find a rhythm, but were prevented from doing so by Neill's abrupt decision that the whole party should number off and adopt an 'in file' patrol formation. Stuck at the back, we decided to let the main group move on ahead of us and sat in the darkness to discuss the events of the last few days. Even with full loads one part of the expedition was moving considerably faster than the other, a state of affairs that Neill could have been putting to good use by allowing an advance party to establish itself in the gully. However, there seemed little chance of that coming to pass in the immediate future, and we resigned ourselves to a slow and tedious slog up to Sayat Sayat. Another particularly annoying thing was the way Neill had made us all get up early to reach the summit, when we could have had an extra two and a half hours in bed, carried all our kit to Sayat Sayat and still reached the top for sunrise before they did. Slightly depressed by the state of things, we shouldered our rucksacks again and within a few minutes caught up with the others at the foot of the roped section.

Neill spoke: 'Where the bloody hell have you two been?' A feeling of *déjà vu* overcame me; the same words that he had used outside the lower hut two days before when we had gone to look for him. His belief in confrontation rather than consensus reminded me of Margaret Thatcher. I looked him in the eye, making no attempt to adjust my head torch, and his illuminated face stood out in the darkness.

Any comment would have been pointless, merely resulting in Pete and me being dragged into yet another futile argument, and we stayed silent until Britt piped up: 'Sir, all the people carrying full loads will meet you at Sayat Sayat.' It was a flat, assertive statement of fact, not a request; Neill agreed without question, and before he could change his mind, we set off at a hard pace to put some distance between the two groups. We soon arrived at Sayat Sayat, dumped our cumbersome rucksacks in a small clump of bushes behind one of the huts, sorted a few essentials into our day sacks and waited for the others.

As soon as we heard them coming, Britt shouted down a welcome: 'See you at the top.' With no further encouragement needed we set out to put some distance between us again, along an almost flat section of the path which, even in the darkness, was well defined. Moving without the weight of our big rucksacks was a pleasure, and we made good time, overtaking tourists of all shapes, sizes and colours, all of them *en route* to the summit, some looking distinctly ill while others enjoyed the exercise and the cold night air. At one point I noticed to my left a small puddle, frozen over by the altitude and lack of cloud cover, and was surprised to discover on standing on it that it seemed to be very solid. Reverting to my childhood, I jumped up and down several times in an unsuccessful attempt to break the ice and then rejoined the path, increasing my pace to catch up with the others and wondering what the temperature was. My pertex-lined fleece was working well, but I wondered how long it would keep me warm if I stopped exercising.

The path took a sharp turn upwards but we maintained our pace, breathing heavily in the thin air as we passed more tourists. The steep section was short-lived, and we continued over flat, bare rock; above and below us all that was visible was a string of torch lights marking the way. The mood lightened as we gained height, but the flat and meandering path seemed to be considerably longer than I had anticipated, and I asked Steve how much further we had to go.

'We've got ages yet.' His Geordie accent seemed strangely out of place, and I was wondering whether altitude affects the vocal chords when a voice came out of the darkness behind us. I turned to see the familiar face of David Powell.

'Hi guys.'

'Morning, Dave. Where's all your crew?'

'They're up on top. I've got a small hut just the other side of the summit. What are the others doing?' I was puzzled by his question.

'We're going to the top for sunrise, the rest will join us there. Why?'

'They've still got their rucksacks with them.' We continued walking as we spoke.

'That's right – they're leaving them at Sayat Sayat, with ours.'

'Well, when I passed them they were well past Sayat Sayat, and still had their rucksacks on.' I stopped walking.

'Did they? Hey, Britt. Wait there a minute.' We caught him up. 'Have a listen to this.' David told Britt what he had just told me; Britt just shrugged his shoulders, not even surprised by Neill's apparent change of plan, and promptly started walking again. The rest of us did some formation shrugging and followed him. David, anxious to get back to his group, bade us goodbye and disappeared into the darkness at what seemed an impossible pace.

The path was starting to become monotonous, the darkness

preventing any view of the spectacular scenery I suspected was around me. Our head torches illuminated only the smooth rock below our feet and as the cold air started to bite though my fleece, I thought of the Hong Kong lads, who had no fleeces. Steve and I stopped to take on some water and chocolate, hoping the extra calories would help warm us. Steve rummaged in his day sack.

'All set?' I asked.

'Bollocks. I'm not going any further. I went to the top yesterday.' He pulled out a sleeping bag, crawled inside and snuggled down. He was not alone in his attitude; despondency was slowly beginning to affect everyone.

'We'll pick you up on the way back.'

'Don't fucking bother, just leave me here. It's too early for all this shit!' He made a final adjustment to his bivvy and closed his eyes. I set off again – he might have been to the top but I hadn't.

The path had deteriorated into large blocks and in places I had to use my hands to pull myself up. I could see torches all over the place; on such steep ground and with the awesome cliffs I'd seen yesterday somewhere in the darkness I wondered about the wisdom of straying from the path, but everyone seemed happy and we made steady progress.

Without warning, I topped out at 13,455 feet. On tourist peaks the world over, the top has to be marked with something just in case anybody misses it, or the views and sense of achievement are not enough. In this case it was a sign, held in place by steel ropes. In front of me was a wire fence; I was unsure whether it marked steep ground, or a profound lack of ground, dropping away into the depths of the gully thousands of feet below us. I'd have to wait for the sun to come up before answering that question and consulted my watch. Forty-five minutes to wait; the cold was beginning to bite and I pulled my fleece around my body, trying to conserve heat. Small furry things ran around our feet – the ubiquitous Kinabalu rats, undeterred by either the time of day, the cold, or the altitude from their ceaseless quest for a free meal.

'I'm bloody freezing!' I said out loud in a vain attempt to warm up, and went to sit in a hollow out of the wind, where I was soon joined by some other people. I was unsure if they too wanted to get out of the wind, or whether they were trying to escape the now considerable overcrowding on the summit, and wondered if anyone else appreciated the irony – one of the prime reasons for climbing is to experience the solitude of the mountains.

I shivered, willing the sun to rise faster. There was the odd flash of a camera and excited shouts came from people reaching the top. I wondered how far behind the other party was. The sun peeped out above the eastern horizon. There were more flashing cameras and I posed for a photo next to the summit sign with the dark red of the sky behind me. There was still no sign of the others and I wondered if their slow progress would cause Neill to fly off the handle again.

'Come on, sun.' I whispered encouragement to hurry it into the sky. At last the other group arrived, out of breath and, despite the exercise, feeling the cold every bit as much as the rest of us. The sunrise wasn't particularly spectacular and we who had been standing around wanted to get going, but Neill wanted to have an expedition photo at the summit, so we all waited until the sun was high enough, pressed an Australian tourist into the role of official photographer and posed next to the sign. Formalities over we set off back down to Sayat Sayat, gradually warming up as the sun rose in the sky, revealing the expected spectacular views. Coming down off the summit was difficult initially, due to the sheer number of people trying to move simultaneously down steep, boulder-strewn ground, but by jumping across the boulders we quickly lost height and soon found ourselves back on the path. My thoughts turned to the next task in hand, that of setting up an exposed abseil. If Neill wanted a *really* exposed one, the best place would be over the edge of the Cauldron and down into the very start of Low's Gully. This was not the most practical of ideas; we had neither the time nor the four thousand feet of rope that would be necessary. I decided to use the slabby bit of rock to the left of the gap: I would be able to solo up to fix the belays, and could also move easily alongside the Hong Kong lads to give them pointers on technique. It wouldn't be very exposed, but it was all that was safely and easily available, and there would be more than enough exposure on the other side of the mountain when we eventually got there.

As we made our way down, I kept an eye out for the rear party's rucksacks, trying to work out where they might have left them; they hadn't had them at the summit but had been wearing them when David saw them at Sayat Sayat.

The party adopted its usual formation with our little group out in front, and we reached Sayat Sayat within an hour of leaving the summit. The sun was by now doing its best to bake everything in sight so we loosened our warm clothing in fear of overheating and tried not to expose ourselves too much to the sun's powerful rays. The rucksacks lay as we had hidden them in the bushes; I sorted out some ropes and gear and walked the short distance to Cauldron Gap. The slabby cliff was much as I remembered it – not particularly steep and with a large flat area at the bottom where the party could mill around in safety when not engaged in abseiling. I carried on up towards the gap in search of a suitable abseil point, and before long came to a large ledge furnished with good belays and in view of the rest area. I set up the abseil and lowered myself down using the rope as a handrail. I wasn't sure how Neill would react to my choice of site, given its lack of exposure, but the deed was done and I descended back to Sayat Sayat to join Britt, Steve and Pete. I laid my Karrimat out in the shade of one of the twisted thorn bushes and nodded off to sleep in the heat of the morning sun.

Some time later I heard voices and, expecting to see the rear group arriving, left my bush, only to find Britt and Steve discussing where the other group had got to. It was 10.30 and there was no sign of them.

'We got here at 8.30. It only took us an hour to get back. No way is it going to take them more than two hours. It's downhill.' I had the feeling I'd just repeated what Britt and Steve had been discussing. 'I'm off to sleep. Wake me if they bother to turn up.'

I returned to my personal bush. The sun was nearly overhead, beating down hard. I closed my eyes and drifted off into the vertical world of my dreams, now inhabited by enormous granite spires, merely a sign of my dedication to climbing, although I suppose Freud might have interpreted it differently. When I woke again at 12.30 the sun was past its highest point and there was still no sign of the rear group. Munching on a fruit biscuit, I toyed with the idea of going back up the mountain to look for them, but my head felt heavy and it was far too hot to move. I dozed off, to be woken again by excited shouting.

'Get out the flysheet.'

'Get them under the shade.'

'Someone break out the water.'

'Where's Mayfield?' My bush was twenty yards away from the

main party and I hadn't been spotted yet. I looked over to see Britt, Steve and Pete busy putting up one of the flysheets, and I guzzled half a pint of warm water in an attempt to clear my woolly, dehydrated head. I saw Britt point in my general direction and Neill looking for me. I wriggled out from under the bush, wondering how on earth it had taken the rear group five hours to get here, and turned to look eastwards; despite the time (1.30) there didn't seem to be any serious build-up of cloud yet. I turned back to see Neill striding purposefully towards me, wearing a straw hat held in place by a check shirt wrapped around it; he looked like a bizarre cross between the Elephant Man and Yasser Arafat, but there was still a Thatcheresque air about him and I had to force myself not to smile at the thought that one man was reminding me simultaneously of three such disparate characters.

'Had a good morning, Corporal Mayfield?' I rubbed the sleep from my eyes and tried to focus on the strange sight in front of me.

'I've been asleep.'

'Where's this exposed abseil then?'

'It's half one. We ought to get moving before the weather breaks.' I was hoping that he might suggest skipping the abseil.

'Yes, but only after the Hong Kong lads have gone through some more rope work, they need it. I want you to be happy with their ability.' It wasn't their ability that was troubling me, it was his. I pointed to where the rope hung down and turned to look again at the weather. Light, wispy clouds had started to accumulate lower down; not, in themselves, a problem but a worrying indicator of what was to come.

I packed my bag and walked over to join the rest. Chow and Lam were lying under the flysheet, still in their green Gore-Tex waterproofs, being force-fed with water. I studied them for a few seconds and turned to Ron, who was drinking from an almost empty water container: 'What's up with them?'

'Oh, they're just a bit tired.'

'Looks like exhaustion and the effects of heat and dehydration to me. Have they not been drinking?'

'Yes, but they only had one litre of water with them.' He didn't seem bothered that these men had come close to being very seriously ill.

'Where have you been? We've been waiting down here since half eight.'

'We've been looking around the summit area. You should have come with us. Spectacular views.'

Yet again, I couldn't believe what I was hearing; we were now thirty-six hours behind schedule, already short of food, and they had gone sightseeing, wasting the whole morning and picking up two casualties into the bargain. There was nothing to be said and I quickly put my harness on. 'I'll wait for everyone at the bottom of the abseil.'

Not waiting for a reply, I walked off in the direction of the gap, but turned when Neill spoke: 'Corporal Mayfield. Have your group done this?' They hadn't. I looked at Britt, sitting behind Neill, and he gave a short, frantic nod of his head.

'Yes, no problem there.' As I moved slowly uphill I heard Neill order someone from the front group to give their water to Kevin. We would not be able to re-supply until we reached water on the other side, which because of the delay would be at least tomorrow; they were going back to the hut tonight and would be able to replenish their supplies there, while we might be left short. I found a smooth flat rock, made myself comfortable and waited. Bob, keen as ever, was the first one up. He offered me his ascenders.

'Set them up yourself, Bob.'

He did so without hesitation and was ready to climb before me. I placed my shunt on the rope above his Crolls and we set off up the slab. Bob climbed smoothly and we quickly covered the hundred and fifty feet to the belay, where he changed over to a figure of eight and slid off to the bottom. Next was Kevin, who had learned fast and didn't need any prompting, but he wasn't concentrating, instead persistently asking me to excuse not only Chow but all three of them from the expedition. I repeated that there was nothing I could do, that he'd have to talk to the Colonel himself, and saw a different side of this normally easygoing Corporal as he insisted that I fight his corner.

I tried again to explain to him: 'He knows how I feel about taking you, and he's not taken a blind bit of notice of me so far. You're going to have to talk to him.' Kevin was not happy with my answer, but there was nothing more I could say.

By the time Chow and Lam were waiting at the bottom Ron had moved up the broken path to watch them working; they ascended and descended without undue difficulty, but I couldn't help wondering what would have happened if I had set up a really exposed line.

Ron seemed hesitant at first and I wondered if his experience, which as far as I knew consisted solely of our two training days and the top roping and abseiling course he'd been on with Neill, was insufficient to give him confidence, but his first comment showed me that he had done a bit of homework.

'The manufacturers recommend that a shunt should not be used on 9mm ropes.'

'So don't use it, Ron!'

'You shouldn't be using yours either.'

Who rattled his cage? This was the man without an opinion. However, he was actually right, but I pointed out that it was common practice among climbers to use it on 9mm ropes, and that despite the manufacturer's recommendations I had never heard of anyone having any problems. He clipped on his shunt and started ascending.

Last in line was Neill; like everybody else, he offered me his ascender and, as I had with the others, I suggested that he do it himself. While he was setting it up I noticed something odd about his harness. The main buckle on the belt was correctly fastened, but his leg loops were twisted inside out so that one of the buckles was resting in his groin – not dangerous, but uncomfortable whenever he sat back and put any weight on it. I was reluctant to tell him as I was unsure what his reaction might be, and for a few moments the thought of his discomfort gave me a little stab of pleasure, which soon gave way to the depressing realisation that I was behaving in a rather petty manner.

He arrived at the belay red-faced and uncomfortable, but I still refrained from telling him about his leg loops as he had shown no signs recently of taking advice from anyone. He abseiled down and, once he had reached the bottom, I stripped the belay and soloed down.

I checked my watch: 3.30p.m. – only three hours of light left. I coiled the rope quickly and ran down towards the rucksacks. Easy Valley Col was still clear, but the clouds were building up rapidly, and I was packing the kit as quickly as possible when Neill came over.

'I want you to met us at the col at 1400 hours tomorrow.' I wondered about his choice of time – surely it wouldn't take more than two or three hours at most to get there from Sayat Sayat, but I was in too much of a hurry to raise any questions.

As the other six walked off towards the path and the relative comfort of water on tap at the hut, we headed uphill fully laden, picked up the line of cairns and started following them around the base of the rhino horn. Britt, still suffering from headaches, was slowing fast, and by the time we reached the col he was lagging behind by some distance. I wondered if the effects of sleeping in the sun for so long while waiting for the others had aggravated the effects of altitude; I remembered feeling very thirsty when I woke and thought that perhaps he hadn't drunk enough water. We decided to slow down as he was one of the strongest team members and to lose him to sunstroke or heat exhaustion would be a major problem.

Hardly stopping at the high point of the col, we carried on down the initial steep section, intent on clearing it by dusk so that at least we could have a comfortable night. Pete was walking some way off to my left and I shouted across that there was the edge of a large cliff over there; he waved a hand and altered his course, but remained some distance away from the rest of us. He was probably feeling the frustration of the last few days as well as worrying about what was ahead, and was taking advantage of the solitude to clear his mind.

Thankful that our luck had held out and the cloud hadn't come down while we were at the col, we stopped to wait for Britt, now some way behind again and becoming increasingly grumpy at our shouts of encouragement. Realising that by the time Britt reached us it would be nearly seven in the evening and darkness would soon engulf us, we found a relatively flat area close to the sound of water to settle down for the night. I grabbed the flattest bit and laid out my bivvy bag. Helping Pete move some large stones increased the space. Steve, anxious that Britt still hadn't arrived, was about to go and help, when Britt stumbled around the boulders that formed the outer edges of the site. Steve took charge of him and the immediate crisis was over. I turned my attention to the water situation. Neill's orders, leaving us short of water while the other half of the party had it on tap at the huts, angered us all. We were all sick of having to carry the excess kit, and giving away our food and now our water had served only to aggravate our mood. I left the bivvy site in search of water and some solitude.

I followed my ears, wearing my head torch but walking by the light of the ever brightening stars. For the time being the weather seemed to be smiling on us. Fifty yards on I came to a dense patch of vegetation, and cutting a path with a parang, I arrived at the foot of a cliff face several hundred feet high. The water I had heard sounded like a small stream but in reality it was only a few drops dripping down from the rocks high above, the noise amplified by the closeness of the walls. I placed as many containers as I could and a plastic bag to try and collect as much water as possible, but we would have to find a more suitable water source tomorrow.

I returned to the bivvy site, watching the stars, and realised I should have looked into the different star formations this far south – I didn't recognise anything. I checked my altimeter: 500 feet below the col, which meant another thousand to go tomorrow to my low point, but there was no water there either, only dense jungle about three or four hundred yards wide. There was bound to be water further down; the vegetation and top soil would soak up any rain and release it slowly, I hoped. Before long we were all asleep.

I awoke early the next morning. Although the valley was light the sun still had a long way to go before there was any risk of the hazards of yesterday. Reluctant to leave the warm confines of my sleeping bag and venture into the cold morning air, I admired our bedroom. Impressive cliffs: the one with the water dripping down it was larger than I had at first thought last night – I estimated at least 2,000 feet and totally sheer apart from the odd overhang. These enormous cliffs weren't even on the map, and I wondered what other surprises might lie ahead, shifting uncomfortably in my bag at the thought.

'Is anyone awake?' I asked out loud to anyone listening.

'Yes,' came back three answers. They were all doing the same as me. There was no sense of urgency, as the others were going to have to catch us up before we could make any real progress.

'I think we should carry on to try and find water – I've only got enough for half a day.' Britt was right.

'I'll go and check the containers I put out last night.' The time had come to brave the cool air. The containers were full, enough water for all our breakfasts, and I returned to the sound of stoves roaring into life. My watch told me it was seven in the morning, and feeling the cold through my fleece I wondered what time the sun might get down here.

With breakfast finished, and what spare water we had left carefully stored away, we packed up and headed off down the path I had followed on my last visit. Britt was feeling a lot stronger and put it down to the loss of altitude. We made good time and before long we arrived at my low point, the steep ground into the jungle, where we had the first rest of the day. There was still no sense of urgency as there was plenty of time before I had to be back at the col to guide the others down to our bivvy site.

We found a way down into the jungle and Britt, regaining his sense of humour, left a note at the top for the others written on an old compo packet. This part of the path had been marked by sticks stripped of their bark, and was well worn, but it hadn't been cleared for the passage of people with such large rucksacks. Britt, well prepared by virtue of his jungle training, produced what looked like a canoe saw and promptly started felling trees. We dropped our rucksacks and took it in turns to clear a path, gaining a hundred yards before we came to a clearing. Returning to the rucksacks, everyone took the chance to add comments to Britt's note, and we set off down the newly cleared section of path; even though we had cleared it well, it was still hard going. My rucksack was far too high and snagged on branches, and the others, with the added width of side pockets, found the going even harder. After a long struggle we emerged into the clearing, slightly bloodied and panting, and had a short rest before round two. The ground seemed to be getting steeper and we could see from our vantage point that off to our left the ground fell away into the gully; in places the jungle spilled over the edge into oblivion and we decided to stick as far as we could to the right.

Pete spied another white stick, but this time we had to pass the rucksacks down in a line over a short drop of fifteen feet broken by two ledges to stand on. From this point the path seemed to follow a stream bed, which was mostly clear, with the occasional fallen tree providing interesting and strenuous challenges. The sun finally came into view and the temperature soared; in the clearings the heat was overpowering and we kept in the shade as much as possible. This little patch of jungle was proving to be a pain in the neck. After a further hour of struggling, the nature of the vegetation changed and I noticed, climbing over roots (or were they branches?) that the ground seemed to have gone.

'Britt, I'm not happy with this. Did you see how close part of this came to the edge?' Everyone stopped, dropping their rucksacks to rest on the branches.

'Yes, we need a vantage point.' We looked around us. It was

impossible to see further than a few feet, and looking down, trying to see the ground, I guessed it must be ten or twenty feet below us, if you could call that pile of rotting debris ground. I started to feel slightly claustrophobic. Off to my right was what appeared to be a boulder, the top of which might provide our vantage point and some open space. Taking the parang I cut my way through the vegetation, which fought back with some vicious thorns until, by forcing myself through the smallest of gaps in the tangled mass, I arrived at the granite wall of the boulder. There was no obvious way up, so I started to climb a tree resting against the boulder, and after a twenty-minute struggle I found the top – large, flat and spacious after the solid wall of plant life below me.

I viewed the top of the canopy to see how much progress we'd made – not much, about half-way there. To my right and just on the edge of the jungle was a very large and obvious boulder I remembered seeing from further up; it would make a good place to bivvy, and being so obvious from above would also provide a good rendezvous. Further over to the right, less than one hundred yards away, was the gully. If we walked or climbed in that direction we wouldn't know that we'd gone over the edge until we looked down.

The disembodied voice of Steve drifted up to me: 'What can you see?'

'Everything!'

'How close are we to the edge?' Pete had had the same thought as me.

'Hundred yards or so.' I looked towards the boulder again. 'I can see a large boulder off to the right. I think we'll head for that – it'll make for a good bivvy.'

'Rich, what about your RV with the others, have you seen the time?' Britt this time. It was midday; if I turned back now I'd be able to make the RV, but it wasn't safe to leave the others in here.

'Yes, I'll have to miss that. It's not too bad; they'll be able to see us from just below the col, and besides the path's very clear, especially after we enlarged it so much.' I wasn't overly concerned for the rear group at this point; they couldn't get themselves into any serious situations and I would be more use here, particularly with us blundering around in thick jungle so close to the edge of the gully. 'I'll be back with you in a minute.' Twenty minutes later I squeezed my way through to the others.

'Don't like this. It's so thick you can hardly move.' Half an hour on, bewildered, and grazed in several places, we stumbled out onto a slimy slab fifty yards from the edge with a massive sigh of relief.

'Am I glad that's over.' I hadn't enjoyed my first taste of jungle. With great care we slipped and slid over to the large boulder, and found to our relief a small stream running either side of it. Britt organised things in characteristically blunt style.

'Right. Drinking here. Shitting and pissing down there by that tree, and washing there.' He pointed to a spot just down from the drinking area. Did he know something we didn't? It was probably his jungle training coming into play again. We set up bivvies and were settled into our camp routine by 2p.m., needing only something to make our site really visible to the rear group.

'Britt, have you got that small air panel?'

'I've got some thing better than that. I found it amongst the crap that Ron gave to Dave Powell to take down for him.' With that he produced a five-foot-square air panel, metallic on one side and orange on the other. 'He wasn't going to take it, so I said I'd have it.' He spread it out on the part of our boulder that conveniently faced up towards the col. 'If they don't see that they're not in the same valley as us.' This was the contingency in case of missing the RV – to find a prominent rock and make ourselves visible.

'Do you think the others will catch us up today?'

I looked up to the col. 'They should be able to see us now.' I strained my eyes trying to see into the distance.

Steve was expecting a negative reply to his question. 'I can't see them.' The resigned tone in his voice was all too apparent.

'Maybe you're right.' I paused. 'They should be able to make it down, though.'

By four in the afternoon the sun had disappeared behind the towering west flank of Easy Valley and there was still no sign of the other group. We made the decision to wait there until tomorrow morning, as any attempt to go back would mean having to negotiate the jungle section in the dark – not too hard now that we knew the way through, but something that no one fancied.

The mood was one of quiet expectancy, but we were still unsure of what lay ahead, and the apparent lack of level ground in front of us was starting to play on my mind. Having a water supply helped to relieve some of the tension of the immediate situation, however, and if the others caught us up tomorrow, preferably first thing, things would improve markedly.

With the sun gone the temperature fell rapidly, and wearing our fleeces we climbed into our sleeping bags, discussing yet again where the others might be. They should have had no problem meeting up with us – we were less than a day's walk from the huts and they'd had the benefit of only having to carry half loads for part of the trip. I tried to assess the amount of time it had taken us to get here with full kit: one and a half hours to Sayat Sayat, an hour to the col, one and a half from there to our last bivvy. An hour to the jungle and, after we had cut the path, forty-five minutes to get through that to our present position; rounded up, a total of five hours – surely, given a whole day, they should have been in sight by now. Although I'd missed the RV they should have been able to find the way down Easy Valley as the path was obvious and Neill knew that section from his last expedition. Why hadn't we seen them above us? Were they in the valley or not? All would, no doubt, become apparent tomorrow.

After two shortish days no one was tired and we stayed up talking about nothing in particular and everything in general. I mentioned that all the stars were in the wrong place, and though we spent some time examining the sky, no one else could recognise any constellations, either. Several hours and umpteen alphabet games later I drifted off to sleep with an image of Dennis the Menace, constructed from the shadows of the overhangs above, indelibly imprinted on my mind.

When I woke the next morning I half expected to see Neill's bunch of merry men descending into the jungle section. From my bivvy I could see most of the way up the valley, but in the still dim light there was no sign of movement; looking down into the gully, a sea of cloud stretched, smooth and unblemished, as far as the eye could see. With no reason to move and the cold morning air outside my bivvy I dozed until 8.30, when the others started to stir. Remaining in my sleeping bag I cooked and ate my breakfast, keeping a watchful eye on the valley above for signs of the rear group.

Looking around, I began to recognise features that Neill had pointed out during the slide show back at the TA centre in Plymouth: on the edge of the hanging valley was the very obvious 'Lone Tree', and just before that I could see 'House Boulder', the place where

Steve Pinfield and Rob New had spent their first night on their ill-fated expedition in 1991. Beyond that was still a mystery to me; even from my vantage point on top it was impossible to see the nature of the access to the gully. I decided to go on a recce over to Lone Tree, from where I should be able to see the access into the gully floor, and by the time I returned the others should have arrived. I might even be able to set up the two abseils – if, that is, there *were* only two.

'Who wants to come on a recce into the gully with me?' I spoke loudly, so that everyone could hear, but nobody replied, preferring instead to examine their fingernails or study the sky; anything but look in my direction and commit themselves to getting out of their sleeping bags.

I tried appealing to their consciences: 'Come on, I don't want to have to go alone.' I made a last attempt to engender some feelings of guilt: 'Looks like I'll be going alone then.' That didn't work either and I braved the cold to pack my day sack, resigned to another solo reconnaissance.

'Who wants to give me their rope? I'll see if I can set up the two abseils.' It was as if I had shorted a hundred thousand volts across their terminals; an unseemly scrabble ensued to be the first out with a rope and thereby rid the lucky victor of a few extra pounds to carry. A grinning Britt handed over his rope, and after a short briefing on my plan I started out. I could see only as far as Lone Tree, 200 yards at most, and the ground looked tricky, but not too dangerous. It was what lay beyond that concerned me; if I could find and set up the descent, then when the others finally showed up we would be able to move that much faster and perhaps claw back some of the two and a half days we'd lost.

I descended from our boulder, crossed the stream and moved on towards my target across the slab, which was coated with a thin layer of green slime and demanded careful footwork. With the bivvy site to my back the ground dropped away steeply to my left, and I felt exposed and not a little lonely, apprehensive as to what lay down there.

The damp section behind, the slabs changed in character, steepening and forming a series of broken corners five or six feet in height; climbing over these corners was unnerving as the granite, although rough to the touch, offered little in the way of handholds to pull on or to reassure an increasingly timid Mayfield. To my right was some vegetation, not as thick as before, but I wasn't prepared to venture in there alone. I reached the comparative safety of House Boulder and, a few yards later, Lone Tree; from this position the ground dropped away on the left and in front for several thousand feet to the gully floor. Over to the right, on the planned access route, the ground dropped almost vertically for 150 feet and levelled out into another thick patch of the green stuff, which ran for a further few hundred yards to some large sweeping slabs that ended in a sharply defined edge and reminded me of a giant ice-cream bowl with half the contents scooped out. Looking back, I was still able to see the bivvy site above me, but there were no shouts that the others had arrived or even been sighted.

I traversed around the top of a small scoop to take a closer look at the way down the first steep section. The canopy at the bottom looked every bit as dense as the previous section of jungle that had spooked us all, and although the ground above was passable with great care, the risk of someone falling would be greatly increased with our large rucksacks, so an abseil was the order of the day. At the head of the scoop was a short face with some solid spikes of rock, over which I placed two eight-foot slings. Butterflies assailed me as I prepared for my first abseil into the unknown.

Come on rope don't tangle. Clip in. Did you tie a knot in the end? Yes. Check those belays again. Don't throw yourself off with the rope. Did you clip in yes you know you did. Now drop nicely rope and don't get caught up in the trees. Good. Time to go I suppose. No! Check the belays again stop prevaricating you've checked everything at least three times just get on with it!

Having given myself the ritual, staccato talking-to that accompanies the preparation for any abseil, I lowered myself gingerly over the edge. Ten feet down I began to relax and take in my surroundings; the rock was solid, handsome granite and in other circumstances would no doubt offer some good climbing, but at the moment I was more concerned with getting through the approaching canopy. I reached it and lowered myself through the initial greenery only to be faced with thick branches barring my way, necessitating a bit of aggression to punch a hole big enough to get down.

Standing on what passed for the jungle floor I peered into the emerald depths, trying to pick out a viable route, until a loud commotion broke out in the undergrowth nearby; it was probably some fascinating example of the Kinabalu fauna, but any aspirations

I might have had to being David Attenborough deserted me as visions of tigers and water buffaloes sprang to mind and sent me prussiking back up the ropes to the open hillside. There aren't any tigers in Sabah, of course, and as far as I knew, water buffaloes weren't particularly well versed in the art of abseiling, but whatever it was had sounded large and powerful enough to put me off the idea of solo exploration for the day.

I assumed that this had been the first of New's abseils, and although I had been unable to see any more ground, my suspicions of there being several large abseils increased; if that was indeed the case then our retreat in an emergency would be blocked and we'd be totally committed to the gully. When I got back to the others I'd voice my fears to Neill – not that I felt he'd listen, but as an exercise in covering myself if anything did happen. Rounding House Boulder, I set off back to our bivvy site. From this lower point I couldn't see anyone unless they stood up, but I was sure the rear group would have finally caught us up. Having found the easiest way through the small corners I made good time, and jumped up on top of the bivvy boulder to be confronted by the same three faces I'd left earlier, trying in vain to shelter from the blistering heat.

'Where are the others?'

'Don't know, we saw someone on the other side of the jungle a while ago, but they made no attempt to come through and join us.' Steve's look of despondency said it all. I headed for the small tree over which Britt had draped his flysheet to provide additional shade. We briefly entertained the idea of going back to see what was holding the others up, but Britt, as usual, summed up everyone's feelings with a flat statement that he wasn't going to carry their rucksacks again and promptly went back to sleep. After replenishing my water bottles, I squashed into Britt's small patch of shade; acutely aware of the dangers of falling asleep in the sun I set my alarm to wake me every hour so that I could have a drink and check that I was still in the shade, and nodded off.

The day passed slowly and then Pete's voice woke us: 'There they are, look.' Three figures on the middle horizon.

'That's got to be them, at last.' I was eager to find out what had delayed them so much; we heard shouting, but due to the acoustics of the valley it was indecipherable. We shouted back, but had to resign our-selves to the fact that communications were impossible and that we'd just have to wait.

'Should be with us in half an hour.'

There was a distinct lightening of the atmosphere, but our optimism proved to be unfounded when, after only a few minutes, we saw two of them retracing their steps back up the hill. I voiced my disbelief as we all stood and watched.

'Now what are they doing?'

'Are they wearing rucksacks?' Steve with his sharp eyesight had spotted it first; they must have merely been on a recce. My heart sank and I resigned myself to another night on Alphabet Rock.

We lapsed into our routine of the last two nights and were discussing what the others were up to, when we heard a distant but audible cry: 'Rich!'

'Who said that?' I turned to look in the general direction from which the cry had come. The others were unsure if they'd heard anything at all.

'Riiich!' the cry came again, drawn out and plaintive.

'That's Bob! Listen.' This time everyone had heard it. We all stood up and strained to see into the dense jungle before us.

'Over here, Bob.' Relief flooded over me at the realisation that at last my partner and I would meet up, and the mood on Alphabet Rock lightened and relaxed at the thought that at least we would have some idea of what was going on.

'Riiiichh!'

'Yes, over here Bob!' I replied, while the others, laughing and joking, attempted to help.

'Bob, shake a bush.' The vegetation in Bob's area shook.

'We can see you now, keep coming.'

'Bob, keep shaking the bushes. There are some big drops in there.' I was concerned for their safety.

'OK.' His voice was still muffled by the jungle, but he sounded closer. I reduced the volume as they approached and we started to rearrange the top of our rock to make space for their impending arrival.

Another cry came and I glanced over to the shaking jungle. My throat was becoming sore from all the shouting and I didn't answer. We all knew what that patch of jungle was like – we'd done it when we cut the path, and knowing we didn't have to go back through, we all took great delight in Bob's obvious confusion. However, his next cry had an edge of panic.

'It's not like Bob to panic.'

'Hat!' Britt voiced his opinion, as loudly as he could.

'Riiicccchhhhh!' came Bob's reply.

I turned to the others: 'Do you think he's by himself?'

'We didn't see all of them turn around, did we?' Pete said, echoing some of my concern.

'He might be,' Steve said with a big grin on his face.

'Bob, are you alone?' I bellowed it out, more concerned about my partner's safety than any sore throat.

'Yes, Rich. Where are you ?'

'Bob, keep shaking the bushes! I'll put my boots on and be down there in five minutes.' I remembered my reluctance to go through that place by myself, my feelings of claustrophobia and the fear of walking over the edge of the gully. The joking taunts stopped.

'Rich, I've lost the path!'

'You're alright Bob, keep coming in that direction.' Boots on and parang in hand I climbed down from our boulder, jumped the stream and moved as fast as I dared over the steep, slippery ground. Britt guided me towards Bob from his vantage point on the boulder and we were soon reunited. Meeting up with Bob after what had seemed like a week brought a big soft grin to my face.

'You alright mate?'

'Fucking hell, Rich, I didn't like that!'

'Give us your rucksack. We're only a hundred yards away. Where are the others?'

'Make me a coffee and I'll tell you.' I could hardly contain my curiosity as we jumped back over the stream and climbed Alphabet Rock to join the permanent residents.

'Where have you been? Where are the others?' Bob laid his bivvy out next to mine, I started to make his coffee and we made ourselves comfortable, ready to listen to his story.

CHAPTER 6

Bob's story

I'd been following the Grand Old Duke of York for the last three days. He was 9,995 men short of the full complement, of course, but I couldn't help laughing when I thought of that old song, especially as the Colonel was from York; it was definitely a case of up to the top of the hill and down again – several times over. However, things had started to go awry earlier than that – I was worried from the moment we got to the Sayat Sayat huts during the initial walk up to the summit. The plan had been to dump the half loads we were carrying in the vicinity of Sayat Sayat (12,000 feet) and then proceed to the summit at 13,455 feet, where we would join the four lads in the front group, who would have dumped their full loads at Sayat Sayat. It didn't work out that way. We plodded past the huts, the Colonel showing no signs of calling a halt, and I began to wonder what was going on. I ran over in my head what he had told us the evening before, just in case I'd made a mistake.

'We will all go to Sayat Sayat as a group, place our kit to one side of the track and then carry on up to the summit. No need to carry our kit all the way to the top, as we've got to come back down that way to pick up the trail that goes over to Easy Valley.' I couldn't have mistaken such a simple plan.

'Excuse me, boss – weren't we going to dump our kit here, with the others'?'

'Oh, we're alright. Do us good to have the extra exercise.' I shrugged my shoulders and carried on, figuring that it must be some sort of test to see how fit we were. Just before the summit, at about 13,100 feet, we stopped and dumped the kit a little way off the track. By that time Chow, who was one of the weaker members of the team, wasn't looking too good and Kevin and Lam didn't look very happy. I was glad that it was still early morning and that the sun hadn't risen – it was hard work anyway and I hated to think what it would have been like if the sun had been at its fiercest. I was still trying to work out the reason for the change of plan. There seemed to be no need for it, but he obviously had a good reason – I was just too stupid to see it, that was all.

We met the front group (minus Steve Page) and did the touristy thing – group photographs and videos of the sunrise – before they left to set up the practice abseil down at Cauldron Gap. The only people left on the summit were ourselves and a young German couple, about whom there was a general feeling that they'd gone to the summit for the benefit of their sex life. I was in favour of hiding behind a rock and videoing the whole show – it would have provided some amusement back at my unit – but I was voted down five to one.

I assumed that we'd follow the front group down, but the boss and Ron wanted to study the gully from our lofty vantage point and pick up some information about the terrain we were likely to encounter. I followed them out to a ledge above the gully. There was a sheer drop of 3,000 feet to the gully floor and a granite wall towered some 600 feet high to my left. The enormous drop gave me a really nasty turn – I was having trouble keeping my balance and realised that an adrenalin rush definitely comes out of one's bum, so I went back to join the Chinese.

Kevin, their senior NCO and spokesman, pulled me to one side and spoke to me in his broken English, asking me to try and get them off the expedition: 'Tell the Colonel, Bob, we not very happy. We not fit.' I looked over to Lam and Chow. It was a bit of an understatement – they all looked really down and very tired.

'If you don't want to go, you'll have to speak up and tell the Colonel yourselves.' I was trying to explain to Kevin that I didn't think the Colonel would listen to me; I'd already been told to wind my neck in at the O group when I suggested the restructuring of the expedition to take into account the differing abilities of expedition members. I'd been shot down in flames on that idea and if I now started to tell the boss that the Chinese didn't want to carry on I'd put my foot in it again. I told Kevin that he'd have to inform the Colonel to his face and that he'd have to be firm.

'Don't carry on if you feel so strongly about it, but you must tell him as soon as possible or we'll have gone too far to turn back.'

'No, Bob, you tell him. You a sergeant. He will listen to you.' He was correct in a way; under the usual military chain of command Kevin, if he had a problem, would bring it to me, and if I could not deal with it, I'd take it to the next rank in the chain of command. I might have been a senior NCO, but in the present circumstances, as far as technical qualifications were concerned, I was a novice just like Kevin, and I was also a guest on a Regular Army expedition. I did know, however, that half the battle is having men that want to be there, and that if they weren't motivated it was going to cause problems.

'Look, Kev, if you're going to see him, do it, but don't moan to me. I've already told him you don't want to go, we all know that. Just try to get through to him.' It was no use; I couldn't get through to him that the Colonel wasn't going to listen to me.

Eventually, photographs and sightseeing completed, we went our merry way back down the mountain to join the front group. On the way down, I thought over what Kevin had said and, as tactfully as I could, repeated it to the Colonel. His response was exactly as I thought it would be: 'Until they come to me in person they'll carry on.' Well, I thought, I've done my bit. I shrugged my shoulders again – a gesture that was going to become a little overused during the next few days, along with head scratching.

By the time we arrived at the abseil down at Cauldron Gap the Chinese were in a bad way, especially Chow, who was close to collapse again – no doubt the exercise of carrying his kit nearly all the way to the summit and back again had got to him – and we had to rig a shelter so they could get out of the sun. After an hour in the shade, drinking plenty of water, they perked up sufficiently for us all to have a go at the abseil that Rich had set up. Once that was completed we stashed our half loads by the track so that we could pick them up on the way past in the morning and set off for the Gunting Lagadan hut, leaving the four lads in the front group to continue to Easy Valley, where they would look for a water source. Rich was to rendezvous with us at the col above Easy Valley at midday the following day. The walk down to Panar Laban went quickly, and I arrived at the hut feeling very fit and well acclimatised.

Later that evening Ron asked me if I would go down to the lower hut to retrieve his video batteries, which were being recharged by two squaddies down there who had an electric socket in their room. I went down and introduced myself, and we started chatting about the expedition; I said that I'd take Ron's batteries back up, sort out my kit and return later on to buy them a beer. My real reason for returning was that I'd spotted a large box of rations in their room and hoped there might be a chance of acquiring some for the Chinese, as long as it wasn't going to cost me too many beers.

I returned wearing my 383 Commando T-shirt, bought three beers and joined the two lads in the corner of the bar. One of them pointed to the dagger on my shirt.

'Commando unit?'

'383 down in Plymouth. We're attached to 3 Commando Royal Marines.'

'You mean Logs Regiment?'

'Something like that. We're the TA equivalent.'

'You're a STAB!'

I didn't want to start an argument over the insult as I hadn't got their spare rations off them yet, so I did the next best thing: 'It's better than being an ARAB!' This was TA slang – arrogant regular army bastard – and it seemed to break the ice. I don't think I'd have got very far in any sort of serious argument, as they both looked extremely fit and capable, and I would probably have ended up having to have my teeth fixed again. They were at the Jungle Training School in Brunei and were occupying themselves during a leave period by climbing Kinabalu. I asked what unit they were from.

'Oh, we're just radio men.'

It didn't take me long to work out that they were 'sneaky beakies', or SAS, as they're more commonly known. After a few more beers I asked if they had any rations to spare and they gave me half a bin liner of Gurkha rations, expressing some surprise that we were short

'First time we've heard of the Royal Logistics Corps being short of food. I thought their new motto is "We sustain."' They started to ask me about the details of our expedition. Who was the leader? How many men? Were we jungle trained?

'We're going down the gully, not through the jungle.'

'I thought your escape route was to the east. We've seen most of that area from the summit. It's jungle. On both sides.'

The questions continued: What maps did we have? Well, we didn't have actual maps, just photocopies – the Colonel had the originals – and some aerial photos. They stared at me. I felt I had to defend the expedition.

'We'll be alright.'

'What radios you got?'

I was a bit embarrassed. 'They wouldn't work in the gully, it's too deep and narrow.'

'Flares?'

'We couldn't take them on the plane, and we couldn't get any out here.'

'Panels?'

'Yep. Got them.'

'Radio beacon? Weighs two pounds, sends out a signal if you get into trouble?'

'No.'

'I'll tell you now, Bob. I don't know you from Adam, I don't give a fuck whether you live or die, but I'm telling you, go to the Colonel and tell him you're ill. *Don't* go over the col, into a place where noone's ever been, without proper maps, without radios or flares.'

'I told you – we'll be alright.'

'In that case,' he said, 'I'll be reading about you in the papers.'

That really got up my nose. 'The only thing you'll be reading is about Bob Mann achieving a world first and you can post it on your fucking door. Thanks for the rations.' If only I had known how much I would have to eat my words later. I left and sat by a lamp post for a fag and a think, feeling, for the first time in ten years, like a Stupid Territorial Army Bastard. Why had I got so uptight with those two lads? Because I felt I had to defend the Colonel? Or was it because their words had more than a ring of truth about them? I ran over the events of the O group two nights before. What Rich had said to the boss was right – there was no way he could get nine non-climbers out of the gully – and if he had been more of a diplomat he might have got the Colonel to listen to him, but he was about as diplomatic as a nuclear weapon. I wished Paul Hughes was here to give me some advice. I really needed someone to talk to. Finishing my cigarette, I headed uphill, pausing only to wonder how the hell that lamp post had got up there.

Back at the upper hut, their gift of food turned out to be less useful than I had hoped; being Gurkha rations, it consisted mainly of curries, which the Chinese wouldn't eat, but Ron took a bit of it. Before we went to bed we all ended up sitting around the table. The Chinese were expressing their doubts about carrying on, which were countered by the boss and Ron describing Easy Valley and emphasising to them that they were all capable of completing the expedition.

'What do you think, Sergeant Mann?'

The Colonel's question interrupted my train of thought. Shit! I was being asked for back-up so that the lads would feel more motivated, and if I told them my true thoughts, complete with doubts, they would pack their bags and go home. That would put me in the firing line and probably end my ten years in the TA. I didn't really know what to say. I tried to convince myself that everything was going to be alright. After all, the Colonel had been into Easy Valley, *and* part of the way up the Penataran – the only bit he hadn't seen was the middle section – and he'd surely made a sensible judgement about it all. On top of that, Ron seemed to think that everything was tickety-boo. What was I worried about?

The next day we got straight on with it and carried our half loads up to the stash at Sayat Sayat. We walked on past it, so I reminded the Colonel that we had planned to pick it up and take it with us to Easy Valley Col.

'We're going to pick it up later,' he replied.

'But boss, it's there – I can see it!'

'No, we'll get up there with half a load and come back to pick it up later.' I looked at Kevin, Lam and Chow. They were all looking fit enough. I said nothing, but shrugged and scratched; we continued on towards the col. The path was marked at regular intervals with cairns, and it was these that led to the boss and me having our first (albeit very minor) confrontation. I was leading, following the cairns, and I noticed him starting to lag behind, looking pale; he also seemed a bit ratty. At one of the rest stops he told me to stack a few extra rocks on each cairn as I walked past – standard mountain practice, he said. I knew that, but felt that stacking more rocks on them was likely to result in a rockfall at a later date and, exasperated by what I saw as an attempt to further slow us down, I muttered just loud enough for him to hear and with some feeling: 'Fucking hell, boss, I'm a soldier, not a brickie!' He didn't respond.

I decided that discretion was called for and did as he said, building up each cairn as I arrived at it, although it seemed pointless as each one was clearly visible from the preceding one. It reminded me of my Commando course ten years before at the Royal Marines Commando Training Centre at Lympstone, in Devon. The Physical Training Instructors there have a game that they like to play, called 'It pays to be a winner'. They claim that it's character building, but having experienced it, I would describe it as heart-breaking. There is a steep hill with a selection of large boulders at the bottom; everyone on the course has to pick up a boulder and run up the hill. The first man to the top is allowed to stand to one side while the rest are sent back down to the bottom to repeat the process. Unfortunately, not only was I the oldest, but by a long way the smallest, and in the battle to reach the top I kept on getting elbowed to the back. Thirty-six men. Thirty-six times up and down that bloody hill, and each time it became longer and steeper. I wasn't a winner that day and I feared that in this game, on this mountain, no one was going to be a winner.

I reached the col about twenty minutes before the boss and set about sorting things out. I told the Chinese lads to sit in the shade of an overhanging rock and have some food and water – although they were looking pretty strong at that stage, I didn't want them going down with heat exhaustion again. I was itching to get back down and retrieve the remaining kit, particularly my video camera. I had the protective 'yellow peril', along with spare batteries and all the ancillary equipment with me, but the camera itself was with the rest of my kit back down at Sayat Sayat. There hadn't been many opportunities to use it so far, and I was keen to start recording the expedition in glorious technicolour, particularly our first sight of Easy Valley. With Rich and me due to pair up again later that day, I needed other important items such as fuel for the stove. I had just started to sort out my rucksack in preparation for returning to the stash, when the Colonel arrived.

'Have you seen Mayfield yet?'

I hadn't, but there was still an hour to go before the RV. 'Not yet, boss.'

'I need him to show us a water source.'

'It's OK, boss – I've still got well over three litres and the lads have got over a litre each.' Ron had also said he had water.

'We need more.' How much more did we need? He scanned the valley, obviously looking for Rich, and I started to unload my rucksack. He asked me what I was doing.

'Sorting out my Bergen so that we can go back down to get the rest of our kit.'

'We're not going back down.' It was only forty minutes away.

'We're going down Easy Valley now. We'll collect it tomorrow.'

'Alright.' I was becoming used to sudden changes of plan – we must have had at least three in the past twenty-four hours – but it didn't make them any easier to accept and I was concerned over what these sudden changes indicated about his state of mind. He wasn't well, I could see that; he was very pale and moving slowly. I had a feeling that he was going down with altitude sickness, but didn't know enough about that particular malady to be sure, and I certainly had no idea if it could affect your mental state. I asked Ron if he thought the boss looked unwell; he said that he'd probably had a bit too much sun but that he was OK. (Later, at the Board of Enquiry, Ron had no recollection of this conversation.) I decided to keep my eyes open and my mouth shut.

Rich never made the RV; he was involved in some serious lumberjacking and lost track of time. The boss asked me to recce forward and find a route down Easy Valley. I went off on my own, enjoying the solitude and looking for signs that the front group had left. I was surprised to find the signs indicating that they had gone down the west side of the valley – on earlier expeditions the boss and Ron had gone down the east side – but I was sure of my findings and the western route certainly seemed the easiest. After about half an hour I returned to the rear group; we picked up our rucksacks and started to make some progress down into Easy Valley. I led, each step weighing heavy on my mind as I realised that for every step forward there were going to be two back to retrieve my stashed kit. At three o'clock the boss decided to stop and fill our water bottles from a tiny spring that trickled out of some rocks.

'We'll spend the night here.' He looked as if he could do with a rest, but I still felt pretty good and asked if I could do another recce forward to look for more signs of the front group. The boss agreed and I set off, following the western route while Ron scouted further to the east. I was glad to be off the leash and, without the weight of my rucksack, able to set a fast pace from cairn to cairn until I came to a drop of about thirty feet with some really thick jungle at the bottom. I found a route down but was unable to find any signs of the front group and sat down for a fag. While I was contemplating the events of the last couple of days I noticed something white on a rock about twenty feet away. It was a note written on an old ration pack: FOLLOW TRAIL THRU JUNGLE UNTIL YOU COME TO DRY RIVER BED. THEN FOLLOW DRY RIVER BED.

The trail took only five minutes to find and was quite unmistakable – a three-foot swathe cut through the thick jungle. I laughed to myself, for it looked like they had used a chainsaw; Britt's little canoe saw had obviously been working overtime. Some of the branches and trunks they had cut were at least eight inches thick and its clearance must have taken a considerable amount of work. I followed it for five minutes until I came to a clearing beside a big rock and started to look for the dry river bed. I saw something below the trees, but wasn't sure if that was the dry river bed the note had indicated, so I spent a good hour looking in other directions just in case I was wrong.

Nothing else materialised and I decided that that was indeed the correct route to take. It was now half past four. I was tempted to carry on, but I was unsure how far I'd have to go before I found the front group, and the terrain in the dry river bed looked very intimidating, so I decided to climb the big rock in the hope that I would be able to see something. After a good bit of climbing I reached the top and looked around. *Got you!* Half a mile away was a big rock which, I was later to discover, had been christened Alphabet Rock by the front group. I could just make out the tiny figures of Pete, Steve, Britt and Rich around one of the big red panels, which had been laid out on the flat top of the rock. I waved my arms, shouted, screamed, but to no avail – there was no response and I assumed they couldn't hear me. Still, at least I knew where they were. I retraced my steps up the mountain wondering why, even though the terrain was so difficult, nobody had returned to see what had taken us so long.

On my return the rear group were occupied trying to erect the silly tents that the boss had insisted we bring along. They were having difficulty finding either a level spot or something to secure the guy ropes, but eventually managed to put up a form of shelter in some shrubs, a pointless exercise as they could easily have slept in their bivvy bags. While they laboured, I collected some rocks to build a hearth so that we could have a fire for the night, and when the Chinese lads had finished their shelters, I told them to collect some wood and plenty of it.

The boss came over and I explained what I had seen on my recce. He seemed annoyed.

'Why haven't any of them come back? *And* I want to know why bloody Mayfield didn't make the RV at the col.' He seemed to calm down when I said that at least we knew where they were and how to get down to them. I was trying to play up the good points and deter him from dwelling on Rich missing the RV – he was my partner after all, and I felt I had to defend him, at least until I'd spoken to him.

I took my sleeping bag out of my rucksack and set about making a bed by the fire. Once I finished, I put some water in a mess tin and was waiting for it to boil on the fire when Kevin came over and asked why I wasn't using a stove. I explained that it was down the mountain with my partner. He very kindly offered me the use of his when he finished, and then asked if I would like to share his food

'There's enough for two.'

'What are you having?'

'Rice and sardines.'

If there's one thing I hate more than a curried fish pastie, it's sardines. 'Shove it up your bum, Kevin.'

He looked a bit insulted until I explained it was just our way of saying no thank you – I kept forgetting that he was from Hong Kong and the culture clash was sometimes a bit embarrassing.

'You want tea?'

I didn't want to insult him again, so I agreed. He offered his mess tin and I took a large swig. It was a big mistake. He'd boiled the water in the same mess tin that he'd used for the sardines and rice. It was bloody awful – all I could taste was sardines – and I spat it out over the mountainside.

'You not like my tea, Bob?'

'Er, yes. Just a bit hot, that's all.' When he turned his back I threw it into the shrubs. 'Nice that, Kevin. Cheers.'

By the time I'd fed myself it was getting late. I was worried about the fact that Rich and I were still split up. I could borrow odds and ends from the lads, but it wasn't an ideal set-up, and I was also worried about the food situation; Rich and I had already given some of our food to the Chinese lads, and on top of that we were now running some days behind schedule. If things didn't speed up then we would be having a few problems.

The others went off to their tents, fifty yards up the hill, and I put some wood on the fire before settling down to sleep. I lay in my sleeping bag, looking at the splendour of the enormous cliffs in the moonlight, and drifted off to sleep, only to be woken some time later by the sound of a boulder being moved close by. At first I thought it was Kevin getting his own back for the episode with the tea, and told whoever it was to stop pissing about playing games and get back to bed, but there was no reply. I looked at my watch;

it was twenty past two. I figured that it must have been someone having a pee, so I put some more wood on the fire and snuggled down into my sleeping bag again. There was a loud 'crack' as if something heavy had stood on a piece of wood; I got out my head torch and had a good look around. Nothing. I put some more wood on the fire and settled down again, this time pulling my bivvy bag over my head. No sooner had I made myself snug than a scratching started on the outside of my bivvy. Whatever it was sounded really big and I was completely spooked. I lay there, paralysed by fear, for at least ten minutes, listening to the scratching getting louder, before plucking up the courage to take my knife from my belt. I shot out of the sleeping bag like a rat from a drainpipe, knife in hand, shouting at the top of my voice: 'Come on, you fucker!'

My neck crawled as I saw a large ape-like shape disappear into the tall shrubs on my left. I've never been so scared in my life; I knelt there for ten minutes, knife in hand, too petrified to move. I must have looked really stupid. Some Commando, getting spooked by an animal. My mind raced, recalling stories of yetis and suchlike – did they live in Borneo? Eventually, I willed myself to move. I put some more wood on the fire, which by now was lighting up almost the whole mountain, and stared into the flames. I remembered the story I'd heard about the gully. The local tribes believe it to be the last resting place of departed spirits: when someone dies, their soul goes to the gully for peace and tranquillity, and they are guarded by the dragon spirit that lives in the gully. If ever a tribe journey into the area, they make a ceremonial offering of eggs and chicken to appease the dragon. Failure to do this will result in the dragon preventing them from leaving, as a punishment for disturbing the peace of the departed souls. I sat there, knife in hand, for the rest of the night, staring into the flames and thinking of dragons.

By the time the others awoke I was ready to get moving, and while they were sorting themselves out I went over to another high point and confirmed that the front group were still at Alphabet Rock. I informed the boss and he wondered aloud if any of them would come back to see where we were. We left our equipment at the campsite and set off up the mountain again. It took about two hours to get back to the remainder of our kit at the stash above Sayat Sayat, and when we got there the boss told us to put up a flysheet to give the Chinese lads some shade. I was anxious to get going, but the boss and Ron wanted to go up and have a look at Commando

Cauldron. I decided to go as well – I'd never seen it and Paul Hughes had told me so much about it.

We eventually arrived back at the Easy Valley bivvy site at about three. I packed the rest of my kit in double time and was just strapping down the yellow peril on top of my rucksack when I noticed the lads milling around and the tents still up.

'Aren't you going to pack the rest of your kit, boss?'

'No. We're going to take half kit down to the front group, come back up here and join them with the rest of the kit in the morning.'

It was too much. I didn't know what to do or say. I was confused – why didn't Ron say something? He'd been keeping a very low profile whenever there was a discussion about plans or a decision to be made. I wanted to be away from it for a while. Rich had half the stuff I needed and anyway, I was buggered if I was going to make pointless trips up hill and down bloody dale just because the Colonel wanted to carry half loads everywhere, especially as I felt fit enough to carry a full load. If I stayed, my frustration would only get the better of me and I would end up saying something I'd regret and which might cost me my TA career.

'I'm not being funny, sir, but I'm not doing that. I'm not walking up and down this bloody mountain like the Grand Old Duke of York. I'm going to join the front group. I can be of more use there.'

He must have heard the resolve and exasperation in my voice, for he didn't argue; he obviously wasn't feeling well and his answer betrayed his listlessness. This wasn't the officer that Paul had told me about back in Plymouth. 'Yes, you carry on, Bob. Ron and I will come with you with half kit and drop it off – you can stay with the front group.'

The three of us set off. I picked up the trail again and led down to the path that had been cut through the jungle. The yellow peril started giving me all sorts of problems – it kept snagging on branches and the extra twenty pounds weren't helping either, so I decided to dump it about half-way to the front group. We arrived at the clearing by the big rock and the Colonel, worried about the approaching dusk (still at least two hours off), told Ron that they would leave their kit and return to the Chinese. He said that, although they had time to reach the front group, he was concerned that they would not be able to return in the dark and didn't want to leave the lads alone overnight. He told me to tell Rich that they would be down in the morning and we said our farewells. I dropped

The authors

Our first view of Mount Kinabalu from five miles away

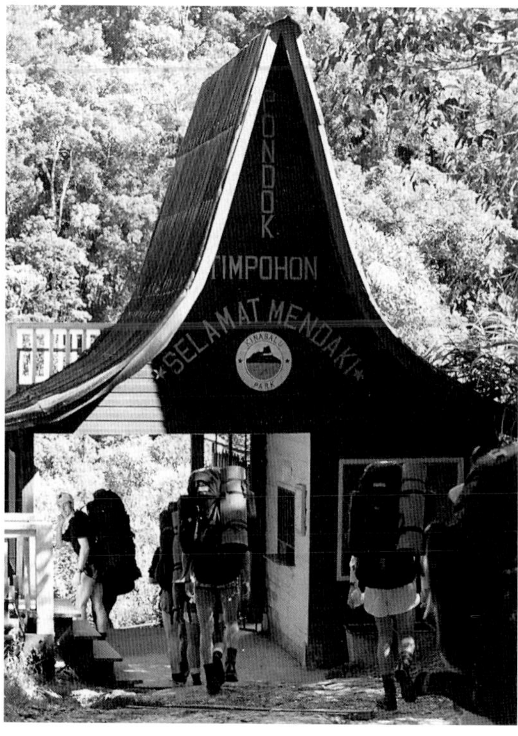

Start of the tourist trail at Park headquarters

Pete Shearer on the Panar Laban rockface on his way to the summit

A cold Rich Mayfield at the summit

The team at the summit. *Standing, from left to right:* Britt, Bob, Rich, Neill. *Sitting:* Ron, Pete, Lam, Chow, Kevin

South peak from the summit

Looking up towards cauldron gap.
In the foreground, emergency shelter for victims of the sun

View up Easy Valley from Alphabet Rock.
The cliffs on either side are up to 2,000 feet high and were *not* on the map

Looking back from Lone Tree. Rhino Horn centre, with Cauldron Gap
just to its right. The cliff on the right is nearly a mile high

In the mist on the big abseils

View down the valley from the bivvy site at the foot of the abseils

Above: Pete Shearer at the top of Robert's Falls the day after his fall. Despondency setting in

Robert's Falls. Bottom left, Steve can just be seen swimming in the pool

The authors at the foot of Robert's Falls. Already losing weight

Drying out after the swim. Here Bob recorded his message for Sue on video.
The last picture we took

The hut at Kampong Melanghkap Kappa

The original medicine, complete with snake

The authors at Melanghkap with the villagers on the day of escape

down into the dry river bed and started to follow the trail, but within fifteen minutes I was lost. I tried shouting to the front group, but they must have been too far away. I was all alone in the thick rattan jungle trying to shove a seventy-pound rucksack in front of me while clearing a path without a parang, which was hard work. At one point I looked down to see, below the interlaced branches on which I was standing, a drop of at least a hundred feet. I was very scared and worked my way back to firmer ground for a rest. When I found the front group, I decided, I would retrace the route, marking it again so that the rear group would have no problem following it; I had to go back anyway to retrieve my yellow peril. For the moment, however, the priority was finding the other end of the trail and the front group.

Covered in cuts and bruises, I began pushing in a different direction. I had been lost for over an hour and the first touches of panic were starting to nibble at my nerves. I tried shouting again and this time thought I heard a faint reply to my right. I shoved for another ten minutes and shouted again. This time the reply was distinct: 'Over here.'

I gained a few more yards, still worried that I was lost, and needing the reassurance of hearing a voice again.

'Rich?'

'Over here, you stupid stab.' I fought my way another few feet, trying unsuccessfully to keep the panic at bay.

'Rich!' There was no reply. 'RICH! You stupid bastard, keep shouting. I'm lost in this fucking hell hole!'

'Over here, Bob. Keep going in the same direction – I'll come and give you a hand. Hold on.' I burst out of the jungle on the wrong side, landing on a slippery ledge which ended, twenty feet away, in an enormous drop. I was lucky not to have been travelling any faster.

'What are you doing over there, Bob?'

'I just thought I'd have a good look around, you idiot!' The panic was subsiding, but I still felt very shaky and was relieved to see Rich emerge from the jungle. He took my rucksack and we carefully made our way to the safety of Alphabet Rock.

The welcome was less than sympathetic: 'Where the hell have you been, Bob?'

'If you were all so concerned, why didn't you come back to see where I was?' I thought they were going to jump down my throat.

They explained that they had been exploring forward and that they had already set up the first of the abseils. I decided not to argue.

'OK, Rich. Get some coffee on and I'll tell you what we've been doing.'

CHAPTER 7

Waiting and waiting some more

We discussed Bob's story and its implications, particularly with regard to the food situation, but came to no decisions about what to do. Bob said that he would have to go back up the next morning to retrieve his yellow peril, and that he'd carry on up the hill to see the Colonel, tell him what we'd been doing and, if possible, find out what he wanted us to do.

We drifted off with our respective partners and got on with the routine of cooking the evening meal. I was glad to have Bob around – his presence was reassuring and he had a large bag of pasta.

'Big eats tonight, Bob.' I filled the cooking pot three quarters full and waited for it to rehydrate before cooking.

After the meal and washing up had been finished we settled down for another long night; with no real work done the others weren't tired, and the usual alphabet games ensued: A-Z of Songs, Films, Music groups, and last (and easily the hardest), the A-Z of things related to the mountain. With Bob's introduction to the pastimes of our boulder only half finished, we moved on, pointing out the large fish a few thousand feet high on one of the walls and Dennis the Menace next to it. As we looked, other shapes started to emerge and the discussion of what they were continued for hours.

Feeling tired after my walk earlier on, I lay on my back and listened to the others laughing and joking. The occasional shooting star traced a fiery passage overhead. All the stresses and strains of the last week played on my mind, but what was giving me the most cause for concern was the food situation. I felt we might well run out; here we were on day five of the expedition, but we we had only covered approximately one day's ground according to the original plan. At this rate we would need at least fifty days' food, perhaps more. By the time the others reached us there would be no way we could carry on – we just hadn't got the food. I tried to rationalise my thoughts, running through the sums again. It would, at their rate, take a further day to reach us, which would leave us with less than half of our food and nowhere near the end of the planned second day. I resigned myself to the potential failure of the expedition, but decided not to voice my opinion as Britt would only call me a hat anyway. I drifted off into an uneasy sleep with Bob at my side.

Dawn broke. Light drifted in over the soaring cliffs, but down in the depths, as usual, we would have to wait for the sun to clear the surrounding walls before the temperature started to rise. From the warmth of my bivvy, I looked optimistically uphill for any sign of the others; there was none, so I rolled over and waited for the air to warm up.

Bob, eager to retrieve his video, was first to rise. I felt a prod in my back: 'Get the cooker out, I'll start breakfast.'

My watch told me it was seven o'clock. 'Are you going to see Neill when you go back up?'

'Suppose I'll have to.' A task he wasn't looking forward to and one I didn't envy him.

Breakfast in bed, not something I'd be likely to see again on the expedition, and he was on his way. I watched his small frame disappear into the jungle. The others were awake and slowly, still in their sleeping bags, started their breakfasts. I kept track of Bob's ascent by watching the shaking bushes and, after thirty minutes, saw him emerge on the other side; he turned and waved, and then set off at an alarming pace up the hill. Wishful thinking told me that the others must surely catch up today.

As nine o'clock neared I heard a shout from above and looked up to see Bob on his way back already; from the speed he was moving we all took it for granted that we'd soon be moving off. I looked at what had been our home for the last three days, kit untidily spread out after breakfast, and realised we'd better do some sorting out. I packed my kit, moved on to Bob's rucksack and, just as I was finishing, saw Bob's Norman Wisdom figure, carrying his large yellow video box, burst out of the bottom of the jungle. A violent rotation of his head to regain his bearings and he was off again at speed in our direction, slowing down only when it came to climbing the boulder.

'What's happening, Bob?' I was intrigued by his speed and the obvious motivation it implied.

'Let's go!' He looked around the boulder for his rucksack. 'Great, you're packed up. Rich, help me put this thing on the outside of my sack.' He held up his yellow video box and handed back my parang.

'Where are the others then, Bob?' We were all somewhat nonplussed by his apparent sense of urgency.

'They're coming. It only took me forty-five minutes to get back.'

'Forty-five minutes! Bloody hell, Bob, did you sprout wings?'

'If we don't hurry then he'll catch us up.'

The penny dropped. We didn't want to walk with the others and become part of their slow-moving convoy; better to move on and get some more abseils set up, so that when they joined us they would be able to go straight into the descent. Within ten minutes of Bob's arrival I found myself carrying the full weight of the expedition rucksack again, which, after the prolonged rest, seemed heavier than before. Climbing down off the boulder, something that was easily accomplished with no kit, took on a whole new meaning. We crossed the stream and moved carefully across the slabby section towards House Boulder. I glanced over my shoulder, half expecting to see the others hot on our trail, but there were no trails of dust, not even a patch of jungle moving.

The short corners provided a distraction, and two hundred yards passed quickly as we reached House Boulder and moved on to Lone Tree. We were covering a hundred yards in about ten minutes; not quite up to Linford Christie's standard, but at least we were moving for the first time in three days.

We reached the belays I'd left on the previous day and Pete asked if we could avoid the abseil by walking round it. I sat at the belay while they viewed the surrounding hillside, and waited for a decision.

'Rich.' I turned to see Britt putting his harness on. 'The more abseiling we have to do, the less walking downhill there will be, and besides I'm not walking down that, look how steep and loose it is.' The others, having come to the same opinion, climbed into their harnesses; I told them to leave the rope in place for the second group and set off down. As I neared the canopy, I strained my eyes looking for whatever had spooked me on my first visit. The distinctive orange and black pattern of a tiger skin was nowhere to be seen as my feet found the ground again and I shouted up loudly that the rope was free, hoping the noise would scare anything off. I looked around nervously, willing the others to get a move on, and within minutes we were reunited, standing in the light of the hole I'd made in the canopy.

'Which way, Rich?' This was the furthest I'd been. What was Pete asking me for?

'Downhill, mate!' We dropped our rucksacks, Britt produced his saw in preparation for the inevitable lumberjacking and, leaving another note for the rear party, we commenced path-clearing operations. This patch of jungle was about 500 yards long and we hoped initially to come out on a river bed to our right, rather than the gully itself. After a good ninety minutes' hard work, we came to a natural clearing in the vegetation and a short drop of fifty feet to the river bed. After the horrors of our last taste of jungle this area was relatively tame, apart from my imaginary tigers. Having no climbing kit with us, we returned to our rucksacks and carried them down to our low point.

Due to our position in the clearing there was a shortage of belays in the immediate area, small bushes being the only ones available. Through a careful balancing act of self-equalising slings, I was able to construct a very strong multi-directional belay from next to nothing, but had to discard it as it used too much equipment, and ended up lowering myself from two bushes. The rock was covered with a vertical mess of what had once been living things, into which my feet sank up to the ankles. Debris fell as my passage continued: brown clouds of dust and leaf mould, which rained down in a continuous stream from beneath my feet. I landed on the steep slab at the bottom and lowered still further on the rope to get clear of the avalanche that would surely accompany the next person down.

One by one they descended the disgusting wall, and with everyone safely down, we left our rucksacks and started to explore the river bed. It was only really a stream, but the lack of vegetation and the smooth, water-worn rock indicated that it must flood frequently and with some force. The odd tree, felled in its prime, bore witness to the power of the river and, given that this was only a tributary, I worried what the actual gully would be like if it flooded. Our stream had carved out a smooth green chute that turned and twisted into deep pools of icy cold water, and having been on the hill for five days, in all that heat and without a proper wash, Britt and I decided to take the plunge before the rear group caught up. We stripped naked to cheers from the others, who declined to join us on the grounds that it was freezing. They were right; there was only enough time to wash the important bits before hypothermia set in, and we jumped out rapidly to dry out and relax in the sun.

The cloud that we had watched over the last few days from Alphabet Rock was almost at eye level after our loss of height, but showed no signs of moving towards us, and we munched dinner waiting for the rear group to catch up. We sat around waiting for a further three hours.

'I'm bored! I'm going to see what's ahead.' I didn't bother to ask for any company this time. 'I'll take three more ropes.' Another mad rush ensued to give weight away, and fully laden with ropes and my rack of hardware I tottered off to the edge. Looking over, I could see a short step leading to a rock pool, before the water took its next inevitable plunge towards the sea; looking out, I saw that the cloud had risen and was now level with me, two hundred yards away and closing slowly. I tied a bowline around a fat tree, threw the rope over, clipped in and tiptoed over the rounded edge; looking down I could only see fifty feet before the rock was engulfed in a sea of solid, white, living cloud. The two other ropes hung from my shoulders and I felt like a diver about to descend into an unknown ocean. The rock became vertical, and the stream next to me fell free and silently into the cloud below. I followed it. The temperature dropped as I entered the cloud and I shivered, wishing out loud that I'd brought my fleece, but it seemed that my voice was threatening to awaken the gods of this unreal place, so I shut up and quietly got on with the job in hand. The single 9mm rope was becoming damp and slippery to the touch, and I moved cautiously until, with only ten feet of rope left, my feet found a long, narrow, flat ledge. I voiced my thanks to anyone listening. Remaining safe on my Shunt I looked for a belay for the next abseil; a large detached pillar weighing several tons and within easy reach of the ledge was the obvious choice.

Drips were landing all around me, some exploding on the ledge, others falling further to become absorbed into the cloud. I looked up into the whiteness, trying to see the top, to find a reference point, regain some equilibrium and make sense of my surroundings. The cloud above thinned in places and I peered into the diffused shafts of light, hoping to find some orientation. What I thought was sky was rock, and thousands of feet above me. It was abstract in the extreme – no sky, no floor. I reeled dizzily inward to grab the belay tapes for support. As quickly as they had appeared, the holes in the cloud filled in, leaving only my ledge, the corners of which faded out into white. My whole world was defined within a twenty-foot radius. I tried to pull myself together, talking loudly to myself, not caring if the pagan gods, or the dragon that was said to live in this dark and forbidding hole, heard me, and threw the next rope over the edge. I continued into the mists, down the bare rock. Water dripped incessantly on me and I hoped it was just spray from the stream rather than rain – the last thing I wanted was for rain to turn this stream into a raging torrent and to have to fight my way back up it. However, the flow showed no signs of increasing and I decided to carry on as far as my diminishing stock of rope would let me; if, after the next abseil, there was no sign of an easing of the ground, we would have to give up anyway. The end of the rope came into view at an easing of the angle, where I was able to stand and look around for belays. There was nothing of any use in sight, so I continued to the end of the rope and unclipped. The angle was now sufficiently shallow that I could walk carefully around, but the bare rock still yielded no belay, and I continued gingerly down the damp rock until it started to increase in steepness again. I squinted into the gloom, but was unable to gain any impression of just how big the drop was, and traversed along the lip until I came to the stream; five slimy feet away, on the other side, was a small bush and a submerged block. I took a deep breath and jumped, landing heavily in a knee-deep puddle, my legs buckling under the impact, leaving me sitting up to my waist in cold water.

Sorting out my slings, I made a belay, threw over the last rope and started the next descent. The angle of the rock had decreased but was still far too steep to walk on, steeper than my supposedly exposed abseil of the other day. I reached the bottom of the abseil and stopped short of the end of the rope, looking hard into the gloom beneath me. Nothing.

I replaced my abseiling device with a Croll and, using it in conjunction with my Shunt, ascended as fast as possible, trying to work out whether we'd be able to continue, and soon found myself standing knee-deep in the cold water of the stream. Fairly sure that we'd reached an impasse, I pulled up and coiled the damp rope, re-crossed the stream and started the next climb. I stopped half-way for a rest and saw the clouds beneath me start to clear. A brief study revealed that at my low point I had been thirty or forty feet at most from a large section of comparatively level ground, at the end of which there was another drop, but the size of it was impossible to tell without something in the distance to indicate the scale. I completed the climb, coiled the rope and climbed the last pitch back to join the others, who were relaxed almost to the point of indifference.

I attempted to whet their appetites for what was ahead: 'Hey, you lot, you should see what's down there.' My enthusiasm didn't catch on.

Bob spoke: 'Rich, I'm not being funny, but I'm not looking down until I reach the bottom. I'll look down then, no problem.'

Everyone seemed happy to stay where they were; there was no sign of the rear group and nothing to suggest that they would be catching up in the near future, so we settled down for the night. I was concerned that we were in a river bed, thirty feet wide. Although the river was no more than a bubbling stream, a few feet wide, the cloud through which I had abseiled was now high above our heads. If it rained on the summit, the first indication we would have was when the flood came, and we could all too easily be washed over the edge before we had a chance to get out of our sleeping bags. No other bivvy site was available, so I set up a Tyrolean traverse using sixty feet of the last abseil rope, anchored at each end and stretched across the site; we would have to sleep in our harnesses, with our Crolls attached to the rope, ready for a quick exit if the worst happened.

Bob's big yellow video box came in handy as a not so portable kitchen table for cooking the night's meal, and with the rope stretched across the river bed and harnesses on, we turned in. The power of the river in spate had carved out shallow hollows in the hard granite bed and these provided an uncomfortably hard mattress for the night. Before sleeping, we discussed who would have to go back up the hill tomorrow to find the others if they didn't turn up. Bob stated that he went last time, and besides he had cracked a tooth and was in a lot of discomfort, too busy munching on pain killers to contribute further to the discussion. Britt was still suffering from headaches, Steve said he'd only slow me down and Pete pointed out that I would be able to climb the fixed ropes faster than anyone else. Their logic was flawless, of course, and I resigned myself to what should be a short trip up the hill – the rear group couldn't be much more than an hour away. My mind wandered and before long I was asleep, waking periodically to adjust my uncomfortable position.

Morning arrived without incident; the small stream was still bubbling unthreateningly away to its heart's content, and by seven thirty we were ready to push on, but there was still no sign of the rear group.

'I'll give them until nine.' I was trying to put off the inevitable trip back up the hill.

'What we did yesterday should only take them an hour if they follow the path we cut for them.' Britt was right – surely they'd be here before I had to go looking. Milling around the camp, I repacked my small day sack, glancing up every once in a while to look for any movement. None came and the time ticked on.

Nine o'clock; the time had come for some exercise. I set off, still expecting to see them descending towards me. I climbed the first short abseil and continued as fast as the path would allow. My anxiety rose as I approached the second rope, for there was no sign of life, not even a movement in the rope to indicate that someone was preparing to descend. I clipped my Crolls onto the rope and climbed to the belay which was deserted. I had hoped that there would be someone in evidence, perhaps with the words 'End EX' on their lips; a decision to retreat now would be sensible and welcomed by everybody.

Untying from the rope, I started running back to Alphabet Rock. I passed House Boulder, seeing some red dive sacks in its shadow, but no other sign of the rear group. Muttering to myself, I looked up the valley. My patience was fast running out – I could spend the rest of the morning looking for them.

I returned to the abandoned sacks and found a note: 'RV here at 1200 urgently.' There was only one logical interpretation of this – End EX; we'd lost so much time and were so low on food that Neill had had no choice but to call it a day. It was 0930.

I resumed my muttering: 'I'm not waiting around here for two hours. If I blow my whistle they should be able to hear me, and at least that way I'll be able to get some idea of where they are. What the hell!' A deep breath and the long shrill blast echoed around the confining cliffs of the upper reaches of Easy Valley.

A return blast came. I looked through the shadows, into the jungle, over rocks, scanning frantically for the source of the sound, and eventually saw four people standing up on Alphabet Rock. I waved a hand, and as I did so a third blast echoed around the valley, this time off to my left and probably from Britt.

I set off at an angry pace, faster than was probably safe, wondering why on earth it had taken them a whole day to cover a distance that had taken Bob forty-five minutes.

'Richard!' I turned to see Ron standing above me no more than ten yards away.

'Ron, what's happening? They're still on Alphabet Rock.'

'Where?' Ron was not familiar with the nickname, which had resulted from the interminable games we had played to pass the time.

'Over there, look!' I pointed in the direction.

'Yes, that's right. Colonel Neill isn't well.'

'Why, what's wrong?' I couldn't wait to hear the news, even if it was bad; any information was preferable to being kept in the dark.

'I think it's the altitude, he keeps having mood swings.'

I smiled. It was a familiar scenario, with echoes of what had happened on the other side of the mountain; however, the first of Neill's mood swings had occurred lower down and I didn't think that they could be blamed on the altitude. Maybe he had been more worried than we had realised and, unable to admit it (even to himself), the mood swings had resulted.

'OK, I'm off to see him.' I didn't want to waste time talking to Ron. He'd proved to be less than useful on the other occasions when I'd had to confront the Colonel. Five minutes later I was jumping the stream and climbing the boulder.

'Corporal Mayfield!'

Was this going to be another bollocking? The smile on Neill's face unnerved me. Kevin and the others came over to greet me, shaking my hand and also grinning from ear to ear. Not quite what I was expecting. Neill climbed out of his sleeping bag, clutching a cup of coffee.

'Corporal Mayfield. How far have you got?'

'Er, I think we're at the start of New's abseils.' I decided not to say too much and sound out what he was thinking before committing myself.

'Good, excellent! So how far is that from the gully floor?'

'I don't know. Yesterday I abseiled down three more pitches and still didn't get to the bottom.'

'Where did you sleep last night?'

'It's nine forty-five now.' I paused to see his reaction; half of the morning had gone and soon the heat of the sun would hinder our movements. 'It's taken me forty-five minutes *uphill* to get here.' I held his gaze. Surely he couldn't assume we'd be able to carry on?

He offered me his coffee. 'Good, so we're not too far behind, then.'

I couldn't believe it. He wanted to carry on. My face hardened. 'We're running out of food, sir.'

'That's OK. Ron and I have two days' extra.'

'You have four days' food, between you.' I wanted to get my facts straight before this started to get nasty.

'Yes.'

'That's, what?' – a quick calculation in my head – 'eight hours of extra food you have.'

'No, four days' worth.' I could tell my tone of voice was annoying him, but at this stage I really didn't care.

'You have eight hours of food if you split it down between everyone.'

'Well, if you look at it like that . . .'

'What other way is there to look at it?'

Sensing my agitation, he changed tack. 'So what's between our two camps?'

I explained the route to our camp in detail and then the new ground that I had covered yesterday. 'At least four more abseils.' I paused to allow what I'd just said to sink in. 'That's six altogether, and we're still not at the bottom. If we carry on we'll have to pull the ropes through as we go down. That means we'll be totally committed – no escape back up as was planned.'

'Yes, that's OK, Corporal Mayfield.'

Had he heard what I just said? 'This is day six! We've only got four days' food left.'

'Yes, but *we've* got day five left.'

I didn't quite understand this statement, but was afraid to ask for clarification. 'According to the expedition outline we're still only half-way through the second day's walk!'

'It's OK, Corporal Mayfield, we've got extra food!' Our voices had started to rise.

I made one last-ditch attempt to get him to abort: 'Bob's done his tooth in. He's in a lot of pain and we're running out of pain-killers.'

I'd seen people evacuated as casualties from expeditions for ailments less serious, but this was no ordinary expedition.

'That's OK – we'll give him some of ours when we catch up.' Bob had been right. He was going to do this thing whatever the consequences. 'You're only forty-five minutes ahead?'

'Yes, but that was going uphill. Downhill it should take you half an hour at most.' I couldn't argue any more. My mind was occupied with the thought of what it was going to be like having a ten-strong party spread out over six pitches. Moreover, the rear group would be in the charge of somebody whose technical expertise was in doubt and who (it appeared) was not in touch with the reality of the situation. It made me angry and frustrated; I was in an impossible situation and there was no way that Neill was going to listen to me.

'So what's the ground like?'

I had just explained that to him; the way was well marked and all the belays were set up, so I fired back a question of my own: 'Where's the next RV, sir?'

'We'll all meet up at the gully floor tonight.'

There was no chance of them making it by nightfall; however, I had no choice but to go along with what Neill proposed and tried to speed the process up.

'I'll take four of your ropes to help lighten your load and leave two in place on the first of the big drops. Pull them through as you pass.'

'See you at the RV.'

'OK, sir. We'll wait until tomorrow morning.'

'Yes. Wait at the bottom.'

'Until tomorrow.' The air around us almost crackled with tension.

'Yes. We'll meet up at the bottom.' He wasn't listening.

'We'll wait until tomorrow morning. Then we will go. We will have only three days' food left. We can't afford to wait any longer.' I spelled it out as clearly as I could; his decision had committed us and the thought of battling through the jungle I'd seen on the way up to Park HQ without food scared me. How many days would we have to go without?

'I'll meet you tonight at the bottom, Corporal Mayfield.' That was my cue to go, so I turned on my heels. Neill was later unable to recall the last part of our conversation.

'OK, sir – see you tonight.' Before any more could be said I picked up four ropes, descended the boulder and jumped the stream. If we were to make it out of this place then we were going to have to move fast.

'Richard, what happened?' I stopped in my tracks. Ron had been waiting for me to return. He'd done this often. When there was an important decision to be made, he was nowhere around, whether through a dislike of conflict or a fear of compromising himself in front of a senior officer, I didn't know. Whatever the reason for his absence, there was no way I was going to repeat all that I'd just said.

'Talk to Neill!' I bellowed and continued on my way. I half expected to get dragged back by my hair, but the paper tiger didn't even stir. Oddly, Ron later had no recollection of this conversation, or the one we'd had before I talked to Neill. Thirty minutes later I rejoined the front group, to be met by a barrage of questions.

'What's happening?'

'Where are the others?'

'We're going for it. Get ready.' It was all I could bring myself to say, but was enough to galvanise everyone into a frenzy of activity.

By midday Bob was by my side at the top of the abseil and finally looked down, intimidated by the exposure and the sheer grandeur of our surroundings. The large tree I was using for a belay needed a sling around it to ensure that the rear group would be able to pull the rope through when the time came. It went against the grain, leaving gear behind, and could have implications further down if we ran short, but the alternative was the time-consuming business of having a rope jam.

Ten minutes later four nervous figures were standing next to me on the wide ledge at the foot of the abseil. I set up the next belay and launched off. This abseil was the one with the steep finish, followed by the prospect of jumping that stream to reach the next belay; with the weight of a full rucksack it didn't bear thinking about. Yet. The others followed, ending up standing awkwardly on the steep rock, apprehensive of what was to come. Britt, Steve and Pete moved down gingerly towards the stream, leaving Bob and me standing at the foot of the rope, our last link with safety. I had left the ropes on the previous abseils, as I had promised Neill, and his group would pull them through as they descended, in order to use them again. We now needed to do the same. It was time to burn our boats.

'This is it, Bob!' I pulled the marked end of the rope, pulled again, and the other end climbed up towards the tree, ending all hope of retreat. As it cleared the belay and fell back to me, I felt like a child who was out exploring, had gone too far and was lost. I started to coil the ropes, remembering being late home and getting shouted at for missing my tea. Something in the back of my mind told me this was more serious than a childhood adventure.

Lower down, the others were being heckled by Britt to jump the stream, which this time, with no cloud to obscure the drop, was going to be considerably more intimidating. The extra weight made for an interesting time, and the smooth, algae-covered rock narrowed the margin for error even further; heart in mouth, I made the jump and set up the next belay. I set off, knowing the ropes ended thirty feet short. I reached the knot at the end and started to pendulum, running from one side to the other in order to reach a belay, eventually managing to stand on some stringy and unstable foliage. The others came down one by one, and as they arrived I pulled them across to join me balanced on my small patch of debris. It became a little crowded and Steve departed to find a way down; half scrambling, he started to fall the last ten feet and jumped, landing hard. This appeared to be the only way off, and the rest followed while I pulled the ropes down and coiled them. As last one down I found that the passage of the others had worn away the vegetation and made the descent more difficult. I joined them to find Bob standing in a clearing made by the water course, looking like the cat that had got at the cream – he was obviously pleased to have completed the abseils.

We had a short break for dinner and discussed why we hadn't seen the others above us on the first abseil. Someone voiced his concern: 'What if something has happened to the rear group?' I felt that the whole conversation was academic, as if they did have an incident we'd be powerless to help – to climb back up with the gear we had was just not feasible and Neill had said that he was as qualified as me.

'It's too late to start going back.' My voice sounded hollow and my thoughts turned to the Chinese lads. Kevin, Chow and Lam were no longer volunteers – they were here under duress, all feeling that the risk involved was unacceptable, and we had left them. The thought played heavily on my conscience and a host of 'what ifs' crowded in on me.

Britt was the first to break camp and, shouldering his rucksack, he set off down the wide, water-worn path, jumping from boulder to boulder. I watched as the rest followed, trying to resolve my feelings, then looked up one last time to study the top, where 500 feet above me the ropes we'd left in place on the upper abseils were motionless and not a shadow stirred.

I placed my rucksack on a rock to steady it, climbed inside the straps and set off. From time to time the boulders were interrupted by large fallen trees, mature specimens that were far bigger than the ones we'd seen in the upper stream bed; the river, when in flood, was becoming even more powerful. The dense green on either side looked uninviting and dark, but if it rained that was where we would be heading.

After only fifty yards I heard shouts from the front: 'Where's Rich?'

'I'm coming, I'm coming.' Crawling on hands and knees to negotiate a felled tree, still with green leaves on its branches, I caught up.

'What's up?'

'More abseiling.' Steve's broad Geordie accent still made me smile; a reminder of normality in these surroundings.

'I think this one's yours, Rich.' Britt was in high spirits now that we were moving again.

I stood next to him and peered down. 'Shit.'

The watercourse had narrowed to only a few feet and what little water there was fell right down the line of abseil. The force of the current had turned the rock into an eighty-foot chute, smooth and clean-cut. The top had a mass of things to belay from, but as far as possible I really did want to stay dry, and chose instead a tree off to my right, from where it was possible to stay out of the waterfall. I placed a sling high on the tree for my anchor, in a position where it would be easily visible to the rear party. This was the steepest abseil so far and as I descended I was grateful for my chest harness, which kept me upright as the full weight of my rucksack came to bear on the rope. Half-way down the rock started to become wet, and the danger of slipping into the watercourse increased so I leant to my left and, walking in that direction, continued down. Ten feet from the ground, ankles straining under the pressure of the angle needed to keep me dry and with the chute some twenty feet to the right, my right foot slipped on a damp patch. My left foot was at too great an angle to stop the impending swing and off I went, flying through the air rucksack first, out of control. I let go of the rope and my weight fell onto the shunt, stopping any further descent, but not my wild pendulum; rock rushed past my face and I kicked out in an attempt to swing clear, but the damp rock offered no friction and my blows glanced off. There was a sickening, crashing jolt. All movement ceased and water gushed around me. I looked up to see where the rope had come to rest. Would there be any more movement, any swings? Had the rope been damaged as it ran over an edge? I turned to face the rock and check my gear; all seemed in order. I was unhurt, probably as a result of swinging backwards – my rucksack had cushioned the impact. I looked down between my legs and saw a deep blue pool of water no more than five feet in diameter, but inescapable around most of its circumference due to the smoothness of the rock. Just downstream, however, was an area where I might be able to pull out onto the bank, the only drawback being the prospect of a short swim. The water falling on me from above had already soaked through my clothing, so I pulled the release on my shunt and lowered into the cold water. It quickly penetrated my boots and socks, cooling my legs and bringing on the first twinges of cramp. As the level passed my groin and moved up to my chest, the cold took my breath away. I rested on the shunt to regain my breath and decided to swim for it. I threw off my rucksack into the water and releasing myself from the rope I dropped, submerging for an instant before surfacing. Pushing, gasping and swimming all at once, I made it to the bank and scrambled up, pulling my rucksack behind me. I sat for a few minutes in the warmth of the sun, composing myself, until a dis-embodied voice floated down.

'Rich, you ready yet?' Bob and the others were obviously unaware of my epic descent.

'Wait one.' I pulled the rope clear of the water and held the end: 'Next!'

The rope stretched as the weight was taken up and someone started the descent; as each one arrived I pulled them towards my dry piece of rock.

'Fucking hell, Rich, you're all wet. What happened ?'

'Don't ask.'

With everyone down and dry (apart from myself), and the soaking wet ropes pulled through and coiled, I started to relax. Too soon.

'Here's another one.' I felt dwarfed by the cliff towering thousands of feet above us; we were still nowhere near the bottom, and I could see at least another two pitches, maybe three, before the jungle swallowed the view.

We made two more abseils from what Britt called twigs and I found myself at the end of the rope with no belays. The eighty-degree rock was broken and loose, and any movement dislodged a shower of vegetation which flowed downwards to be stopped only by other small plants balanced in the chaos. To my right was a small tree – too small, and I couldn't reach it anyway. On the left, under a large overhang, the vegetation became more substantial and the only option was to start another pendulum, the danger being not from wet rock but what the rope might displace from above me. I started swinging, trying to jump out as far as possible to keep away from the rock, using the Shunt to hold my weight and thereby leaving me with both hands free to grab the tree. Every time I came close the overhang pushed the rope away and left me motionless for a fraction of a second, until gravity intervened and sent me back the way I had come. Several swings later, my arms clamped around the desired tree, so thick my hands were unable meet at the back. I made myself comfortable in the branches and looked down. At least another two abseils to go, how many did that make? This was the bit that Neill had thought we could have walked down.

'Next!' The impending rock above acted as a sound-proof wall between us and no reply was forthcoming, so I just had to hope that they had heard me. I sat tight and waited. The ropes went tight and I was faced by a worried looking Steve.

'How did you get over there?'

'With great difficulty.' As I pulled him over, the rope rubbed on the rock above and I began to worry about the abrasion they were undergoing. A frightened Steve grabbed the tree, hugging it for dear life and unable to make himself safe for fear of letting go. Eventually he managed to free a hand, clipped himself on, and one by one the rest of the team arrived: the five of us ended up perched in the tree, like a brood of bedraggled fledglings ready for their first flight. It must have presented a ludicrous spectacle and would have been funny if our situation hadn't been so serious.

The rope jammed on the steep rock overhead, necessitating some hairy climbing and another abseil to free it. This further depressed us – spirits had deteriorated with every abseil and our initial optimism and relief at being on the move again had evaporated.

There was no end in sight to this difficult section, and although nobody voiced their thoughts, the concern was there, unspoken and inescapable – if this was the easy section, as Neill had led us to believe, then what was waiting for us ahead?

Reluctant to be caught in the same situation as had occurred on the last abseil – having to pendulum with a large rucksack – I took a spare rope on the next abseil and 'volunteered' Steve to carry my rucksack. Again I found myself at the end of a rope with nowhere to go, not even a far-off tree to aim for. I looked up, left and then right.

'Come on, come on.' I was willing something to materialise, but couldn't see anything, and was almost at the end of my tether when I noticed a shallow ledge no more than six inches wide and only marginally less steep than the surrounding rock; above it were several plants. I climbed to stand on it. Testing the plants was rather unnerving – they could not, by any stretch of the imagination, be described as strong, but strung together and loaded equally they might just do. I tied on the spare rope and threw it down. I couldn't see if it reached the ground, but the angle eased about a hundred and fifty feet down and I hoped for the best. I joined the rope to the bottom end of the previous rope; this would safeguard the rest of the party and I could supervise their passing the knot – a tricky business that none of them had experienced before. Unfortunately, when it came to my turn I would have to do without the benefit of the other rope in order that we might retrieve it for later use, and I would have to rely solely on what looked suspiciously like a collection of cabbages. Solitary figures arrived next to me, horrified to see my belay, and I talked each one past the knot and sent them on their way. The last one went past and I tried to strengthen my anchors, putting off the moment when I would have to trust my cabbages. I stood in balance and pulled through the ropes above me, before gingerly, and with my heart in my mouth, starting to descend. Thankfully, there were no stressful swings and I soon found myself with feet back on ground that was still steep but walkable with care.

Britt and Steve had started off and were now out of sight. Pete helped with the coiling of the ropes, and carrying two over his shoulder set off, leaving me with the last to coil. Unnerved by my last effort, I sat down for a couple of minutes' reflection. This was way beyond what I considered safe and I was certain that if I got out of this I'd have some things to say to Neill. Then it struck me – I was thinking 'if' instead of 'when'. Psychologically, it was a crucial moment, the point at which I first realied that all our efforts would be directed towards survival. With all the others now out of sight I felt very exposed in this awesome place; tiny, insignificant and more than a little frightened.

I moved before the fear had a chance to take hold and made all speed to catch up with the rest. The steep rock demanded care – it was loose in some places, wet in others and my heightened senses detected hidden dangers everywhere. I followed next to the stream and soon came into earshot.

'You fucking wanker!' I was within sight now and even at a distance I could see the veins standing out on Britt's neck; he was absolutely furious. Pete made a clumsy attempt to calm him.

'Shut up, Britt.'

'I'm going to kick your bloody face in!' Britt and Steve had somehow crossed the watercourse and were standing on the edge of yet another abseil.

'Britt, it was just an accident, nothing to get upset about.' Pete was standing with his hands on his hips and doing nothing but aggravating the situation. Bob clung to a tree close to the edge, pale-faced and unmoving. Britt made an attempt to cross the water but the fear of falling stopped him.

'Fucking come here, you twat!' I watched this disturbing sight, not really wanting to get involved. It wasn't like Britt to lose his cool – OK, we were all on edge, quite literally in the case of Steve and Britt, but this wasn't helping.

Britt was still trying to cross the stream from the precarious position that he and Steve occupied. I was worried about his safety and the likely consequences if he managed to reach Pete, so I put on my best sergeant major's voice.

'Britt, STAY THERE!'

'That fucking arsehole.' He pointed to Pete, who shrugged his shoulders. I was unsure why he was so upset and still unwilling to be drawn into the confrontation.

'Britt, calm down. What's happened?' Before he could say anything, the explanation dawned on me. 'Pete, where's your rucksack?'

'I dropped it.' From Pete's position fifty feet above, a falling rucksack would have missed Britt by inches, and after fifty feet in free fall it would have been moving very fast. I could understand why Britt was a bit shaken.

'All because you had to carry an extra rope!' Britt paused and tried to cross the stream again. Keeping these two apart had to be my first priority.

'Britt, stay there!' I attempted to change the subject. 'Anyway, how did you get across there in the first place?' He was taken aback by my question.

'Up there. Why?' He pointed to a narrow section of water. I passed Pete and dumped my sack next to Bob.

'You OK, Bob?' He nodded. From my new position I could see how close Steve and Britt were to the edge, standing on a steep slab damp and slippery with moisture, inches from the final drop to the gully floor seventy-five feet below.

'Britt.' He was still shouting obscenities. 'BRITT, stay there. Don't move, I'll make a belay here and throw you a line.' I pushed Bob off his perch on the tree that was the only good anchor point and set about extricating us from this mess. Twenty minutes later, we were all standing in the gully floor enjoying the light relief of looking at Pete's broken rucksack, split at the seams by the impact and with most of his equipment damaged including his compass; the mood was lightened by his misfortune and even Britt calmed down. As Pete tried to repair the damage, Britt and Steve found a bivvy and Bob and I did the same.

I made a mental note that it had taken us five hours to complete 1,800 feet of descent in twelve abseils. Although I had left belays in place all the way down, and ropes some of the way, I doubted whether the rear group would be able to do what we had just done, but they were beyond our help. We could not retreat. We were committed.

CHAPTER 8

Tough going

We settled down to our by now mundane routine of eating, washing and preparing for the next day. Steve and Britt collected some old dried-up wood with the intention of starting a fire. The sun had long since departed; above, the summit was still illuminated by its powerful rays, but down in the shadows of the gully floor, the evening air was cool, still and quiet, with only the soft noise of the small stream encroaching on the silence.

Occasional moans came from Pete's direction as he sifted through his broken equipment and made what appeared to be a very good repair job on his rucksack with the limited materials at his disposal, while the rest of us lazed around, each lost in our own thoughts. Bob voiced his thoughts, speaking for us all, wondering if the rear group would make it down tonight; I looked back up the gully, not expecting to see anything.

'Listen!' Steve shot to his feet, closely followed by everyone else, and five expectant faces turned upwards.

'Can you see them?' I only half believed he'd heard something and after several minutes we sat down, disappointed.

'Let's get this fire going. If they do come down at night it will give them something to aim at.' I was glad to see that Britt had returned to his usual self after the incident of the falling rucksack. The dried-out wood, which lay all around us, burned beautifully and we soon had a good fire with flames reaching high into the darkening sky. I voiced my concern for the rear group.

'It'll be dark soon. They should be well on the way down.'

'I wouldn't like to spend a night on that!' Steve's comment met unanimous agreement – a night spent on the steep section down which we'd come would be unpleasant, to say the least. The light faded further, and in the slim arc of sky visible between the gully walls we could see the reds and oranges of the sunset. The fire threw out a flickering circle of light, illuminating the surrounding rocks, but its warmth and the sense of security it gave served only to accentuate our isolation as daylight silently slipped away, and outside our little sphere of light the imprisoning walls soared into the darkness.

Periodically, one of us would imagine we heard something and we would give a single whistle blast, but there was never any response. The intervening time was occupied with flickering shapes and faces.

Britt broke one of the silences: 'Rich, what exactly did the Colonel say?' I knew where Britt's question was leading – why didn't we just go for it?

'He said we'd meet at the bottom of the gully tonight.'

'And if they don't show – what then?'

'I said we'd wait until tomorrow morning, then we'd have to go.' The discussion of the ins and outs of what I had said, Neill had said, and how we could or should interpret it, carried on for hours. Britt was all in favour of leaving first thing while I felt that we must go and go soon, but was unwilling to leave at first light – if the rear group had been benighted, then they might join us early in the morning, in which case it would be worth waiting for a while in order to have the whole expedition together. Unresolved, the conversation moved on to consideration of other factors.

'Rich, we've already used the best part of our food.' I realised the situation could get much worse.

Bob, the senior person in the group but a relative novice in this sort of situation, contributed little, but did accurately sum up the situation and our dilemma: 'Two things could have happened. Firstly, the Chinese have reached the point where they have confronted the Colonel and told him that they're not going on. In that case, the rear group will have had to go back. Secondly, there could have been an accident at the top. Either way, we can't get back. With the amount of food we've got left, we have no choice but to go on, and as fast as possible, but I'll go with whatever Rich says.' We were moving towards a consensus – Pete, partnerless and probably feeling further isolated by the friction he had caused earlier, agreed, and we came to the conclusion that we would wait until ten the next morning. If we hadn't heard or seen anything by then, it was a fair assumption that they'd backed out when they had the chance – something I wished I could do. Warm and snug inside my bivvy watching the fire and still hoping to see five descending head torches above, I slipped off into an uneasy sleep.

Cold morning air and the smell of woodsmoke from last night's embers. Oats and apple flakes, and a pregnant silence, full of false hopes. Not this morning or the next would we see the rear group; once we started to move fast, we all knew they stood no chance of catching us.

The morning routine finished, we stood around waiting for our self-imposed deadline to expire. One hour to go; I mulled quietly over the events that had led us to this desperate situation. There had been times in my life, especially when climbing, when I'd been scared stupid, but only on one other occasion had I not been able to see a way out, not been able to see myself sitting at home, safe after the day's adventure. Now . . . what? If the next section wasn't too hard or dangerous, and we moved with the speed of a hundred gazelles, the chances were that we'd be OK. If it was to prove hard or dangerous, or both, what then? And what of the others? Would we be accused of leaving them, of disobeying orders? What if they died? I sat alone on my boulder, watching the rest sitting about, and Pete still trying to repair his rucksack.

'Come on, Rich, stop trying to wind yourself up.' A little bit of moral support sometimes goes a long way, but this time it did little to quell my fears.

'It's twenty to ten, Rich.' Britt was keen to get away. One last look back up the cliff. Still no sign.

'I suppose we'd better move.' No use trying to delay the inevitable. We set off, slowly at first, as the rocks had taken on a new feel, permanently wet and very slippery. Pete walked off ahead, still feeling sorry for himself after yesterday's events. Two hundred yards down from us, he started to slip and, both feet together, lowered himself closer to the easy-angled but slippery rock in an attempt to slow down. He gathered speed. Stood, and sat again. In front was a short drop into pale blue water.

'He's going in.' The four of us stopped in our tracks and stood shoulder to shoulder, riveted by his strangely majestic progress. He disappeared over the edge and a fraction of a second later – Splash! A plume of water shot skyward.

Days of tension dissolved and we exploded into fits of laughter. We saw him surface, short of breath, but the weight of his rucksack and the uneven pool bed combined to pull him over again. It was too much. I sank to my knees laughing, not concerned as to whether he'd hurt himself – it was just too funny. One role that Neill had not assigned was that of expedition clown, but it looked as if Pete was assuming that mantle. We caught him up as he scrambled out onto terra firma.

'That was cold.' His broad Scots accent was thick with self-pity, and his comment merely served to enhance the absurd event. Daft grins and soft comments did nothing to repair his soggy ego.

Most of the morning was spent making good time. The sides of the gully were steep and offered little or no chance of escape; we had come to descend the gully and so far it was giving us no choice in the matter.

Stopping for lunch we sat in the sun and looked back up the route we had taken down to the gully floor, picking out the ropes we had left in place. I dangled my feet in the cold water of the river, which at this point was thirty or forty yards wide. With the deed done, no one, myself included, really wanted to talk about the others; we moved off, indulging in some light speculation as to why the ropes were still in place as we hopped, jumped and in places waded down towards safety. Large boulders, green with slime, forced us to remove our rucksacks and jump ten, sometimes fifteen feet to the floor, and then lower or drop the rucksacks. The possibility of twisting an ankle or a knee was very real. As the boulders increased in size, we used slings, hand-held and knotted, to help lower us further. Human ladders came into play, standing on each other's arms and heads – not all that serious or difficult, but time-consuming. Time we might not be able to spare soon.

Mid afternoon; Bob was watching from on top of a boulder the ropes we'd left behind.

'There they are!' A mad scramble ensued to clamber on top of the boulder. In turn we viewed the figure through Bob's binoculars; from this distance of three or four miles away it was impossible to tell who it was, but he was definitely coming down one of the first abseils.

'He's not wearing a rucksack!' The person disappeared into the green patchwork of the forest and the rope became invisible again. Speculation continued for the rest of the day, but we all came to the conclusion that it must have been someone on a recce coming down to tell us to abort. Why else would a lone abseiler without his rucksack be seen, and so high up – at a point that had only been thirty minutes ahead of them more than thirty-six hours ago?

We hadn't agreed with many of Neill's decisions, but it seemed that at last he had made a good decision, given their fitness and the speed at which they were moving. Maybe he had seen sense; it was too late for us, but not for them.

The conversation moved again to food, a subject that was now arising every time there was any discussion. We were down to four days at half rations and the rear group must have been in a similar situation. If we moved as fast as the original plan dictated, we would have six days of hard walking ahead; we were convinced that the rear group, with only two full days of food left and still on what was the planned second day of the descent, would have retreated. It was obviously suicide for them to carry on. They would have absolutely no chance of getting out if they pulled the ropes through.

A few short abseils of thirty or forty feet slowed us down again and, assuming the others were no longer following us, we left no messages or belays in place. As the sky dimmed and the cloud moved in above us, Bob and I found a large flat boulder the size of a double bed and laid out our bivvies side by side. I felt guilty that I hadn't managed to phone home from Park HQ, but didn't think Sandy would be too worried as she was used to me not phoning or writing for long periods of time. We fired up the cooker and rehydrated the pasta, not eating as much as I would have liked, due to our now twice slimmed-down rations. Bob made up for the lack of food by smoking more. Water, on the other hand, was no problem – there was an abundance of it and we'd stopped carrying it in order to save weight. The vegetation was damp and our attempt to build a repeat of last night's roaring fire failed, much to everyone's disappointment, as our clothing was damp and uncomfortable, and a fire would have been most welcome. A few drops of rain sent us all to the dry sanctuary of our Gore-Tex bivvies, and as darkness fell, we lay content in our sleeping bags, warm and safe.

The next day brought with it fresh hopes of progress and an end to this misadventure. Bob and I were working well together, our friendship strengthening as our fears grew, and we set off in high spirits which were soon dashed by another short abseil. I became absorbed in the problems of belays and retrieving gear – the less we left behind now, the better. I kicked myself, thinking of all the gear I had left behind for the rear group, never to be used.

I found a log wedged between two boulders and passed the rope around it, hoping that it would pull through without jamming. One at a time we descended. Most of the boulders we had passed overhung dramatically on the downstream side and this one was no exception. As we lost height, the boulders became greener and the jungle canopy almost touched above our heads, giving the impression that we were in a tunnel. I was coiling the ropes again when I heard excited shouts.

'It's New's Pools!' The point from which New and Pinfield had made their escape in 1991 by climbing out up the east face of the gully – we recognised them from the newspaper article and photograph. New and Pinfield had decided that to continue down the gully from here would be too difficult and dangerous for a two-man team, which suggested that this was going to be make or break time for us; our team was bigger but less experienced, and we were about to find out for ourselves if their assessment had been correct.

The gully banks had taken on a new perspective. Gone were the steep slopes with their dense blanket of forest, and in their place were high walls of bare, damp rock, crowding in on us and cutting out the sunlight. It was still only mid morning, giving us most of the day to battle it out with this hard section. We tried to walk around the pools but the steepness of the rock forced us back; the sides here were vertical for several hundred feet, green and with loose rock everywhere – a nightmare to climb, which increased my admiration for New and Pinfield.

The first pool was no more than a few feet wide but forty feet long, and although it appeared to be only chest deep, the water was very fast-flowing. The lower one, only twenty feet below us, started narrow but then expanded to several yards wide; its depth was hard to tell but it looked deep enough to require a swim. Beyond, the ground and water dropped away around a spur and out of sight. The sides further down seemed to get higher as the river dropped.

We resigned ourselves to getting wet, stripped down to the minimum of shorts and trainers, and started to prepare our rucksacks. Steve had never done a river crossing before and stood in his shorts shivering while Britt gave him a crash course in how to keep your gear dry whilst swimming with it: take one Gore-Tex bivvy bag, insert rucksack, inflate and tie knot in end. Result: an ungainly but buoyant object that looks not unlike a barrage balloon. Steve was not entirely convinced that the knot in the end of his bivvy would stop the water, but had no other choice.

By unspoken consent, I was first into the cold water, letting the current carry me forward; reaching the edge, I braced my arms against the smooth rock and glanced down. The initial idea had been to jump, but the jagged rocks at the bottom put paid to any such heroic ideas.

'We're going to have to abseil, it's too dangerous to jump.' The four faces on the bank strained to hear over the roaring of the water. I forced my way back to dry land.

'We can't abseil down that, it's a waterfall.' Steve's voice of reason fell on deaf ears.

'There's no other way.' Everyone looked concerned.

'What about the rucksacks? We can't wear them, not if they're inside the bivvy bags.' Steve had a good point.

'We'll throw them down first.' The obvious solution. Not so obvious was the belay point; I made one more trip to the edge, this time with a rope, but no anchor points came to light, not even the smallest of cracks for conventional hardware. Not a thing. The current pulled the rope out of my hands, tangling it up in the rocks of the river floor, and ten minutes later I was still struggling in vain to free it, the current having further wrapped it around and under submerged boulders.

'Someone give us a hand.' A little prompting, but still no one moved; they were all warm and unwilling to spend any more time in the water than was strictly necessary.

'Britt, give us a hand.'

'You're doing okay as it is, Rich. Carry on.' I felt my temper starting to fray; it was impossible to stand in balance against the force of the water and free a jammed rope at the same time. I was also getting extremely cold.

'For God's sake, Britt, give us a hand.' He smiled sweetly but made no further response.

'Hang on, Rich, I'll get it.' Steve slid down the rock and braved the water. Minutes later we were standing on the side with the rope coiled. I avoided saying anything to Britt – his reluctance to help made me feel uneasy and just a little angry.

'There's nothing to use as a belay down there.' I looked upwards, hoping to see some vegetation of substance and saw, high on the right, a tree, surrounded by what looked like ferns. Pete accompanied me as I climbed up to it. The pale green tendrils of the ferns stretched out around us, at first trodden underfoot, but as we neared the centre of the clump the ferns thickened, deploying razor-sharp barbs. I wished I'd put on my trousers. Finally, bloodstained and stinging, we reached the tree. Using the half rope that I had cut the day before, I tied a bowline and we lowered ourselves back to join the others.

The extra weight of climbing hardware I was carrying gave me cause for concern – would it float? I untied the knot in the bivvy bag and blew some more air into it.

'You going first, Rich?' I was still angry about the lack of help earlier and the automatic assumption that I would go first stung me further.

'Not if you want the pleasure.' I launched my bivvy bag in silence and followed it to the edge, then clipped into the rope, pushed my bivvy-bagged rucksack over the edge and followed it again, lowering myself as fast as I dared, water pounding on my shoulders and head. I unclipped, jumped the last few feet and swam, my large olive-coloured bivvy happily floating downstream ahead of me. The cold threatened my limbs with cramp; my only defence against it was to swim faster, and with the aid of the current I soon found myself on the far bank, wet but safe. One by one, Bob, Steve, Britt and Pete took the plunge. I moved forward, apprehensive as to what lay ahead, and my fears were confirmed by more waterfalls fifty yards on. I returned to the landing site.

'Don't bother getting out the rucksacks, there's more swimming yet.' Long faces and moans. I picked up my bivvy bag and carried it like an oversized baby in both arms to the next pool – an easy wade no deeper than my waist. The water dropped away on the far side; looking out horizontally I could see to the next spur and my heart dropped. Spur after spur interlocked for as far as I could see, the steep sides soaring on in all directions. This could mean only one thing: the river was getting steeper and with it more dangerous.

I found a way down, hopping from boulder to boulder and managing to keep dry, but then came across a small drop down which the only way was by rope. Anxious to preserve our remaining ropes, I remembered the last abseil – it had been only twenty feet but I'd left far more rope than that in place.

'I'm going back to cut the end off the last rope, we're going to need all the gear we've got.' I retrieved the parang from my rucksack and started back, passing Steve and Pete, who were wrestling with sinking bivvy sacks. Knife in one hand I entered the water but the two-foot blade hindered me and I was forced back to the bank. Forty feet away hung the rope, battered by the water. I put the parang in my teeth and threw myself into the water, swimming as hard as I could; a small eddy gave me the chance of a rest, but not wanting to hang around too long I kicked out at the rock, pushing myself towards the rope against the ever strengthening current. I managed to half lift my body out of the water and the reduction in drag enabled me to cover the last few feet. I grasped the rope, the waterfall pounding again on my head, pulled the rope tight and ran the parang over it. It parted first time and deposited me back in the pool; I coiled the rope and drifted back easily on the current.

We pulled the rope through after the short abseil, adding one more degree of commitment to the many we'd already accumulated. I felt strange: uneasy and scared. If the gully stayed like this we could do it but we'd run out of food shortly and still have a long way to go. We picked up our bags and walked.

'Shit, another one.' There was little conversation; we communicated in terse, frightened phrases. A long search for belays revealed nothing, so I climbed out onto a ledge for a better view. I could see the water chute, which looked like a massive kids' slide, the water working its way down the smooth rock via a series of small pools, and at the bottom was a short drop of no more than ten or fifteen feet into an indigo pool. I studied it for hidden dangers – rocks or undertows – but could see no sign of anything untoward. Britt and Pete tried to join me but were unable to do so and settled for bombarding me with questions.

'What's it like?'

'Can we do it?'

'Hurry up, we're getting cold down here.'

'No problem, just watch out for the last pool.' Pete set off first, pushing his bivvy bag off ahead of him. It stopped in the first pool and Pete kicked it hard as he splashed into it. He stood up in the knee-deep water and looked back at us.

'This is great! Come on, you lot!' He was enjoying himself immensely and there was an almost tangible lightening of the atmosphere. I wondered whether to point out which was the last pool, as from where he stood he couldn't see any further than the next pool down. I made myself comfortable and watched. Pete reached the pool and, not realising it was the one about which I had warned him, tried to walk through it. He stepped off and disappeared into the hole, surfaced a second later gasping for air, hauled himself over the edge and fell down the last drop into the pool. Much to my amusement, I was able to watch the others make exactly the same mistake. As they swam the last stretch of water I climbed down from my vantage point and followed them down. Pete had been right. It was fun. The slide turned one way and then the next, momentum pushed me high up on the outside of the bends and I was stopped only by the clear, cold pools. Knowing that the last one was a swim I was prepared as I hurtled down the last chute and dropped the last fifteen feet into the pool; it was much larger than the rest and as a consequence slower, making the going harder as I could no longer rely on the current for momentum.

We regrouped at the other side of the pool. Bob's bivvy bag gave up the ghost; it just fell to pieces, the rucksack inside falling out in a soaked heap next to his feet. Wordlessly, he discarded it and carried on.

Our progress grew faster as the angle eased. There were several small pools, and short jumps offering little resistance. My jaw chattered with the cold, and my fingers became numb. At one of our short breaks, perched on top of a boulder, I ate some precious chocolate and offered some to Bob. I was concerned for him – his slight frame had little body fat and offered no protection from the cold. I noticed that his fingers were becoming clumsy and he was shivering almost uncontrollably – classic symptoms of the onset of hypothermia.

'Got any more, Rich?' In any other situation I would have ordered a stop and put him in a bivvy with some hot food, but here all I could do was break open another bar of chocolate from our diminishing supplies. I wasn't very far away from Bob's condition. I hoped I'd be able to spot the first signs when it hit me and that I'd have the strength to look after us both.

We set off again, boulder hopping and wading through waist-deep water that pulled at our legs, threatening to topple us.

Despite my concern for Bob, I was starting to retreat inwards when Steve's voice, just audible over the roar of the water, jerked me back to reality: 'Fucking hell, did you see what Britt just did?'

Bob and I looked at each other apprehensively and pushed on to find Steve and Pete standing on a narrow ledge.

'Where's Britt gone?'

'He's down there, look.' Steve pointed to Britt clambering out of the water some forty feet below us. There was no obvious way down.

'How did he get down there?' I wasn't sure that I wanted to hear the answer.

'He jumped. He fucking jumped.' A look of bewildered disbelief, followed by a shrug of the shoulders. 'There's no way I'm doing that!' Britt hauled his rucksack out of the water.

'Come on, you hats.' I was still unsure how he'd jumped.

'Jumped from where?'

'Here. He ran out across there, feet slipped there, missed that rock by inches, and into the water.' I moved as far forward as I dared. The rock on this side was steep and slippery, while the opposite side overhung and had jagged rocks protruding. The water fell in between and because of the narrow passage had increased its speed to a raging torrent, propelling the flow in the lower pool to a dangerous velocity; how Britt had avoided hitting anything on the way down was a mystery. Shouts of encouragement came from below.

'What are you waiting for?'

'It's alright for him, he's down.' Steve was annoyed at Britt's shouts.

'I'm not waiting here any longer.' With that, Pete threw off his rucksack. There was only room for two steps before he hit the slippery slab, feet pedalling in order to gain as much distance as possible before gravity claimed him. His momentum carried him towards the fall line, his feet shot out from under him, his hip hit the rock and he slid, out of control, down towards the speeding torrent and out of sight. I held my breath.

'There he is!' No need to swim. The force of the river was more than enough to gain the boulder fifty feet on.

'Sod this. Bye!' Steve was next; he followed the same trajectory as Pete and slid away out of sight. More friendly shouts came from our over-excited Para.

'Call yourselves Commandos? You're last.'

'Rich, I'll go next.' Bob held my arm. 'I've got an idea. Everyone else went high, but their feet slipped after only a few feet. I'll go low but fast. I should be able to get further that way.'

'Bob, just remember you're a Janner.'

'Thanks, Rich. You just watch this.' Down went his rucksack; down on all fours went Bob, like a sprinter in the blocks. A deep breath, three steps and he was gone, not further along, avoiding the rock face but straight off the edge, down towards it.

'Shiiiiiiit!' Concerned for his safety, but overwhelmed by nerves and Bob's hilarious execution of the jump, I broke down in fits of semi-hysterical laughter. A few seconds later he emerged downstream and looked back.

'Didn't like that!' Alone on the ledge, the noise of the waterfall crowded in on me. I threw off my rucksack, watched it fall, disappear,and emerge again. I took one last look up. New had escaped up the right-hand side of the gully, but here both sides had been smoothed by billions of tons of water, over millions of years, cutting a gorge hundreds of feet deep. Was this what Neill had expected me to climb? Here we were: the rear group were safe on the tourist path while we were committed, almost out of food, with no prospect of escape. Jump or wait. I looked down at the others, Britt and Steve moving on, Bob shouting encouragement.

In for a penny. I take one step back and launch myself off. Little momentum, boots struggling to grip, knees working hard. One last step – too late, my hip hits the rock with a sickening thud. Air rushing past my face is replaced by rock; I roll over onto my back and prepare for the impact, sure I haven't got far enough out and that the jagged rocks are reaching out for me. My feet enter the water and are violently whipped out from under me, turning me horizontal and dragging me down. A breathful of water. Swim. Cold water in my mouth. Swallow and try again. Eyes stinging in the cold bubbles. No light. Rocks jab my legs, arms, back. SWIM! I start to panic, arms flailing to find the surface. My head breaks into the open, lungs fill with air and I realise that the current has already pushed me as far as the boulder at the end of the pool, where Bob is waiting for me.

'Take my hand, Rich.' Hauling my rucksack up was hard work; I examined it, finding that small holes were materialising in the fabric, allowing the water in and soaking everything.

'This is just ridiculous, Bob.' Shivering uncontrollably, he nodded in agreement. 'Better catch the others up.'

We climbed down between two boulders and waded on, before being stopped by yet another fall, this time bigger. There was nowhere dry to stand and we all huddled in the freezing water up to our waists. The water pounded over the edge and out of sight.

'What do you think?' I was shaking uncontrollably and knew that if we didn't get out of this water soon we'd all start going down with hypothermia. Pete threw off his rucksack first and we all tried to see where it landed but the view was obscured. He manoeuvred himself to the edge and slid off, disappearing with the flowing water. With bated breath we all waited to see if he would surface further down.

'It's OK. Come on down.' Pete waded into view.

'Pete, watch your rucksack.' Britt and I noticed it floating towards the edge of the next falls. Feeling like a lemming, I threw myself off. To my relief it was a straightforward slide into shallow water and although my feet hit the river bed hard it was far less harrowing than the previous fall. The rest of the ungainly lemmings followed.

'Pete, watch your rucksack.' Britt was fast losing patience with him. I was all too aware of the next fall, which seemed louder than any of the others; we couldn't even see the pool below, only plummeting cliffs on either side. Pete unwittingly let his rucksack slip over the edge and Britt, touchy anyway about falling rucksacks, lost his cool again, venting his tension. Pete was not about to stand down.

'We're going down there anyway, it's no big deal.'

'Go on then – you jump off first.' They both peered over again. There was no sign of any rucksack or pool.

'What if there's no water at the bottom? Britt, Bob, hold my feet. I'll crawl over further and have a look down, and don't fucking let go.' There were sniggers from them as they grabbed my feet and pushed me over.

'It's no use. I still can't see anything.' They pulled me back.

'What about an abseil, Rich?' Britt looked hopeful.

'No chance – not without bolts to use as belays. Neill told me I wouldn't need them.'

'Do you think you can climb out?' Bob's faith in my abilities was touching but, given the circumstances, unfounded – to our right was the eastern plateau, the direction of escape from this ghastly place, but all hopes were barred by the overhanging rock. To our left was the western plateau and the summit, not as steep but just as impossible. The jungle canopy closed above us blocking out all hope of any sun to slow the onset of hypothermia. I scouted around the back of the pool for a belay, but the rock was totally smooth, offering no anchors, and my anxiety rose in inverse proportion to my hopes. Bob managed to crawl out of the water and knelt precariously on a slippery slab, arms folded and shivering, trying to prevent any further heat loss, and I joined him.

'I think I might be able to climb out.' I didn't think I could, but there was really no choice – I had to try. 'Off to the the left, over there.' I pointed to my chosen route. 'I'll see if I can get over to that.' The jungle, with the promise of plentiful belays in the form of trees, was only fifty feet above us, but to get to it I would have to climb out over the blank, wet wall that dropped down to whatever was at the bottom of the waterfall; with no belays I would be effectively soloing.

'Get all the rucksacks up here.' Battling with the Teflon-coated rock, we managed to get the four remaining rucksacks up to where Bob was sitting and I made everyone sit on them in a tight group. I got out a rope and a handful of slings, and tied on to the end of the rope, a symbolic exercise in confidence building rather than to give any significant protection against a fall.

'I'll pass the rope around you. I want everyone to hold on to it. If I come off, try and stop me.' I didn't fancy my chances
- the consequences of a fall were too ghastly to contemplate.

'Right. I'm off. See you at the top.' I forced a smile out and four apprehensive faces stared back. I edged leftwards, boots smearing on nothing, and hands on inadequate holds. Gaining height, I looked down; water, and a long way off – definitely too far to jump or . . . I tried to block the word 'fall' out of my mind. Half-way up the angle increased – only marginally, but enough to stop me. My right foot slipping, I reached up for a small flat hold, pulled hard and reached further to a miniature quartz crystal. Fingers straining, my foot found the flat hold; all I needed to do now was stand up and, scarcely daring to breathe, I slowly stretched higher. My hand wrapped around a root; I was unsure if it was solid but had no option. I closed my eyes and pulled. It held. I grabbed the sturdy tree above it, threw a sling round the trunk and clipped the rope through it, sick and tearful with relief. I'd done some scary leading before but never anything like that and I now understood what people meant when they referred to naked terror. All the reassurances of civilisation and technology had been stripped away for a few minutes, leaving me with nothing but my fear.

Twenty feet further on I found a ledge large enough for everyone and tied the rope to a thick-trunked tree. The others prussiked up to join me as the light started to fade.

'Rich, help me look for my rucksack.' Pete was dripping, cold and very uncomfortable.

'I'll be with you in a few minutes, Pete.' I was in no hurry; it had probably gone over several more waterfalls by now anyway. I gathered my climbing gear together.

'Oh for fuck's sake!'

'What's up, Britt?'

'My gas canister, it's been pierced.' He held it up in the light of his head torch. 'My dive sack's soaked. Everything's soaked.' He pulled out every last bit of what had been dry clothing and emptied the water out of the dive sack.

Pete and I left Bob and Britt to sort out their respective disasters. We walked along our ledge in the gathering darkness. I found a tree, tied on the rope and passed it to Pete. He handed it back.

'Rich, I'd appreciate it if you went down.'

'Pete, you dropped it.' There was no way I was going down there; besides, this was the man who had refused to support me when I had asked him, back on the other side of the mountain. I handed back the rope.

'Rich, I'm not being funny but I really would appreciate it.' He tried to hand it back, but I wouldn't take it.

'No way, Pete. It's your rucksack – you want it, you get it.' Reluctantly he placed his descender on the rope and started to lower; I placed my shunt on and followed him to the edge. In the fast-failing light I could make out the pool a hundred feet below. I shouted down: 'Can you see it?'

'Yes. It's over in that corner.' He pointed to a spot just at the limit of my head torch. I looked across to the section of wall that I had climbed, and what lay below it; we could have survived the jump, but the house-sized boulder that was acting like a giant bung at the downstream end of the pool would have barred our exit. The rock overhung on all sides, smooth and unclimbable. We would have become unconscious through the cold and drowned. It was a daunting realisation of how close we had gone. The whole situation was out of control and the darkness exacerbated my fears. I felt utterly spent. How would we get out?

Pete's voice intruded on my black reverie: 'I've got it, Rich.'

'OK then, up you come.'

'Pull me up, Rich.'

'What? Use your ascenders.' The very last thing I felt capable of was setting up a rescue.

'Rich, I can't do it.' I left him there for a few minutes.

'Rich, are you still there?' His voice had a panicky edge. 'Rich, I'm cold.' I muttered obscenities under my breath and returned to the tree belay, to set up a hoist on the abseil rope. I started to pull, making progress at first until the rope buried itself in the vegetation at the edge of the ledge and the resulting friction became too much for me. I added a further turn to the system to gain extra purchase and pulled again, but it just buried the rope further.

'Britt, Bob, Steve – give us a hand, quick. Pete's got himself stuck.' A bit of brute force might do the trick. They came tumbling into the pool of light thrown by my head torch.

'What's wrong?'

'He can't climb the rope.'

'Why?' Britt's anger was only just below the surface.

'I don't know, but he's been down there for almost an hour now, we'd better get him back.' Panicky whimpers came from below. 'Wait, Pete, I'm just sorting out the belay. Right you lot, pull on that end.' I moved to the edge and looked down.

'We'll have you up in a minute.' I turned to the mules. 'Pull!' The rope sank further into the damp soil, all the way down to rock, but kept moving, and ten minutes of hard work saw Pete ascending over the lip to join us.

'Thanks, lads, got a touch lonely down there.'

'Fucking hat.' Britt was something less than pleased at having him back. We returned to our soggy gear and left Pete to coil the ropes.

Bob's camera was, miraculously, still dry and he took some photographs. His wet sleeping bag, being filled with down, had lost all its insulation properties and I didn't envy him the prospect of spending the night in it. My dive sack was still in one piece and its contents – clothes and spare food – were dry, while my sleeping bag, although not inside the dive sack, had remained dryish due to its compression sack being so tightly packed and water resistant. It was slightly damp, however, and I put it inside my even damper bivvy, which by now had several large holes. It would offer only minimal protection against the elements, but was better than nothing.

'Listen!' Steve's sharp ears had picked up something again. 'I can hear a helicopter.' Everyone strained their ears.

'It's just the noise of the water, playing tricks.'

'It's a jet chopper, listen.' Britt was adamant.

'Maybe they've started to look for us.' Steve – ever the optimist.

'No-o chance of that.' The general consensus, as tomorrow was day eleven, was that people would start to look then; we'd be twenty-four hours overdue, but I doubted that anyone would come. It had been made more than obvious on several occasions that there was no mountain rescue service in Sabah. The only way of getting us out would be by helicopter, but I wondered if we were we too high for one to reach us. I dug out my altimeter. 8,550 feet. We hadn't lost as much height as I had hoped. Could helicopters fly that high?

'So what's the plan for tomorrow?'

I wasn't sure how to answer Bob's question, but Britt stepped in. 'Rich is going to climb out.' I just lay in my bag, watching small insects flying around in the blue light of the cyalume. Could I climb out?

CHAPTER 9

No escape

A fine mist soaked everything. The holes in my bivvy bag leaked water very effectively. My stomach was knotted with anxiety and hunger. As day broke I could see through the thin canopy the vertical rock that lay above, another reminder of our precarious position.

I had not slept well; the responsibility of being the only climber was weighing heavily, and I had spent most of the night running through our situation again and again. The decision-making process within the group was changing as we progressed. In the early stages there had been discussion, leading to a consensus but now there was little discussion and the others were looking more and more to me, not only for decisions, but also for their execution. Their support (particularly Bob's) was re-assuring, but their belief in my abilities was becoming something of a burden; I wished desperately that we had another climber with whom I could share the load, and who could take over if I became injured or otherwise incapacitated. As things stood, a serious injury could mean that we would have to sit and wait – for a rescue that wouldn't be coming.

'You awake, Rich?' Bob's voice, keen to speak to someone.

'Yes.'

'I'm freezing. This bag's soaked and it rained last night.' I looked over at his drenched sleeping bag and remarked that he shouldn't have brought a down one.

'Bit late for shouldn't haves, isn't it?'

'Shouldn't be here, I know that.' Was that despair in my voice? Emotions kept on creeping out, unbidden.

'I'll start breakfast, what do you want?'

'Got any apple flakes and oats?'

'Yes, we could have some of them for a change.' The tension

receded temporarily, only to return as I prepared to lead the first pitch of the day.

I scouted around the ledge, examining the vertical, vegetated rock, which was loose and threatening. As far as I could tell we were on a spur, at its steepest point – if we stuck to the crest of the spur, the angle should become more friendly and we would also have the advantage of being able to see the surrounding terrain more easily. I thought back to yesterday, relieved to be away from the gully and the threats of hypothermia and drowning – whatever lay above couldn't be any worse than going back down there. As I saw it, climbing gave us two options: gaining the summit plateau, 4,000 feet above, and then striking back for the tourist path, or (more likely) gaining sufficient height to enable us to contour round the west flank of the gully and bypass the difficult section before dropping back to the lower part of the gully, which we knew to be easier.

'Rich. Over here. This looks like the easiest way up.' I'd looked at that bit first and dismissed it, but hadn't found anything easier, and I was pleased that Steve was willing to make a contribution.

'I think you're right.' I returned to collect my rucksack and, as I racked the gear up on my harness and tied in, laid out a plan:

'Bob, you hold my ropes and second me. Britt, you come up next with Steve. We'll leave all the rucksacks down here; Pete, you go last, tie on the rucksacks and Britt and Steve can haul them all up.' That way I could concentrate on the climbing and not become sidetracked by having to think about the gear. 'I think that's the fastest way to do things.' Everyone just nodded.

'Right then, see you at the top.' I smiled at Bob, but he couldn't manage to return it. A deep breath to calm my nerves, one step up, and I was absorbed; easy going for the first forty feet, but no protection against a fall. The little vegetation that existed was too small to offer even a handhold, but as I passed a small bush I placed a sling around the roots and clipped the rope through it, a purely psychological exercise of no real value in terms of holding a fall. The rock became steeper and looser, so I pulled off some of the loose stuff, revealing a damp crack, and after a bit of cleaning (a slow process with only one hand free) I managed to insert a small wired chock, on which I gratefully dangled for a rest. Using a sling attached to the wire, I was able to stand up higher and reach another crack. In went another wire; I burbled happily to myself to relieve the tension. Another sling to stand in, and easy climbing until the crack petered out, leaving me to fend for myself once again. Above was a large tree, and fifty feet of steady climbing later I was safely tied on at the top of the first pitch. The rest followed me up and as they began the tedious business of hauling the rucksacks, I started on the next pitch. It was not quite so steep and the greenery, although more abundant, still offered little in the way of protection but did everything possible to hinder progress. I battled my way through bush after bush, while over my shoulder the gully opened out and at every angle the ground seemed to drop away violently. The climbing eased but, as if to spite us, the hauling became more difficult as the rucksacks were no longer hanging free, and I was forced into time-consuming back climbing to free a jammed rucksack. At the top of pitch four, after what must have been a good 400 feet of climbing, the ground yielded to a more acceptable angle and I untied.

'We'll walk from here.'

Bob looked apprehensive. 'It still looks a bit steep.'

'You'll be OK, Bob, just follow the group.'

I set off on a recce, returning twenty minutes later: 'Let's get going, it's not too hard.' We donned our rucksacks and set off slowly. Patches of steep rock barred our progress from time to time, but we managed to skirt them by staying, as I had suspected we would, on the crest of the spur. The ground on either side dropped perilously into rock bands interrupted by overhangs and the odd vegetated ledge. We climbed occasionally with the rope, but mostly solo. The plants at this altitude were dense, like thick thorn hedges, interspersed with odd specimens of the 'bastard tree', as Britt had aptly named it, for its tendrils were wiry and difficult to see until the barbs embedded themselves, ensnaring us, ripping clothing and lacerating skin. The branches, having very little weight, were impossible to chop with the now blunt parangs as the foliage just moved with each swing.

'This is hard going.' I stopped for a drink, sipping only a small quantity as being away from the river meant we now had a very limited supply. With most of the afternoon gone my arms and legs felt heavy. I was exhausted.

'Britt, want to take the lead?'

'No, not really.'

'Well, I'm knackered. I'll take an hour's rest here.' Reluctantly, Britt took the parang and pushed on. The continued unwillingness to help and blind faith in my ability to force a route out depressed me. I couldn't do it alone and was unwilling to be the sole decision maker.

We decided to try and traverse to the north, away from the summit and towards the foothills, small villages and safety, but every recce just revealed another rock face of massive proportions; I hadn't remembered so many cliffs being marked on the photocopied map and I stopped to study it. According to the map this area should have been easy-angled and free from cliffs. I swore under my breath, recalling the unmarked rhino horn near the summit – the contours were probably guesswork or the product of the cartographer's imagination.

I caught the rest up. The time was starting to worry me; it was mid afternoon, and we had planned to be back in the gully by then, having bypassed the dangerous section, with a clear run to the kampongs and safety, but instead here we were, still on the wrong side for any escape and unavoidably gaining height with every step. The temperature had risen and I finished off my first water bottle. Only two pints left. I started to ration it, as if we couldn't get down off this spur, there would be no replenishment tonight.

'Rich, your turn.' Britt handed back the parang. I set off with a new earnestness, eager to get down to business and the gully. The spur turned into a ridge, slowing us further as pinnacle after pinnacle had to be overcome.

Six in the evening and no prospect of finding enough level ground for even one person to lie on; we were forced to carry on, the ridge now heading in the wrong direction – south, and back towards the summit. I came to a vegetated impasse, the ridge buried under the accumulation of a millenium's long-dead vegetation. The only plant able to colonise this tangled mass was a bastard tree; not just any bastard tree – this one was twelve feet tall and a formidable obstacle. I made an attempt to pass it, but was easily repulsed.

'Britt, it's your turn mate.' I handed over the parang and watched his reaction.

'Ohh, cheers Rich!'

'You're welcome, Britt.' He made a concerted effort but to no avail. I started to look for an escape route off our escape route. The right side was no option – it would only lead back to the gully, or the awesome mile-high cliffs below the summit area. To the north, the ground dropped away abruptly but had an abundance of large trees and would, with luck, bring us out in the easier lower section.

'We can get down there, no trouble.' I pointed out the potential escape line. 'But not tonight.' Abseiling into darkness, unaware of what was below, was not a prospect I relished. 'Let's find a bivvy.'

Britt was still trying to hack his way through the bastard tree. Bob wandered back the way we had come to try and find a bivvy site but with no success.

Steve shouted up from the left side of the ridge: 'Down here. We can sleep down here.'

Britt finally gave up: 'I hate these fucking plants!'

Steve's bivvy site was a narrow ledge, which he had already bagged, leaving Bob and me with a fallen tree's roots. By no stretch of the imagination was it going to be a comfortable night. My battered stove took some coaxing before spluttering into life. A quick food count showed thirty-six hours left at half rations, but I dared not reduce it further for fear it would cause an exhaustion casualty.

'My sleeping bag's useless – it's still soaked.' Bob wrung it out and water pattered to the jungle floor. I took a deep breath; he was my partner, after all.

'You can sleep with me tonight Bob.' He was unsure at first how to take my offer, but was unwilling to spend a cold, sleepless night.

'You sure?'

'Yes, on one condition.'

'What?'

'NO tongues.' Daft giggles engulfed us as we packed away and prepared for the fast approaching darkness. The bivvy would have been cramped for just one person. The roots formed a cave; red soil fell at the slightest movement and the floor was made of the same red soil criss-crossed with roots. I folded my Karrimat into four in an attempt to cushion our behinds and placed a cyalume up in the roots to conserve the head-torch batteries. We snuggled up to each other in the sitting position that was all that the available room would allow.

A debate ensued as to in which direction to mount the next escape bid. One thing was undeniable, and that was that although we were out of immediate danger, the overall situation had continued to deteriorate. I longed to be back in the UK, having an epic on

Snowdon in winter, or even listening to Des O'Connor records – anything would be desirable compared to this. I mentioned that the summit could not be too far away, but sensibly my suggestion was turned down. I studied my altimeter. It still read 8,500 feet – the needle must have been stuck, and no amount of shaking and tapping would persuade it to move. I placed it back inside my rucksack. Perhaps it would work tomorrow.

Steve voiced the unthinkable: 'How long do you think we can go without food?'

Britt tried to make light of the situation. 'You, you big fat hat, you'll last for ever.'

'No, seriously. How long?'

'Bobby Sands went months, but then he was in a hospital bed and on a drip.' My comparison cheered me up – I would never have thought that Bobby Sands, the IRA terrorist who had died on hunger strike in the Maze Prison, could become a role model for me.

If we got down safely, then we would follow the gully to the River Penataran and the kampongs. There was one question lingering in the back of my mind. One I didn't want to voice. How long would it take?

My watch was irritating my wrist and I turned on the torch. Britt looked over. 'What's that?'

'Looks like a leech to me.'

'Yerrr, get it off quick, Bob, before it bites me.'

'I'm not touching it. Here – use the parang.' Britt was enjoying every second of my panic: 'It's already bitten you – look at the size of it.' I sliced it off with the big knife and launched it into the bushes.

After a long discussion it was decided to abseil down the line I had seen earlier. Bob and I drifted off into an uneasy, cramped sleep. Every time one of us moved it would wake the other. The sleeping bag covered only the lower half of our torsos and offered little insulation for the upper, but our combined body heat ensured that we remained relatively warm.

The stove was on its last legs, becoming increasingly difficult to coax into life, and with only three days' fuel left, I made the observation to Bob that if we had to swim again, having lost the ability to make hot drinks, the onset of hypothermia would be inevitable. I pushed the thought to the back of my mind and concentrated on making breakfast, the only food we would have until evening, reduced to a single sachet of oats and apple flakes. It didn't do much to fill me up. My stomach ached. I thought of home and tried to ignore my discomfort.

Bob had decided to ditch his sleeping bag. It was unlikely that he'd be able to dry it out and, being down filled, it was worse than useless when wet. Even if he could get it dry he'd lost his bivvy bag and the moment it rained again . . . From now on we'd be sharing.

By seven we were back on the ridge, looking down. It seemed steeper in the cold light of morning. I chose a sturdy tree on which to belay and set off, punching a hole in the undergrowth and dragging the tangled rope down with me. After one pitch I found myself standing back on level ground. Maybe today we'd have some luck. The others lowered themselves through the tunnel of foliage and we scouted around; the jungle was open, making for easy going, and the weather was fine. My hopes rose – after all, the kampongs were only four or five miles away, so we might even get out before nightfall. I had a good feeling about today.

'I think there's a way down here.' Britt stood on the edge and waved everyone over. The drop was not too steep, but still needed a rope; I set off, the openness refreshing and the speed of movement exhilarating. I got as far as I had been able to see and looked down.

'Shit!' My grip tightened on the rope. At least a thousand feet to the gully floor and from here impossible to tell if it was passable; any attempt to negotiate it would mean running out of hardware before we reached the bottom. Not an option. I prussiked back up. Britt was unsure why I had come back.

'What's up, Rich?'

'That's a non-starter.' I shook my head in disgust. 'It's far too big, we'll have to find a different way off.' I coiled the ropes as the others continued to scout around. They came up with another possible descent – this time only a single pitch to another ledge, and we repeated the process: abseil down, regroup on the ledge and scout around.

'Here's another short step, Rich.' With the full rope doubled and what remained of the other rope on my shoulder I set off, encountering at the end of the rope the old problem: no belay. I started the usual ritual of swinging to find one, the ground no more than sixty feet away. To my left a small waterfall over bare rock stopped any further swinging, but just out of reach was a small dead tree. I wished I was wearing my rucksack, as the extra weight would have stretched the rope just enough to allow me to stand on it. Hanging on to the last few inches of rope, I managed to get one foot on the tree, and let go of the rope, which returned to its usual length, leaving me balancing one-legged in the tree. Even if I had wanted to get back the rope was now out of reach; I had to carry on. I sorted out the anchors – if everyone treated the tree with respect it should hold. I gingerly lowered off to the ground.

'Next!' I watched as Steve, carrying two rucksacks, came into view.

'How did you get down there?' I pointed to the second rope.

'So how do I get over there?'

'Swing!' I was going to enjoy watching everyone do this. With the extra weight of two rucksacks the rope stretched that little bit further and Steve stood on the rickety tree.

'Oh shit, I don't like this.' He shuffled around to get onto the second rope.

'BELOWWW!' I looked up to see a large blue object plummeting towards me; a massive jolt of adrenalin hit me and I dived to my right. There was the sickening thud of a soft object on rock, and turning to look where I had been standing, I saw my rucksack, distorted by the impact, lying on the ground.

'You OK, Rich?'

'Yes. Better luck next time, eh?' I inspected my damaged rucksack and made some light repairs while Steve descended. Bob and Britt made the tricky change-over and Pete brought up the rear. Britt led off again through the jungle while I watched Pete make the change-over and stand in the tree; he had one foot in close to the rock and the other pushing out, making the tree strain under his weight. He was doing well, retrieved the first rope and let it fall to the ground. I found the end and started to coil the rope. I was about half-way through when I heard a terrified scream and turned to look upwards.

The tree was giving way. Pete, still with his rucksack on, grabbed at it, but too late. He fell, his feet catching on some vines, which toppled him over, and I could only watch in morbid fascination as he tumbled, out of control, limbs flailing like a rag doll. There was a small ledge at half height and I hoped for a moment that he might hit it on his back, his rucksack absorbing most of the impact. I stood, transfixed. He hit the ledge, bounced back up and plunged again, headlong and helmetless. With only a fraction of a second to think, I dived to my right to avoid him hitting me.

There was a tremendous crash, accompanied by the fricative grunt of air pushed out of compressed lungs, and followed by a horrific, gasping wheeze which lasted long after the noise of the initial impact had died.

I stared in disbelief. I'd seen people fall ten feet and be hospitalised for months. Surely he was dead. I went to turn him over but stopped, picturing ribs sticking out, sucking chest wounds, a fractured skull. If he wasn't dead we couldn't carry him. Did we finish him off? Who would do it? The train of thought took seconds while my mouth opened in a silent scream; I couldn't get my breath, let alone act.

'CASUALTYYY!' I heard the panic in my voice, the sound of rucksacks hitting the ground, heavy footsteps steaming back uphill, the crashing of undergrowth being forced out of the way. Pete started to stir and I carefully removed his rucksack. Shakily, with bloodied hands, he steadied himself and lifted his head to look at me. His face was a bloody mask and blood lay in pools on the rock, accompanied by teeth.

Britt burst into the clearing: 'What's happened?' I looked over to him, dismay and horror written all over my face. I was still unable to turn Pete over for fear of what I might find. Britt sensed my inaction and pushed me out of the way.

'Get the first aid kits out!' I felt useless, paralysed by shock, and fumbled through my rucksack, handed my first aid kit to Britt and turned away. It was the only way I could handle the situation. The others arrived.

'What's up, Rich?' I couldn't speak, just nodded in the direction of Pete, who was still lying where he'd fallen. I coiled the rope to keep myself busy while Britt sorted out what was left of Pete.

An indeterminate length of time later, Britt spoke: 'Right, OK. Let's go.'

'What?!' I turned to see Pete looking like an Egyptian mummy, unsteady on his feet, but on his feet none the less, face plastered in blood, which was congealing in his hair, his eyes and mouth. I loaded the rope and we moved on as if nothing had happened. I took one last look up and left the clearing.

CHAPTER 10

What, no food?

I watched as Pete wobbled along in front of me, dragging his feet and almost falling on several occasions. Our progress slowed to a snail's pace and I hung around at the back, dreading the shout from the front that would signal another abseil for me to set up, but none came and after an hour of watching Pete wobbling we came to the gully floor. By sheer luck we had come across one of the very few places along its length where it was actually possible to walk into it.

Boulder-hopping, with its increased demands on co-ordination between eyes and feet, slowed Pete even further. I was amazed that he was still alive after such a horrendous fall, let alone able to walk, and it had taken its toll on me too – I was feeling nervous and shaky, probably suffering a little from shock – and Britt had taken over the lead without discussion.

'It's five now, we'll look for the next bivvy and make camp.' Britt's decision was music to my ears – after my slimmed-down breakfast I'd had nothing to eat throughout the long day and this, combined with the shock of Pete's fall, had brought me to a point where I felt close to collapse. I wondered how Pete was feeling. Although he'd had no choice in the matter of carrying on, I couldn't help admiring him; I wasn't sure that I'd have been able to cope so well in the aftermath of a sixty-foot fall.

Steve found a large boulder which overhung on one side to form a cave. Large stones littered the floor, promising an uncomfortable night, but it was the only shelter we could find. Britt was preoccupied with Pete's injuries, checking and rearranging his dressings, and the whole group was subdued. Bob and I went straight into our evening routine with hardly a word passing between us; the meal was inadequate and did little to fill our aching stomachs. We checked again how much food we had left in the futile hope of finding the hitherto undiscovered treasure of an overlooked food bag at the bottom of a rucksack, but the result was as we knew it would be: twenty-four hours more at half rations, and then – nothing.

Under the conditions we were experiencing, the body could use as much as four or five thousand calories daily; neither Bob nor I were over-endowed with excess body fat on which to live once the food ran out, and we could only hope that we reached civilisation within the next couple of days, before we started to become too weakened.

'Rich, I've run out of fags.'

'That's OK, Bob – I don't smoke.' I was as sympathetic as I could be, given the circumstances.

'No, you don't understand – when I stop smoking I eat more.' There was real concern on his face.

'It's alright, Bob. We're going to run out of food tomorrow anyway.' We sat in silence for a moment. 'I wonder how much food the others have got?' We looked over to their bivvy site, some fifteen feet away: Pete and Britt were busy making hot drinks and rehydrating food, while Steve was off scavenging unsuccessfully for firewood. They hadn't given any food away to the Hong Kong lads and I knew for a fact that Britt had taken an extra two days'; they were relatively well off compared to us, and I felt an unreasonable stab of jealousy, allied to an altogether more primitive emotion that welled up from deep inside my subconscious. It was dark, intense and frightening, and I decided to change the subject.

We discussed again what might have happened to the rear group. Britt and Steve joined in and the combined conclusion was that they would not have committed themselves – knowing that there were in front of them at least another six days of hard walking, jungle bashing and complicated rope work, they could have made no other decision. If, however, and in the face of all the indications to the contrary they had continued, then we felt it unlikely they'd be able to progress further than New's Pools; we had been stretched to our limits over the last three days and I just didn't feel that the rear group had the ability to accomplish what we had.

The conversation moved on to our predicament. We made a detour around the subject of food and concentrated on developing some sort of plan. In truth, there wasn't much to discuss – the only option was to get out as fast as possible, but I felt there was one way we could improve our chances.

'Let's cut the gear down to an absolute minimum. That way we can move faster. It only took New and Pinfield two days to get out from here.' A sound plan but with one fatal flaw – the north side, up which they had escaped, was cut off by a massive cliff, and for the time being we'd have to be content with following the gully floor, which was an unknown quantity and might well require the use of some of the gear I was suggesting we ditch. The replies were unanimous and in the negative.

Pete tried to do the honourable thing. 'You can leave me here. I'll wait for the chopper.'

Britt quashed his suggestion with brutal logic. 'No one's going to be looking for us yet, Pete. It's only been ten days – no one will start to do anything until after the weekend at the very earliest.' Everyone, myself included, had made the assumption that Neill had arranged a suitable cut-off date – although I hadn't agreed with most of his decisions, I was very confident that he'd done at least the absolute minimum to ensure the overall safety of the expedition. Such was my state of mind, however, that I was starting to doubt even this, and I regretted not having taken Dave Powell up on his offer to act as my cut-off. We agreed on a general plan for the next day: now that the hard bit was completed and we were back in the gully, we would follow the river to the kampongs, two days' walk at the most.

Our granite mattress made sleep difficult for everyone, but Bob and I fared worst, waking each other through the night every time one of us moved in our shared sleeping bag, and again we were the first to rise in the morning. Light streamed into our bivvy as I was preparing our breakfast, and I mulled over my dark and irrational thoughts of the previous evening; I could only think that the shock of Pete's fall had released the tension that had been accumulating over the last few days. I was not able, however, to banish entirely the unease it had engendered – it is never pleasant to have to contemplate the dark side of one's soul – but at least I was feeling more positive.

I decided to treat myself to a change of socks and voiced my optimism to Bob: 'Should be out by tomorrow afternoon.'

'Yes, with a bit of luck.' He didn't sound confident. 'How far down the gully are we from when we left New's Pools?' Bob's question was aimed at gaining some moral support, but I could only be truthful.

I looked up the gully and saw the large boulder that would have blocked our escape from the bottom pool, and which it had taken us two days to bypass: 'No more than 150 yards.' Our lack of progress was alarming; at this rate it would take days, even weeks, before we got out, and I felt the first stirrings of panic. In order to distract myself, I started to pack, but my mind continued to work overtime. It had only taken New and Pinfield two days to escape, and that was from slightly further up the gully; if we could reach the top of the Northern Ridge we'd be in with a fighting chance, but down here we had little scope for escape, particularly as we were on the wrong side of the river and therefore unable to pick up New's and Pinfield's route.

Bob and I were ready long before Pete. All his functions seemed to have slowed down and his co-ordination was not what it had been; his rucksack, never the tidiest of things, was now a complete shambles, and he needed Britt's help to pack. I hoped desperately, for our sake as well as his, that his condition would not deteriorate further – he was relying on us to help pull him out, but we were already dangerously close to running on empty ourselves. I wasn't sure how long we'd be able to continue, and if Pete did go downhill, we might be faced with some dreadful decisions.

We left our bivvy site and set off down towards what we hoped was no longer a gully, merely a river. Boulder-hopping, jumping, occasionally having to drop our rucksacks down first, then gingerly lower ourselves, we crept down the river bed. Pete moved slowly, blood dribbling down his face from his still open head wound.

After an hour of exhaustingly slow labour we came to an impasse and my heart sank – I had hoped that the hard section was over. The river dropped between two spurs and disappeared around a third out of sight. A large fallen tree offered an escape from the gully floor, and although it would lead us out onto the wrong side again, we had no choice but to take the route it offered. With some difficulty Steve and Britt crossed it and, once on the other side, shouted back their usual subtle, witty encouragement. It was no easy option, slimy and with thick branches barring the way, but everyone managed to cross it without incident. We resigned ourselves to the climb on the west side back up towards the summit area and started off, our spirits declining as our altitude increased and we realised that any height gained at this stage would later have to be lost.

The terrain was unforgiving, with no leeway for mistakes, and every foot of progress was hard won. After several hours of extremely hard going I handed over the lead to Britt at a stream bed where the rock surface was steeper and the vegetation less substantial.

'Looks easy enough,' Britt said. He jumped, tottered and promptly slipped several feet. I held my breath – fifteen feet from where we where standing the stream bed dropped into the gully at least a thousand feet below us. Any slip from here and you'd have time to think about it on the way down. Britt recovered his balance and moved to safety at the other side of the stream bed, dislodging some of the vegetation as he went. Pete and Steve managed to dislodge the rest as they crossed, leaving Bob and me standing on the wrong side of a slippery chute that had been denuded of most of its footholds. The others disappeared into the jungle. We opted for the cautious approach, deciding not to attempt running across; the others, in a search for footholds, had come progressively closer to the edge and we wanted to maintain a healthy distance from such a large drop. Bob set off first, timidly testing every step, but as he reached the centre his foot slipped and he started to slide towards the edge. He slammed into a fallen tree, checked his descent and used the tree to pull himself out on the opposite side.

Safe for the time being, he turned to me: 'Come, on Rich – it's not too bad!'

'You're lying.' I eyed the smooth, slimy rock nervously, carefully placed my weight on a small foothold and set off. No sooner had I committed myself than my feet slipped and I started the trip down, lying on my back: 'Bob, I'm going.'

I looked down between my feet, focusing on the edge. It was pin-sharp, this dividing line between me and oblivion, and beyond it all was a blur. Bob's tree glided past, out of reach, and for a moment I had the weird feeling that I was stationary and the landscape was moving beneath me. The rim came up to meet me, my feet hit a projecting rock on the very edge and my legs began to buckle, the momentum of my rucksack threatening to push me over. My shoulders and upper body absorbed the impact, causing me to sit up, and I stopped, feet braced, staring straight down the drop. Oddly, I felt quite detached from the situation and found myself unable to do anything other than try to estimate the depth of the chasm in front of me; I sat, transfixed, until Bob's cry brought me to my senses. I turned my head to look at him.

'I'm OK, Bob.'

'I'll get you a rope.' He started to fumble with his rucksack.

'It's alright, Bob, I'll climb back up.' Slowly, the weight of that enormous drop tugging at my heels, I climbed back up to the fallen tree. It started to disintegrate in my hands, the slippery surface underfoot threatened to send me tumbling downward again and several seconds of frantic scrambling ensued before I ended up standing next to Bob.

'You OK?' His concern was touching, but I didn't want to dwell on the event.

'Yes, let's keep moving and catch the rest up.' I walked past him, not bothering to look back.

Britt, making good progress, had cut a path. The vegetation was not so hostile in this area, but the ground was getting progressively steeper, and the front three had stopped to discuss the options while they waited for us to catch up.

'Do you think we could abseil back to the gully from here?' I looked as far over as possible, but could see nothing.

'I'll have a look.' We had taken to wearing our harnesses permanently – it saved time and meant that if someone had an accident it would be easier to rescue them. Britt handed me a rope and I hunted for a belay.

A deep breath, and I started down. The rope was becoming dangerously worn and in any other situation I would have condemned it. Now, however, I had no choice – it was our last full-length rope. A few feet down the vegetation thickened and I had to kick my way through it, pulling the rope down as it became entwined in the bushes. I reached the end of the rope, but still couldn't see any further, so I tied on our last half length, passed the knot and carried on down. Without warning I emerged from the jungle and found myself staring into space, straight to the bottom of the gully – one, maybe two thousand feet below me. My head spun and, bitterly disappointed, I started the climb back to the belay. I gained the knot, passed it again, untied and pulled the snagging rope up to be coiled. Forty-five minutes later, desperately tired and out of breath, I made it back to the others.

'What's it like?' all four enquired in unison.

'It's a non-starter.' I tried, unsuccessfully, to keep the dis-appointment out of my voice as I explained what I had seen.

I coiled the rope and watched as they disappeared into the green patchwork of the jungle. With the rope stowed away, and feeling rather lonely, I set off to catch them up, pushing myself to the front to talk to Britt.

'Britt, have you seen anything edible?'

'No, not a sausage.' I pictured a sausage tree, or making a sausage snare for the wild ones that ran around in this part of the jungle. The absurd thoughts brought a smile to my face for the first time that day.

'I haven't seen any sausages either,' I replied through daft giggles, and we continued the conversation in soft voices so as to not be overheard by the others.

As the ground became steeper I abseiled down several more times, but succeeded only in depressing myself further – the sides of the gully here were just too high, and with our diminished climbing equipment we had no chance of descending. In my demoralised state I feared that even if I was able to get everyone down we'd be no better off, just stuck in the gully, jumping waterfalls and taking unacceptable risks.

As darkness fell, we stopped on one of the ledges and made a bivvy. I placed a sling around a tree and attached it to my harness to prevent me falling off the ledge in the unlikely event of falling into a deep sleep.

Pete's stove had been smashed beyond repair when he dropped his rucksack and he was cooking with Britt and Steve. Our stove was only slightly better and I coaxed it, protesting and now leaking fuel, into a slow burn so that we could cook our remaining two sachets – one of beef granules and one of mashed potato. I tried to water down the re-hydrated food to make it go further, resulting in a soup of sorts which we ate slowly, spinning out our last dinner to last as long as possible. I put the thought of what the next meal might consist of to the back of my mind as we took alternate spoonfuls out of the pot.

The meal was over all too soon, and to take my mind off my rumbling stomach I turned my attention to my altimeter, the needle of which had remained consistently at 8,500 feet. An initial gentle tapping of it turned into a full-blown bashing on a nearby tree but even this advanced approach failed to free the needle and I slung it over my shoulder in frustration. Britt questioned the wisdom of my actions, but I could see no point in hanging on to useless weight.

I placed a blue cyalume over my head and Bob and I settled down in the damp sleeping bag, bodily warmth our only comfort and protection against the cold and wet. We quietly discussed various plans of action ranging from ditching everything and just going for it, to sitting and waiting for a rescue. Our concern for the rear group was growing; today was day eleven, and if they had got out, then now would be the time they should start some kind of search. The discussion centred on what Neill and David Powell had told us about the lack of any kind of rescue service, and we were forced to the inevitable conclusion – we would have to get out under our own steam. I stared at the blue light and tried to sleep.

A light rain fell relentlessly all night, soaking the sleeping bag and increasing our discomfort. For once, I was thankful for Bob's small frame; my sleeping bag was not the largest, and I briefly wondered what it would have been like if he'd been the 6- foot 15-stone giant I had been expecting.

Our last breakfast: I filled the battered stove with the last of the spare fuel. Oats and apple flakes, just like all our other breakfasts, but I couldn't find it in me to regard it with the usual boredom – from now on our only sustenance would be hot water, and that only as long as the fuel lasted. While I waited for the water to boil, I checked through my kit. The map had turned into a sodden mess, but I wasn't too concerned as its lack of accuracy made it next to useless, and threw it away, resigning myself to navigation by instinct and compass. If we could get to the other side of the gully, we'd be able to escape up to the ridge and then to the hunters' paths that New and Pinfield had used before. It had taken them only two days, and I was sure that we could go without food for two days. Food. Whatever the train of thought, I inevitably came back to the same subject. The water boiled and as Bob started to prepare the food, I glanced through the mist and drizzle to the far side of the gully, no more than fifty yards away. Bob handed me the mug containing the very last food, hardly enough for one man, let alone two, and I ate slowly, savouring every mouthful.

We packed our remaining equipment and I took in my surroundings, trying to decide which way to go. The general consensus, to continue traversing, seemed as good an idea as any – trying to get back to the gully floor from here would be a waste of time. I hoped we would be able to find a route back down at some time during the morning, and cross the river before the rain caused the water level to rise.

I set off, wielding the parang and forcing the route as fast as I could safely go. Several small abseils saw us standing at the edge of a large drop. We had been successfully losing height all morning and seemed to be not far away from our objective.

'I think we might be able to get down here.' I retrieved the rope from my rucksack, secured a belay and set off. The angle quickly increased to well past the vertical and I reached the end of the rope hanging free. Spinning slowly in space, about fifty feet above the river, I tried to come to a sensible decision. Would we be able to jump into the water? Was it deep enough? It was far too clear to be able to gauge its depth accurately, but something told me it was too shallow. We could abseil to the bottom using the remaining half rope, but that would entail leaving all the ropes behind – something that was unthinkable on this terrain. I would have to find another way down, so I started to climb the rope to search for an alternative route. To my right, the gully floor dropped away again and the walls just seemed to get higher. To the left would only take us back the way we had come. I viewed a bastard tree; was it strong enough to take a belay? I gained height until I was level with it, a comparatively small tree looking rather precarious on its perch. It would have to do, but first I needed another rope. I returned to the top and the usual expectant faces.

'Well?'

'Might be able to get down, who's got the other half rope?' Bob handed it over and I departed once more, kicking myself – if only I had pulled the ropes through on the first of the major abseils. As Neill wouldn't be using them, I had wasted them in one last vain effort to help speed the rear group, and two full ropes would have meant that this obstacle would prove no great problem. I lowered myself to the level of the bastard tree and started to pendulum. As my momentum grew, and increasingly large pieces of vegetation rained down, I hastily put to the back of my mind all thought of the abrasion the rope must be undergoing.

I gained the bastard tree, found to my surprise that it was perched at the edge of a bottomless chimney, clawed my way into it with feet braced in opposition to my back and attained a resting position; between my legs the ground fell directly into the clear water some hundred feet below me. I unclipped from the rope and tied on the half rope. The knot was three feet below the level of the bastard tree, requiring a deep breath to launch out of the chimney into space and fall the short distance before the rope came tight. Sitting on the rope I could see that the ends reached the water, which was one worry out of the way, but how was I to get the rest down safely? They had seen how to pass a knot before, but had they taken it in? This one was different – I wouldn't be nearby to offer help, and it was completely free, just hanging on the rope. The knot was only on one rope, and if someone did mess it up and fell then the rest would be stranded, with no hope of getting down. I would just have to hope they got it right.

I lowered down to the clear, fast-moving water, which was nowhere near as deep as I had expected; only up to my thighs. I waded through to stand on the opposite bank and, holding onto the ropes, peered down again.

'Shit.' Another abseil, maybe bigger, then a swim. I turned upwards, my voice straining over the roar of the water:

'NEXT! Leave the rucksacks till last.' I didn't want any further incidents caused by the weight and bulk of the rucksacks; if necessary the last person could lower them on the ropes. Steve was first down. Trying to keep the concern out of my voice I motioned him into the chimney, and talked (or rather shouted) him through the change-over. The technicalities over, and braced in the chimney, he held up the slack rope.

'Now what?'

'Jump!' His look of extreme concern brought a smile to my face, but seconds later he jumped, swinging out wildly, free from the rock and any possible danger, and rapidly descended into the water. I talked down Bob and Britt, leaving Pete at the top to sort out the rucksacks, which was not a particularly good decision after what he'd been through. One by one the rucksacks came flying down the rock, attached to the rope by only a single karabiner and left to slide down. I recovered the bags and watched Pete's descent with bated breath until, with everyone safely down, I could turn my attention to the next abseil. I coiled the ropes while Britt tottered across to where the vegetation became more substantial and he could feel more secure.

I didn't fancy another swim, but there seemed to be no alternative – the water below was dark and uninviting, which could only mean it was very deep. I briefly entertained the idea of jumping, but as usual we couldn't see the bottom, so I carefully climbed down to the edge and set up the next belay. Just as I started down a vision of broken bodies, battered by the water, popped unbidden into my mind, and I stopped to check my equipment, muttering under my breath to get a grip. My fears – the river, the cold, equipment failure, my own fallibility – were feeding off each other, threatening me with all kinds of demons; keeping a tight rein on my emotions, I slowly started to lower myself. Smooth, bare granite towered above and below while to my left the river, spraying off protruding granite blocks, plummeted into the pool. Fifty feet from the bottom I spied a large ledge off to my left and started the inevitable pendulum. I swung into the waterfall and the slippery rock sent me tumbling rightwards, out of control. As I slammed into a shallow corner, knocking the wind out of my lungs and bruising my legs, it became obvious that I wasn't going to be able to reach the ledge, so I resigned myself to another swim, reasoning that the cold might help to prevent any swelling in my knees, which I could feel stiffening after the impact.

As I neared the pool I saw a submerged boulder and a gentle swing landed me on it, knee deep in the bitterly cold water. I retrieved my descendeur and Shunt, attached them to my harness and jumped in, the cold whipping the breath from my lungs as I swam for the bank with my rucksack in front of me. I could feel myself weakening by the second, and trod water in a vain hope I might be able to walk, but my feet found only water, my head submerged and I took a breath of cold water. Gasping, I swam on, thankful for the buoyancy of my rucksack, kicking hard with my legs and paddling with one arm. My feet finally found the shore and I dragged myself out. Shivering, I looked up.

'Next!' They couldn't hear me over the roar of the waterfall so I motioned with my arms. One by one they lowered into the freezing water and jumped in, swimming hard for the shore. Pete was left until last again; he hadn't changed into shorts and had to jump in fully clothed.

The rain was still falling, but at least it was warmer than the pool. I dried myself off as best I could and replaced my sodden waterproofs. Bob took the opportunity to wash his legs, which, like everyone's, were in a bad way – lacerated, grazed and bruised, covered in dried blood and with the odd cut going septic. Pete wrung out his sodden clothing and put it back on; he had no other warm clothing. He was becoming sluggish in everything he did and at this rate I didn't think he'd be able to look after himself much longer. He wasn't alone – the effects of cold and exhaustion were creeping up on all of us.

It was midday and we had only covered a few hundred yards but, more importantly, we had lost several hundred feet in altitude. I was ready to go, but after the morning's adventure the team seemed reluctant and were slow in sorting out their gear.

Bob took out his video. He panned round and, aiming the camera at the waterfall we had just descended, proclaimed loudly: 'I name these falls "Robert's Falls".' His son. He put down the video and took some photographs. Britt, not wanting to be left out, named the adjacent falls 'Sadie's Falls', after his girlfriend. I couldn't help but feel that we were just wasting time. No one seemed to have a sense of urgency. Bob went off to one side and, placing his video on a boulder, started to talk into it, making his peace with his wife and son. The truth hit me: he felt that we weren't going to get out and was, in effect, making his will. It was unbearably sad.

In some distress, and in need of solitude, I set off down the gully, tears burning my eyes and fighting with a rising wave of panic. I talked to myself, trying to prevent the last vestiges of confidence and belief from fleeing, and gradually my walk took on a purpose. I set off down the gully in earnest, sure that we must have passed the hard section by now. Boulder-hopping and jumping small streams, I made good progress, and I began to feel optimistic. In front of me, the spurs seemed less tight, but as I neared a large boulder, I was unable to see any further. I clambered on top and despair dropped me to my knees. A massive waterfall. Four hundred feet, maybe further, and impassable with what little gear we had left. I felt crushed.

I looked back up towards the others, who were blissfully unaware of my latest discovery, and trudged slowly back, not wanting to have to tell them what I'd found. Trying to keep as positive an attitude as possible, I started to look for an escape route. On the west side of the gully a spur came down to the river and looked easily climbable; not the best option, but it was on the right side and might allow us to skirt around the waterfalls. And we *might* get out in only another two days. Two foodless days, but there was hope.

I returned to the others and told them what was ahead. No one seemed to want to add anything and we set off in silence. Everyone looked down over the edge just to confirm what I had told them.

Parang in hand, I commenced cutting my way through the

undergrowth, hauling myself up over boulders on the steepening ground. The parang felt heavy in my hands and my blows started to lose their effectiveness as my arms tired. The ground continued to steepen and the vegetation became more dense.

'Britt, take over for me. I'm knackered.' I sat down, feeling light-headed and unsteady on my feet. I was out of breath, there was a sickly sensation in my stomach and I was unable to focus my eyes. A disgruntled Britt snatched the parang and took over the lead. Grateful for the rest, I watched as the others walked past; the people at the back were having a relatively easy time, while the person at the front was becoming exhausted by the effort of cutting the path, swinging the blade for several minutes just to make a yard of progress, which was quite likely to be lost when he came up against an impasse.

Pete was the last man, and I joined on the end and followed him. The pace was easy after the morning's work climbing up and down ropes and forcing the path. I checked my compass: due south, the wrong direction.

I shouted forward: 'Britt, do you think we could go downhill here? It doesn't look too bad.' There was no reply, so I pushed past Pete and worked my way to the front.

'Britt, we're heading the wrong way.'

'We're on a path. Look, old parang cuts.' My morale lifted, but I still had reservations about the direction.

'But we're heading south.'

'I didn't see anything else, any other way to go.' With that he set off again. I waited for Pete to catch up. Britt had, after the initial first aid, left him to his own devices, and several minutes later he staggered into view, exhausted.

'You OK, Pete?' He looked very ill, sweating and weak. His reply was punctuated by his ragged breathing.

'I'm OK, just slow down a bit.'

'Come on. Let's catch up with the others, you go in front of me.' He carried on, slowly, up the near vertical ground. I tried shouting to the others to slow down, but we were too far behind. Pete struggled on a steep section above me. I watched a black and red beetle, three or four inches long, toiling away at its busy life, unaware of the drama unfolding around it, and picked it up, wondering if it was edible. The thought revolted me and I put it down, smiling as it hid itself under a fallen leaf. I set off again to find Pete hanging on to a tree, exhausted. I started up to help him, pulling through the branches of a sturdy tree, but without any warning he fell, too tired to make a noise. A branch caught his shoulder and turned him face down before he landed chest first on a branch above me with a heavy thud which jarred his body and expelled the air from his chest in a sudden wheezing noise.

'Oh fuck.' I climbed towards him, the branches hindering me, catching on my rucksack and threatening to send me toppling back down.

'Pete? Pete.' I lifted his head and stared into his eyes.

'That hurt!' He was out of breath, but still with us.

'Yeah, I bet it did.' I took off his rucksack and he sat up.

'I'm fucked. You should have left me at the bottom, waiting for a rescue.' I tried to shout to the others again but they were still too far ahead. I blew on my whistle, but there was still no reply.

'Do you think you can carry on?'

'Give me a minute, I'll be OK.' Fatigue and dejection were written across his face and I didn't think he could carry on, not without a long rest; it would only be a matter of time before he seriously hurt himself, or worse.

'Wait here, I'll go and tell the rest to stop and wait.' I knew I shouldn't leave him but I had no choice and so, making him as comfortable as possible, I picked up my rucksack and set off. Climbing as fast as I could, and then running over the easier angled ground above, I soon caught up with the others.

'Pete's had another fall. He's not too bad, but just wait here. I'll go back to get him.' I threw my rucksack to the ground and had a drink, feeling light-headed again. Nobody offered to go back and I needed a break before heading down. Ten minutes passed and my legs still felt shaky. Pete came into view. I studied his walk; his co-ordination was impaired and his morale was at rock bottom. Without saying a word, he dropped his rucksack and collapsed onto it. Britt shouldered his, gave a disapproving look at Pete and set off up the path, closely followed by the others. I chatted to Pete for five minutes in a fruitless attempt to cheer him up.

We trudged uphill for the rest of the afternoon, finding various items of litter and a bag of nails. Much speculation ensued as to how the nails got there; Britt was convinced that they belonged to hunters, and that we were on a path frequented by locals. I was unsure – it seemed to lead nowhere, from the gully to the massive cliffs of the eastern plateau. I briefly entertained the idea of gaining the other side of the mountain, the tourist path and safety, but remembered the terrain I'd seen days before and placed all hope of the other side out of my mind.

Just before dark we stopped and Steve grabbed the only flat area large enough to take a person lying down. Bob and I found a hollow fifty yards further down the path and before we turned in, I checked my compass. We were still heading south.

The rain had started at three in the afternoon, as usual and, if it followed its normal pattern, would continue until the early hours. The light drizzle soaked everything and we slipped our two wet and cold bodies into the equally wet and cold sleeping bag, still wearing our wet fleeces, the close proximity of our bodies the only protection against the cold. Britt's voice came cutting through the white air: 'Do you two want any food?' The mere thought of it was enough to make me smile.

'Have you got any to spare?' Fifteen minutes later, Steve's ghostly figure appeared through the mist, carrying some rice pudding and soup. Reluctant to stay and chat in the cold wet air, he dropped off the food and set off back through the mist to their bivvy site. In the cramped sleeping bag we used the last of the fuel to heat it up. It did little to stave off the gnawing hunger, but did raise our spirits.

Our bed was made from roots and long dead foliage. The path on which we lay meandered along the very top of the ridge and all around us the ground dropped away steeply. In places the jungle parted, with the tantalising promise of fine views, but the mist prevented us seeing into the gully and any potential escape routes. Bob and I tried to formulate a plan, our discussions revolving around the path. At no time had any mention been made of a path linking the north and south sides of the mountain, nor was there a path marked on the map; I had seen the terrain that was beyond the Eastern Plateau and very much doubted whether a path could exist between the two. I wondered if we might be able to descend the west side of the ridge and follow the next river along – because of its distance away from the gully and the mountain it should be less steep and would lead us to the Penataran.

The conversation turned to the amount of equipment we were carrying and we unanimously decided to ditch all but the most essential of gear. First to go would be the tent. This was the only item about which Neill had been adamant and we had never used it; it was to be followed by my trainers and the now useless cooker.

As darkness gathered the rain increased to a downpour and our cocoon acted like a giant sponge. We awoke sodden, cramped and cold, but the sky was clear. Bob and I were unwilling to lie around, keen to get started. I shouted to the others, enquiring how long it would be before they were ready to move.

'We're having breakfast.' Bob and I looked at each other: soaked, cold, miserable and extremely hungry.

'I'm not hanging around watching them eat breakfast!' Bob agreed and we broke camp. With everything packed we walked slowly up to the other bivvy site. They were still in their sleeping bags, staring at the stove slowly heating up the water. We didn't have the pluck to beg for food; if they'd had enough to spare I'm sure they would have offered.

'Britt, how long will you be?'

'Twenty minutes, more or less.'

'Bob and I will walk on ahead. We'll stick to the path and if we come to a fork we'll stop and wait for you.' Not waiting for a reply, we set off.

Britt's voice drifted over the ridge to us. 'Don't get too far ahead.'

Now that we were on top of the ridge, the path had levelled out and our progress was fast. The cloud cover was gone; down to the right we could see the gully, thousands of feet below, and I was surprised to discover just how much height we had gained. To our left the ground dropped away equally steeply into what appeared to be another gully. I took a bearing with the compass: south.

'Bob, we're still heading south, look.' I offered him the compass to confirm my observation.

'It's a path, Rich, someone must have made it. It must go somewhere.' We stopped for twenty minutes and waited, quietly discussing the direction and further possible lines of escape.

Once the twenty minutes were up I shouted for the others: 'Britt!' I paused for a few seconds. 'Steve!' An indecipherable reply came back, but they sounded close, and we shouldered our rucksacks and trudged on slowly. Half an hour later they had still not caught up, so we stopped and shouted again, but this time there was no reply. I got out my compass, checked the direction (still south), and blew the whistle, expecting a return blast, but nothing came. I tried again. Still nothing.

'Pete's probably slowed them down. We'll carry on ahead. There's no way they could get lost on this path.' We slowed our pace still further. Bob suggested walking for another fifteen minutes and then trying again, in the hope that they would have gained some ground on us.

From our new vantage point on the ridge the gully looked very impressive; we'd gained sufficient height to be able to see all of it, right the way up to the big abseils at the end of Easy Valley, and the col. I stopped and stared. It looked so close. In the summit area I thought I could see people milling around, but I doubted whether they could see us among the vegetation. If only we could make it to there. I checked myself – it was no use hoping for the impossible. An excited cry came from ahead of me.

'Look!' I paced out to catch up. In a clearing was a stick cut at both ends and on top an old sardine can. To the right of centre was a fireplace. We made a brief search for any food that might have been hidden, but to no avail. With dread I noticed the path had ended and that above us were the impassable cliffs of the Eastern Plateau. There was no point in going any further, wasting any more time.

Downhearted, we turned on our heels and set off, stopping every fifteen minutes and shouting for the others, but still there was no reply. I was worried and Bob was too, but we were both afraid to talk about our fears. In three places the path split for ten or fifteen yards and then rejoined itself. An hour passed quickly, and still no replies to shouts or whistle blasts. I feared the worst.

'Bob, where are they?'

'Maybe they've gone off the path.'

'Maybe they've gone back down the path. After all, it does go in the wrong direction for escape.' We discussed the options the others had faced. They still had food; our calculations gave them two or three days' – the amount we had given away to the Hong Kong lads. They had said they'd be twenty minutes behind us. We'd just walked downhill for an hour and waited for thirty minutes. The conclusion was inescapable. We were by ourselves. Five minutes later we had formed a plan.

'We'll head north down off this ridge to the next river.' I had noticed on the way up that there was another, lesser spur off to the north. If we could gain that, then there might even be a path on top of it. There seemed to be a slight path leading off in roughly the right direction, so we left the comfort of the main path and any hope of seeing the others again.

Jungle. Cutting paths, and the bastard trees were in abundance. After the speed of travelling on the path, we slowed to the usual pace of the jungle on steep ground. The extra exertion of wielding the parang made me feel unsteady on my feet; I stopped for a few seconds and then carried on, but the dizziness returned instantly. I handed over the parang to Bob, content to take a back seat until I felt stronger, but the dizziness just increased and I started to lose my co-ordination. I was stumbling, slipping, not totally in control, so I took another short break and watched Bob as he tackled another bastard tree, swinging the knife one way, then the next. Left and right, up and down, vegetation flying in all directions, kicking and stomping it down with his boots, anything to get through it.

He stepped forward again and disappeared, swallowed by the jungle. For some reason, I thought of Arnold Schwarzenegger bursting through the undergrowth chased by aliens. I stood and walked un-steadily forward.

'Rich!' A faint cry, too far away to be Bob. But who else could it be?

'Bob, is that you?' I couldn't help but think that he was messing around.

'Riiich! Get the fucking first aid kit!' he shrieked from below me, panic and fear in his voice. I felt the adrenalin starting to pump.

'I'll be there in two minutes, Bob. Keep talking.' I ran forward, all giddiness gone and my strength returned. I headed straight for the point where I had last seen him and peered down.

'Shit!' He was lying down some forty feet below me. It was not a cliff but very steep ground, and he had fallen the whole way.

'Rich I need the fucking first aid kit!' From my vantage point I looked quickly around to see an easier way down but there was none. I watched Bob moving uncomfortably, holding his right hand high in the air.

I jumped feet first and slid, the undergrowth flashing past my face. I grabbed at some bushes and my legs crumpled under the impact of my feet hitting some protruding roots.

'Fuck, that hurt! Bob, where are you?' From my new position I had lost sight of him.

'Down here. Get the first aid kit.'

Not wanting to jump again I lowered myself as quickly as I could, the rotting vegetation occasionally giving way and sending me falling, but never too far. I turned to see Bob sitting on the ground, right hand high in the air and his whole arm soaked in blood. I ran over, dropped my rucksack and started throwing things out to get to the first aid kit. I glanced at his hand.

'What happened?'

Rich was some way behind me as I tried to cut through what must have been the biggest bastard tree in south-east Asia. The more I cut, the more the long thorns ripped into my skin. I was getting really pissed off with this thing, and the more frustrated I got with it, the bigger an obstacle to our escape it became. My mind was working overtime and every blow of the parang came to represent something that had gone wrong on the expedition:

Slash. Chow collapsing on the first day. Another slash. The argument that Rich had with the boss. The abrupt changes in plan from the boss. The cock-up with the Chinese rations. It was as if this tree in front of me was receiving every ounce of my frustration.

Up and down with half loads.

Rich missing the RV at the col.

The ape-like shape that spooked me in Easy Valley.

The split from the rear group.

Pete's fall.

Running out of food.

And now, to cap it all, the split from the other three. Something must be doing this to us – things were getting worse (if they could) by the day – and there just couldn't be any explanation other than some malevolent force, probably the dragon.

I was through. Bits of dead bastard tree lay everywhere. I couldn't keep the grin from my face. Done it. I wiped the sweat from my eyes, stepped over the stump like some sort of conquering hero and was just turning round to speak to Rich when the ground gave way beneath my feet.

'Shit!' I was falling down a steep bank of jungle, lashed by branches and undergrowth. I tried to grab hold of something with my left hand, but whatever I grabbed gave way. Instinct told me to keep hold of the parang – it was all we had to get us out of this jungle and we'd never be able to move without it. As I fell, I tried to roll onto my back so that my rucksack would slow me down, but before I was able to do it my feet hit something and my body twisted round, leaving me sliding head first on my chest. I saw a big boulder rushing up to meet me and instinctively put out my arm to ward off the impending collision; the parang hit the rock first and the impact caused my hand to slide over the handle and down the blade. Desperate not to lose the parang, I gripped it tighter and, as if in slow motion, saw the blade bury itself deep into skin and bone. An instant before my head hit the rock I managed to twist out of the way; my shoulder crashed into it and I carried on falling, the jungle lashing my face again, until I came to the bottom and all the wind was knocked out of me by the impact. I lay there, trying to get some air into my lungs and gradually became aware of the pain in my right hand. Remembering what had happened on the way down, I was scared to look at first but the pain got worse and I turned my head to have a look. My hand was still wrapped around the blade and there was blood everywhere. I could see that the blade had buried itself deep into my fingers. I felt sick. I lifted myself to my knees and started to peel my fingers from the blade. *Shit. Shit. Shit. Not now. Not here in this fucking hell hole. Please.* Two of my fingers were almost completely severed and the top of a third was hanging off.

The only thing I could think was how the hell I would be able to carry on. The blood was really flowing now that I'd removed the parang and I started to panic. I shouted for Rich to get the first aid kit and heard him shouting from the top that he was on his way. I sat down with my arm in the air and applied pressure to my brachial artery to stem the bleeding. I felt as sick as a pig, physically and mentally; every time I tried to come up with an explanation for our appaling luck, I reached the same conclusion. That hostile force that was dogging our footsteps. Why was it doing it? Had we really offended the guardian of the gully that much? Whatever it was, it wasn't going to get me without a struggle. I was tempted to tell Rich about it when he arrived, but thought better of it; things were bad enough already without him thinking I'd gone mental, too. Where was he?

'Rich, get the fucking first aid kit. Hurry!'

As Bob related the event I broke out the first field dressing and bandaged his hand up as tightly as I could. Using zinc oxide tape, I curved his fingers into a hook to increase the compression and stop the bleeding. It would make it difficult for him to climb, but he had to continue. If not, I'd just be leaving him to die; the chances of anyone looking for us this far away from the gully were nil.

No sooner had I applied the dressing than it started to weep blood, so I applied another one on top. I knew the wound needed stitching but I had no equipment to do it with, and wondered, if we ever got out of this place, whether he'd be able to keep his fingers. White-faced with shock, we both stood. I looked him straight in the eye.

'Does that hurt?'

'Yes!' Annoyance in his voice.

'Good, don't do it again.' I smiled, and for the first time in the twenty minutes I'd been there, he smiled back. I searched for the offending parang and made a vow to myself that if I fell I'd let go of it straight away.

I set off with Bob in tow. After the excitement I felt even more unsteady on my legs. My feet seemed unable to stay where I placed them and my dizziness surpassed that of earlier; the exertion was taking its toll. I stumbled, my ankle twisted and I fell over, head first down the hill. I let go of the parang, but my hand slid down the blade, the index finger taking the full pressure of metal on bone as skin and flesh parted. I came to a halt in a bush.

'Oh, fuck.' Excruciatingly painful. I held my breath and smiled. It turned into a laugh. 'Hey Bob, guess what I've just done?'

'What?'

'Get the fucking first aid kit out of my rucksack, will you.' My smile turned to a grimace as I straightened my finger and saw the white of the bone before blood engulfed it again. Not as bad as Bob's, but bad enough. I closed my eyes and hoped for the pain to go away. Bob arrived at my side, grinning.

'Does that hurt?' I smiled weakly.

Ten minutes later we were on our way, fingers almost severed and blood seeping through the white of the dressings. I took the lead, parang in my left hand, and headed slowly downhill over the uneven ground, my knees and ankles permanently at buckling point. Thick bush after thick bush, fallen trees, bastard trees and short outcrops combined to hinder our descent.

By late afternoon we found ourselves staring down into yet another gully, as steep and treacherous as the last. A short abseil saw us standing at the gully floor. On the far bank the sun's rays bounced off the bright granite, so we waded across and soaked up the warmth, laying out the sleeping bag and wet items of clothing in an effort to dry them out. For the first time in two days I started to relax, the pressures and stresses melting away, and drifted off into an easy sleep until a hand on my shoulder shook me awake.

'Rich. You're covered – look.' Bob pointed to my legs. Through eyes thick with sleep, I looked down to see several leeches feeding. One or two of them must have been there for some time, as they were engorged and sat, fat and glistening, on my skin. I shuddered.

'Pass me the parang.' Revolted by the sight I started to pull them off one at a time, but it was difficult to get hold of their slippery bodies. Even when I managed to get a grip on them, the battle wasn't over, for they would stretch to three or four times their original length before detaching themselves with a tiny, rubbery slap and immediately sink their jaws into my fingertips, from where no amount of flicking would dislodge them. Eventually, with cautious use of the parang, I rid myself of the vermin before inspecting Bob and doing the same for him.

I was warm and comfortable in the sun and unwilling to move on, despite the threat of the leeches, although I might have felt differently had I been aware of the existence of the Giant Red Kinabalu Leech, which can attain a length of a foot. The ones we had encountered were mere babies by comparison, but we never found a quick and easy method for dealing with them. We were aware of the folklore that suggested the use of a lighted cigarette or putting salt on their tails, but Bob had long since run out of smokes and due to some appalling social gaffe we had managed to mislay the condiments.

Reluctantly, we packed away the warm, moist sleeping bag. I took some bearings and looked to the north, where the gully sides were high and looked too hard to climb. I had a quick scout around but could find no escape. We discussed the only two real options. Firstly, we could commit ourselves to this gully and start jumping waterfalls again, but after the last few days this option held little hope for us and we weren't prepared to go through that particular trauma again. The only other route was back the way we'd come, in the hope of traversing around the top of this gully and still making it back to the Penataran.

Downhearted, we recrossed the river and started to climb our descent route before breaking out left across the slope. My left arm weakened with every blow of the parang and, gritting my teeth, I changed hands; surprisingly, it didn't hurt too much and I found a little extra energy. The terrain to the right fell steeply away into the unnamed river, and to the left was a mixture of steep jungle, bare rock and vertical, degenerating decay. Either way the possibility of escape was limited.

It was six in the evening and there was still no sign that we had made the right decision in leaving the path. We had resigned ourselves to being alone, but the isolation was bearing down heavily on us both. We stopped on the ever steeper ground for one of our frequent rests and drank some water, the only nourishment we could afford ourselves. The icy cold fluid did nothing to fill my aching stomach. Hungry and tired, surrounded by imposing cliffs and the oppressive green vegetation, I began to feel that our position was almost impossible. The ledge we had been following petered out and we were left with two options: abseil to the river several hundred feet below, or climb higher. The shortage of rope and the thought of having to swim again put paid to the first idea, so it was down to me to climb out. I could see a large tree some fifty feet above me and aimed for that, pulling on rotten foliage, moss, dead trees, throwing off great handfuls of debris which fell out of sight down to the river. I reached a small dead tree and wrapped my arms around it for a rest, looking over at Bob some twenty feet below me and to my right. The ground under me dropped straight into the river; it was a long way down, but my strength was ebbing away and I needed a rest. Folding my arms around the back of the tree, feet hanging uselessly, I closed my eyes; I tried to find a ledge to rest on by moving my feet up and down but succeeded merely in clearing all the vegetation, leaving only bare, wet rock. My feet stopped. I was too exhausted to carry on. I closed my eyes and dozed off.

'Rich!' A panic-stricken voice screamed up to me, waking me from my sleep. 'RICH! Wake up!' My eyes were heavy with sleep and unfocused, but the pain in my arms brought me back to reality. I turned my head and focused with difficulty on Bob.

'Rich! Go on mate, you can do it!' He was still standing in the same place. 'Go!' He motioned upwards with his arms, willing me to climb.

'I'm OK, Bob, just give me a minute.' Uncontrollably, my eyes closed. All strength deserted my body, leaving me like a rag doll. *Get your head down, Rich.* A dim voice at the back of my mind tried unsuccessfully to reason with the sleep demon, but the demon's voice was the only one I heeded. *Sleep.* I relaxed more, my weight fully on the tree, arms interlocked behind it. The pain in my shoulders increased in direct proportion to my relaxation, threatening to rouse me but not quite succeeding.

'Rich!' Bob's voice came like a ghost from the past, intruding on my dream world, and left again.

I'm home. Back in England, back in Plymouth, eating a mammoth steak, smothered in garlic and herbs. My stomach is full, I'm contented, my newly found surroundings are clean, leech-free, warm and dry. My family are around me, smiling, happy at my return. The children are running around, shouting excitedly. I feel quite serene, all feelings of pain and discomfort gone.

'You all right, Rich?' A soft voice in my ear and severe pain in my shoulders jolts me half-way down the road to awareness. I briefly see Bob in soft focus and his words come from far off. The demon returns, stronger. *Sleep. Just relax.*

Pain in my shoulder. Pain in my head. Bob's gone, fallen or climbed past, I don't know or even care. Soon I'll fall. *I don't care. I'll be asleep, it won't hurt.*

'Rich!' Bob's voice again, a million miles away. *Let go Rich, it won't hurt. All this pain will be over.*

'Rich! Get the rope!'

'Rope? What rope?'

'Rich. Climb the rope, use the rope!' *I wish he'd be quiet.*

'Come on, use the rope!' *Now what's he saying?* I look up. Bob's looking down at me from the large tree.

'Use the rope, can you see it?' He waves it around and the end of it whips my face, stinging. Slowly, I come back to reality. Reason and motivation return.

'Clip the rope, NOW!' I released one arm and almost fell. I fumbled with my shunt, attaching it to the rope and then to my harness. I was too tired to double-check and just let go, heart in my mouth. Had I done it correctly? I started to fall. There was a sudden jerk as the stretch and slack in the rope was taken up and my fall was arrested. I hung on the rope, thankful to have the weight off my shoulders, and methodically commenced my climb, with Bob shouting encouragement at me. Ten minutes later I crawled over the edge and collapsed, eyes closed, lying face down on the leech-infested ground.

I have a vague memory of Bob trying to wake me, and of him placing me inside the sleeping bag. Perhaps my sleep demon was talking to him; it was certainly talking to me. I was back in Devon again.

Bob recalls the incident in detail:

I was standing on a pile of loose vegetation, wondering why Rich had stopped, when without warning it started to rain. Hard. It sounded like somebody emptying a lorry load of ball bearings out of the sky. Sheets of water began sluicing down the face and the vegetation on which I was standing started to get washed away. I grabbed hold of a rotten, decomposing root and shouted to Rich: 'Come on, mate, get moving!' He didn't respond. *Shit, what's wrong?*

'Come on, Rich. For fuck's sake start moving!' Still no response. It was at this stage I realized that the one guy who was going to get me out of this mess didn't have limitless resources – he was human, just like me, and had reached the limit of his endurance. He couldn't do everything. The animal instincts took over: frustration and anger welled up inside me, releasing an enormous jolt of adrenalin. I put my rucksack on a ledge and climbed towards Rich, frantically punching and kicking holes in the vegetation to use as holds, shouting all the while in an attempt to bring him back to reality.

'Wake up. Get your fucking act sorted out. Get your ass moving. If you don't move we'll both die.' There was still no response, and when I arrived at the tree I realised that I'd have to resort to something more physical. Holding the tree with one hand, I gave Rich what my father used to give me – a good old-fashioned backhander across the face. His head rolled back. I was ready to duck the expected fist, but there was no response – he was in Never Never Land. It became obvious at this point that it was down to me to get us out of this, so I unfastened the lid of his rucksack, flung it open and grabbed the rope. With the rope over my shoulder I started to climb, initially (and none too gently) using him as a ladder. The face was at an angle of about eighty degrees and covered with loose, rotting vegetation which was already disintegrating under the onslaught of the rain; as I started to climb, my hands and feet accelerated this process and after twenty feet I found myself sliding slowly but unavoidably back down towards Rich. My size six caught him in the chest and for a moment I thought that we were both heading for the gully floor, but luckily my other foot passed on the opposite side of the tree. I ended up wrapped around the tree, face to face with Rich, who still looked vacant and still had the lid of his rucksack on his head from when I'd taken the rope out. Under normal circumstances I would have found the situation quite comical – Rich with a silly hat and my voice an octave higher – but I was angry and frustrated and really pissed off with this hill. I had another go and this time managed to gain thirty feet, tears of frustration pouring down my face, screaming obscenities at the dragon that was throwing these challenges at us. I reached another small tree. It was too small to be of any use and I carried on, raging at the mountain, punching and kicking holes in the vegetation, two steps upward and three back, making another thirty or forty feet, before I slid back twenty hard-won feet to start the process all over again. After what seemed an eternity but was in reality only a few minutes, I reached the treeline and pulled myself over the lip, still shouting: 'Fuck you!'

I had beaten the dragon. I went to tie the rope round a tree but in my haste made a complete pig's ear of it – I couldn't for the life of me remember how to tie a secure knot, so I made do with a Bob Mann special, something you won't find in any book of knots. I tied a knot in the other end, coiled it and threw it at Rich. It caught him full in the face on the first attempt and at last he seemed to come round; with agonising slowness he attached his shunt to the rope and started to come up. When he was about half-way up, I began to have doubts about the Bob Mann special; maybe it wasn't so special after all. I grabbed hold of the knot to prevent it coming undone and screamed at Rich to hurry up. Eventually, he reached the top. It looked as if he was starting to slip away again, but I managed to get him to re-tie the knot for me before he collapsed. I dragged him up the hill for twenty feet, took off his rucksack and put him in the sleeping bag. Aware that I needed to retrieve my rucksack, and still fired up, I made my way to the tree and abseiled back down. I donned my rucksack, changed over from abseiling to prussiking and started back up. Half-way there, my hand burst open again. Blood poured down my arm and across my chest, and suddenly all my aggression evaporated. The dragon hadn't given up; he sucked away all my energy and spirit and I was left dangling on the rope. I felt almost lifeless. My rucksack weighed a ton and I knew I couldn't make it to the top with it on my back, so I took it off and let it fall. It stopped fifty feet lower in a patch of vegetation and I struggled to the top, managing to crawl the twenty feet up to join Rich in the sleeping bag before I passed out.

CHAPTER 11

Losing control

Bob tried to wake me several times, asking me if I could go back down to retrieve his rucksack, which he'd left at the bottom of the cliff when he had climbed out to rescue me, but I was just too exhausted to move. Any attempt at movement made me feel nauseous and I was unable to do the simplest of tasks. I slept on the ground where I had fallen.

Bob roused me enough to get me into into the sleeping bag and made sure I had my head torch, for it was now dark. Later, he made me get out of the sleeping bag to check for leeches – I was covered from head to toe. Bob painstakingly removed them one by one and put me back into the bag. I was asleep in seconds, beyond caring about anything, least of all blood-sucking parasites.

I'd been in Plymouth for a long time before Bob woke me again and joined me inside the damp sleeping bag. His wet body, bloodied and sweating, smelled just as revolting as my own. The crowded conditions did nothing to ease my cramping limbs, and the tightly stretched material of the sleeping bag, dirty with soil and grit, aggravated the wounds left by countless falls and the effects of the bastard trees. It was as if the sleeping bag was lined with sandpaper – every movement chafed and helped to magnify our misery. Despite the pain and discomfort I slept deeply. I woke at one point to feel my top lip swelling, but dropped off to sleep again.

The next time I woke, the swelling had increased and become painful; I touched the inside of my lip but there was no feeling at all. I drifted off again, this time dreaming of the plane home.

A movement in my mouth brought me back to consciousness. It was so swollen that I couldn't talk properly. I touched the inside again, and felt a sharp pain in my finger. I tried to pull it out, but something had attached itself to the tip, and I felt movement again, between my top lip and my teeth.

'Arr phuck! Weeches!' I cried through clenched teeth, frantically trying to peel it off. Reaching inside my mouth I grasped it with thumb and forefinger and pulled at the slimy, saliva-covered thing. It stretched and became thinner, but my grip failed, sending it whipping back inside my mouth like an elastic band. I tried again, this time using my nails to grip it more tightly, and its head parted from its body, sending a spray of my blood over my face. I flicked the disgusting thing away and felt for the head inside my mouth. It was embedded deep in my top lip and, too exhausted to try any longer, I left it there.

We woke periodically throughout the night to peel off the leeches. In the light of the head torch, the ground was a sea of leeches – black, slithering, standing up on one end to sniff the air and heading inexorably our way to feed. The Gore-Tex bivvy with its holes offered little protection. Our exposed faces were the main problem, with the leeches feeding off our cheeks and becoming entangled in our hair. I developed a fear of finding one feeding in my ear, and that it would become too large to slither out, causing permanent damage.

By daybreak our bed looked like a battlefield, covered with leech corpses and blood. There were still hundreds of them crawling towards us and I wondered idly what they fed on in the absence of humans. I crawled out of the sleeping bag, dislodging some newly formed scabs, and blood trickled down my legs. Bob followed quickly and we inspected each other, removing a dozen more leeches. I felt stronger than yesterday, able to carry on.

Bob spoke: 'I had to leave my rucksack at the bottom of the last climb.' We peered over the edge. Fifty feet down, perched in a bush, was Bob's rucksack. We discussed trying to retrieve it, but Bob was reluctant to go down again with his hand in such a state. I checked the knot that Bob informed me I'd tied the night before and lowered off towards the bush. Hundreds of feet below me the river pitched violently through the water-smoothed boulders, and putting myself back in the position of the previous evening brought me close to tears. I tried to focus on the job in hand, with only partial success.

Arriving at the bush I tried to pick up Bob's rucksack but my full strength eluded me and dizziness returned. I rested, eyes closed, exhausted by this small effort.

'I can't do it Bob, I'm too knackered!' Even shouting up took its toll.

'Get my passport, money, Sue's Instamatic and that bug key-ring that I bought at Park HQ – leave the rest.' I didn't question what seemed to me a rather odd selection of belongings, just rooted through the rucksack, stuffed them into my fleece pocket and started the arduous climb back. As long as I moved slowly, I felt OK, but any attempt to speed up just brought dizziness and nausea. Back at the top, we repacked the remaining gear. Using the rucksack and my day sack, we split the load evenly. I tried to sound optimistic.

'We should be able to move a lot faster now.'

The terrain was still no easier: steep, slippery, vegetated and with the odd small crag requiring an abseil. In the absence of a map, a guessed bearing was the best we could do, and keeping an eye on the compass, we headed north.

We soon discovered that without food our bodies were taking longer to recover from any physical exertion. Our rests became longer and our movements sluggish; the continuous left to right slope made the walking arduous, and painful on the ankles. We stumbled along through the interminable, oppressive green, with tentacles of the ubiquitous bastard tree pulling at our clothing and skin.

I sat down to rest my aching legs, watching Bob and the leeches draw nearer. Fascinated by these strange creatures, I watched one trying to climb my boot. It seemed to be smelling the air with both ends of its body as it sought out exposed flesh, and I wondered if it possessed noses and jaws at each end. As it neared the top of my boot, I raised the parang and brought it down as hard as I dared on the leather uppers. I felt the blade strike hard into the leather and expected to see the leech in two pieces. It wasn't – it just shook itself out, stood up on one end to sniff around and resumed its climb towards food. I tried hitting it again, harder. My foot hurt.

'Hey, Bob, have you seen this?' Still it climbed. I placed the parang in its path and watched it slither onto the blade. I positioned the knife next to the heel block of my boot and the leech crawled on; with the advantage of this improvised chopping board, my next blow succeeded in slicing the hitherto indestructible creature in half and took part of my heel block away. I wished we were as robust as these disgusting things.

Bob was unimpressed with both the battle I'd just had and my new-found interest in the phylum *Annelida*. He walked on, and I tagged on behind, across ground which was easing in terms of both angle and vegetation cover. What seemed like hours later we arrived back at the river, although which one it was we were unsure; the terrain, the absence of landmarks and our limited field of view were making navigation difficult. We rested for half an hour and debated the next move.

The river didn't look too hard, but according to the compass it was travelling in a westerly direction. In the absence of anything to take a bearing from or any obvious sign of escape we decided again to walk on a northerly bearing and hope for the best. We filled our water bottles from the fastest moving part of the river, the least likely place for unseen parasites to be hiding, as our ability to sterilise the water, making it safe to drink, was almost gone, our supply of 'steritabs' just about spent. Soon we would have to drink untreated water and the risk of becoming ill would increase with every mouthful.

We climbed the steep, rotting vegetation of the far bank. Branches and roots crumbled in our hands or underfoot, threatening to send us falling back to the river, but the angle soon eased; it was still steep, but not dangerous. The jungle became too dense to even swing our arms, and progress slowed to a literal crawl as we climbed over, through and even under the entwined, impenetrable mass of moss-covered roots, branches and trunks. High above us, the canopy shone emerald green, but down on the jungle floor the prevalent colours were the dark browns and greens of decay. There were few signs of life and even the leeches seemed to have abandoned this area, presumably because of the lack of suitable prey.

I stopped for a rest, drops of rain splattering onto my face, and looked up. No hope of any sun this evening. No hope of drying out the sleeping bag, as even if the sun did come out, down here under the canopy its warmth wouldn't reach us. My bloodied and torn legs started to sting as dirty water ran down them. Bob was out of sight somewhere ahead. I could feel panic starting to set in at the realisation that I was alone and set off in a hurry, still out of breath.

'Bob?' Where was he? 'BOB?'

'Over here, Rich.' A loud, disembodied voice, close, but still out of sight. I called to him to wait and followed the tracks he had left in the thick coating of moss on the trees. I found him sitting, deep in thought, on a fallen tree.

'Let's stick together, Bob.' I feared the ultimate disintegration. The point where it became every man for himself. We had started out ten strong and now there were only two of us; I was terrified that some incident might separate us. I didn't feel strong enough to face the jungle by myself.

The punishing terrain continued. We struggled on, unable to wear our rucksacks and having to push them in front or drag them behind. We hadn't been able to stand for hours, and every movement caused a downpour of dead moss and water, which covered our hair and got into our mouths, ears and noses. It was overwhelmingly claustrophobic and we were soaked. And cold. And despondent. The sun dropped below the horizon, taking with it any hope of warmth and comfort, and all but extinguishing our spirits.

On the jungle floor, our world began to shrink as the light faded. We needed a place to sleep, but the ground – thick roots interspersed with bottomless holes – offered little hope of comfort. Insects of varying degrees of hideousness stalked us on every moss-covered branch. A black and red beetle, which had been following me all day, eyed me malevolently.

We found a hollow in a dead tree which was big enough for us both to lie down, but only if we lay on our sides and moulded our position to the protruding roots. It was comfortable only for a few seconds at a time, and any movement from either of us sent the other into throes of pain, cutting off circulation or opening old cuts. The last of the light departed and we entered our heart of darkness. I had been thinking about the nightmare river journey in Francis Coppola's film *Apocalypse Now* and wondered if mad Colonel Kurtz would come to invade our dreams.

Morning dawned without warning. We lay huddled together in the damp, cramped sleeping bag, my arms around Bob's shoulders. Bob stirred as a spasm of cramp bit into my right calf muscle, but I was too tired to move and just hoped it would go away.

The spasm passed and we struggled out of the sleeping bag. Packing the remaining equipment away, I found myself longing for oats and apple flakes. A week ago I had been bored rigid by the morning ritual of opening the little white sachets, but now they represented the height of luxury.

Everything we possessed was wet and cold. We were down to what we stood in – shorts and a T-shirt, with a fleece (wet, of course) our only reserve. I checked on Bob's hand; it had stopped bleeding, but the dressing had become filthy and of little protection against infection.

'Bob, do you remember back at your house, when we sorted out the first aid kit?'

'Yes.' He seemed unsure of where my question was leading.

'Well, whose idea was it to take the iodine instead of the antiseptic creams?'

'No, Rich. You can't.' Bob was regretting his decision, but there was no alternative.

'We've got to. You can do my finger after I've done yours.' Slowly, and as gently as possible, I unwrapped his fingers. Dried blood stuck the bandages together and I had to use the scalpel to cut the last of the dressing away. Seeing the wound again was horrific: grossly swollen fingers and the two deep cuts which had almost removed them. I was no longer able to see bone, as the scar tissue was already forming a red protective layer, but the walls of the wound were clearly visible and weeping yellow pus. I reached for the iodine. Trying to adopt a light-hearted approach, I jokingly tossed Bob the leather parang sheath.

'Bite on that.' Teeth clasped around it, he turned his head and offered his hand. I opened the small bottle of brown liquid and painted the wounds. Bob hopped a bit and so did I five minutes later when he repeated the process on my finger. We set off.

I paused for a drink, the steep ground in front of me dropping away into dense vegetation. Several leeches were feeding on my legs, so using the parang I sliced them off and checked my crotch for more. Bob was having a bad day. It was his turn to carry the large rucksack and he had been lagging behind all the time. I shouted encouragement in a vain attempt to speed him up. The original plan to ditch everything in an attempt to speed up had merely served to help maintain the same pace. We were definitely becoming weaker – I was moving like a snail, yet the only weight in my rucksack was eight pints of water, my camera and the compass.

I took the compass out to check the bearing. North-west. I peered through the canopy in search of landmarks – a futile exercise – and took a bearing on a tree no more than twenty feet away. Bob caught me up, dripping with sweat.

'You OK, Bob?'

'Yes, just keep going.' He paused for breath. 'Which way?'

'Over there.' I pointed in the direction of the tree and in doing so, turned too fast and lost my balance. I fell against a convenient tree and propped myself up, light-headed and confused. Bob seemed unaware of my staggering. He stared into the green and brown patchwork, waiting for me to take the lead.

I located my tree and headed off in its direction, climbing over and under obstacles, hacking through the undergrowth, fighting to push a path. Ten minutes passed and I stopped for Bob; I remembered passing the tree, but not taking a further bearing to walk on. *Shit. Could be going around in circles.* I checked the compass, eyes struggling to focus on the red needle. North-east. *Good.* I took a northerly bearing on yet another tree. Waiting for Bob was becoming wearing. *Come on.* My patience was starting to run low.

My turn to carry the larger rucksack. Through force of habit, I placed it on a low branch for support and climbed into the harness. It felt just as heavy as when we started, on the other side of the mountain; the straps still pulled hard on my shoulders and my legs felt rubbery.

Struggling under the weight, I watched Bob disappear in front of me. Exhaustion had dulled my senses to the point where I could focus only on Bob and I couldn't work out whether we were going uphill or down. I climbed over some rotting logs, making an extra effort to catch up.

It was Bob's turn to be impatient: 'Come on, Rich. Which way now?' All I could do was point in a northerly direction. He started off again. I followed, the large rucksack catching on foliage and the odd bastard tree.

Mid afternoon. The rain started, soaking my T-shirt in seconds and lowering my body temperature. Massive droplets of colder water fell off the trees as I brushed past them. Bob was out of sight although I could hear him occasionally and I was left to my own devices; I checked my compass and took the chance to have a rest. Bob's rustling became fainter and then stopped altogether. *Stupid bastard. If you hadn't stopped for a rest you wouldn't have been left behind. Left behind. Alone. Don't leave me alone, Bob. We're partners. Bob.*

'Bob!' The seamless green of the jungle ambushed my senses. 'BOB!'

The cold of the river was refreshing after the steaming heat of the jungle, and it was tempting to stay in the water, but I soon found a boulder bank on which I could climb out. No sooner was I dry than I came to another impasse and had to wade across again. The river was still very turbulent and the force of the water passing my legs moved them uncontrollably. The slimy rocks on the river bed caught me out. I stumbled, then fell into the thigh-deep water, trying to use my hands on the river bed, but my arms weren't long enough. My head submerged, I swallowed water and was swept off downstream. I felt a jagged rock brush against my leg, tearing the skin, and it slowed me down enough to regain my balance and find my feet. Being knocked off our feet by the water every so often was becoming commonplace and no longer concerned us greatly. We were past caring.

I took a deep breath, looked upstream towards Bob and then downstream. The river took a turn for the worse, with lots of small waterfalls, and we were forced back to the jungle and the leeches. The going, in places, was getting easier – the river, when in flood, had cut other wide channels through the jungle, down which we could boulder-hop from one smooth rock to another and thereby increase our pace. Under the larger boulders were caves filled with flies and broken vegetation; although cooler, the smell of dead and rotting things made them uninviting places.

The extra speed took its toll. We became dizzy and started stumbling, so we stopped in the sun and took a break. I closed my eyes. Sleep engulfed me.

A dilemma: after walking on a northerly bearing for the past four days, Bob wants to follow a ridge line, heading almost east, in the hope that there might be a path on top. From what I can remember of the map, the kampongs are to our north-west, but that's only in relation to where we were then, almost a week ago. I've no idea how much ground we've covered since then. Bob puts a strong argument across.

'Even if it is the wrong direction we should at least be able to see something, get a new bearing.' He's adamant, so we decide to follow the ridge line for half a day. I fill my water bottle from the stream; small insects are swimming happily in it, the colour a distinctive light brown. No steritabs left to make the water safe. I drink straight from the bottle.

The foothills are still steep and hazardous, but the thought of being on an open ridge line, able to see more than ten yards, is a great motivation. I follow on behind Bob, watching his latest batch of leeches feeding.

'Bob, you've got half of Borneo's population of leeches on your legs.'

He dismisses my observation resignedly. 'I'll get them off later.' I check my own legs to find the other half happily feeding. I pull their elastic bodies off and flick them away.

'Hey, Bob, there must be animals around here.'

'Why?'

'Well, what do all these leeches feed off?'

'Lost British Army Expeditions.' We stop in our tracks, laughing, our mood lifted far away from the situation and our discomfort. We carry on, grinning at the thought of all these leeches waiting in ambush, hoping for another expedition to cock up.

We were walking through fairly open jungle when something caught Rich's attention.

'Hey, Bob. Look at this.' He pointed to a small shrub with a bunch of little red berries hanging on it. 'Do you think they're edible?'

'I don't know. Have they got a sell-by date on them?' We discussed the little we could remember of conversations that we'd overheard about poisonous fruit and how to test for them, but ended up resigning ourselves to the fact that we knew absolutely nothing. We looked at each other for a few seconds, and I spoke: 'Tell you what, Rich. You eat a handful; I'll sit here for four or five hours, keeping an eye on you, and if you die I won't eat them.'

This suggestion received a blunt reply, so I tried a different tack. 'We'll have one each, and swallow them at the same time. That way, we'll go together.' This wasn't an altogether serious suggestion and I could feel myself starting to giggle. I looked at Rich and we both burst out laughing.

'OK. Let's try that.' We each took a berry from the tree and placed it on our tongues. Tongues and berries both disappeared. We both raised our eyebrows questioningly for a few seconds and then nodded to each other. Tongues and berries both reappeared. We spat the berries out and slagged each other off through fits of laughter. The game was repeated and continued until unfortunately, in yet another fit of giggles, I accidentally swallowed my berry.

'Shit. I've swallowed it.' There was a brief silence before Rich was pole-axed by another laughing spasm.

'It isn't funny, Rich – I've actually swallowed the bloody thing!' It took several minutes before Rich was in a fit state to resume speech.

'What did it taste like?'

'I don't know – I didn't get the chance to taste it – it just went straight down.' Eventually, we decided to eat what berries remained on the tree. They were delicious. We spent five minutes looking for more bushes, but none materialised. We headed off, still giggling.

Bright sunlight reflecting off the leaves. Steam slowly rising, hanging on the air. Exhausted, I collapse onto the rucksack and wait for Bob to catch up. Leeches crawl towards me. I wonder how they know where we are; can they smell? Do they see and hear? It's of no importance – they just know.

I wipe blood from wounds inflicted during the latest battle with a bastard tree. My legs are thick with dirt and the front of my thighs one large laceration, some of it bleeding, some healing, healthy scabs next to yellow pus and infected, inflamed wounds. A small trickle of blood weeps down my leg from a parasite I pulled off earlier.

A light rustling in the trees above me indicates the onset of rain; it takes several minutes before the large drops work their way through the canopy and start to fall on me. Looking up to the canopy, the bright sunlight has gone. Hope eclipsed by the cloud, doubts rise from my subconscious and the demon sits again on my shoulder. *You won't get out of this. Why not just give up now? Relax. Have a snooze.* I look around anxiously. *Get a fucking grip, Rich!* I can't see Bob.

'Bob. You OK?'

'Coming.' Just the act of talking to someone is enough to raise my spirits. Bob staggers into view and collapses next to me.

Down the ridge again; Bob's idea of map reading leaves a lot to be desired. He resigns himself to the fact that he's no Francis Drake and agrees to be led by my judgement, for what it's worth. We find ourselves at a river. Which one, we have no idea, but the main thing is that it's heading north, only a few feet wide and the sides aren't too steep. We feel like we're making some real progress and I voice some optimism.

'Might get out today, Bob.' I don't think I've convinced either of us, but blind hope is better than no hope at all, and anyway it's all we have left.

'Yeah, only two more days at the most.' No smile, just a stare.

'Two more days.'

We come to a small drop – no more than fifty feet – and look for a way round it; I take a look to the left and Bob the right.

Alone, I scout around; my mind wanders and I'm too tired to even try to stop it. *Maybe I'll sit down and relax.* In my mind's eye I see the rest struggling unsuccessfully to survive. I wonder what has happened to the officers, the Hong Kong lads, to Britt, to Steve, to Pete. I check the date on my watch: the sixth of March. *We fly back to Hong Kong tomorrow.* I picture the plane: not the plane we would fly on, just any plane. I can't see it; how could a plane land in here? It would have to crash land. You couldn't even land a helicopter in here. It's too dense, the sides are too steep.

My chest tightens and my breathing becomes shallow and irregular. *Where's Bob?* I try to stand but my legs are useless and I tumble backwards, landing heavily, the remaining air expelled from my chest. *Come on, you twat. You're losing it. Get a fucking grip.* My voice sounds alien, my eyes are closed and I've lost control of my breathing.

'Rich, I'm down.' Bob's shout brings with it some kind of normality. I look around at my unfamiliar surroundings, unsure how I've got here.

'Er, OK.' I wander around, disorientated.

'Rich, you coming?'

I follow the voice. Bob is standing in a small clearing fifty feet below me and the sound of a helicopter, almost deafening, suddenly rings in my ears.

'BOB, HELICOPTER!' He starts jumping around, waving his arms above his head, and shouting. A few moments later he stops.

'You sure?'

'I can hear it. Don't stop!' He waves frantically above his head again. 'They're looking for us!' I sink to the ground, listening, and the sound slowly changes to that of the river. My ears have been playing tricks on me.

I unravel Bob's hand, the bandages filthy, sodden from swimming and the downpour. The slashes are blackening around the edges, green and yellow pus weeping out; it smells awful. I bend his swollen little finger for a better look, reopening one corner of the wound, and the pus shoots out under pressure, followed by blood. I paint it with iodine and dress it. We have no fresh dressings left and the only option is to wash the old ones we have left in the river – almost clean and wet dressings are preferable to dirty wet ones. I do the same to my finger. The slash is numb and I'm worried about infection or, worse still, gangrene. I've never seen it and don't know what it looks like, but at a guess it would look and smell like Bob's hand.

'Hey, look.' For the first time in days, I feel like smiling.

'What?' At the bottom of the first aid kit is a small sachet.

'Dioralyte. Food. Well, almost.' Unable to contain my ex-citement I rip one open and pour the powder into my mouth. The sherbet mixture instantly dries my mouth, and the sensation of taste, after days of deprivation, is almost overwhelming.

Seventh of March. The plane leaves today; I'm unsure exactly what time, but I suppose it's irrelevant anyway. It's early morning and the time in the UK must be around midnight – our wives and children will be tucked up in bed, warm and dry. I place my wet sock on the ground and rest, the exertion of sitting up having made me light-headed.

Some time later I open my eyes. What was I doing? Boots. No – socks first. Where did I put them? I scan the ground, find them and slowly pull one onto a sodden, slightly swollen foot. I haven't had dry feet for days and I'm half expecting to find them swelling up like balloons as a result of trench foot, but they seem to be holding up so far. Being unable to walk would be the final straw – we would have to give up and wait for a rescue. What rescue? Neill had said we'd be on our own, because there was no rescue organisation in the area, and that's why I was here, to climb out if the shit hit the fan. Have I fucked up? What more could I have done? I'm on my last legs now. We are out of the gully and into the river section; he said it was only two days to safety from here, but we've gone almost a week and still seen no sign of civilisation.

Bob sits next to me on the torn Gore-Tex bivvy, staring listlessly into the ground. Where did I put my other sock?

Surely *someone* has missed us? Park HQ, for instance – they must know where we are and when we should be out. Walking along the river bank (fairly easy going at the moment), we talk through the likely sequence of events. We should have been out on the second of this month; when we failed to show up, Park HQ would have phoned the emergency numbers that Neill should have left with them. Our units would have sent someone (probably Paul Hughes) around to our families to inform them we're missing. As soon as our families are mentioned we change the subject; it's more than we can bear to discuss them openly. We stumble on, following the river.

Five in the evening: our families will be getting up and preparing for school. A curious feeling of normality sweeps over me, my body involuntarily relaxes and my eyes close.

'Get up you'll be late for school.'

'Where's my shoes?'

'What's for breakfast?'

'Mum where's Dad?'

Get off the ground Rich. Propped up on my elbows. *Where's Bob? I was just talking to him . . .* I turn my head to look upstream, but my eyes won't open. *Stand up Rich. You must get out.* Fired with a newly found resolution I find my feet and force my eyes open.

'Bob!' He's sitting on a boulder upstream, resting.

'Coming.' He stands and walks forward a few paces before sitting down again.

'Come on, Bob, almost there.' I am lying.

At no time did I want to give in, and when we collapsed we'd just lie there until we found some strength; where it came from I have no idea, but it always came. If I was to die, then at least I would die trying. All I could do was keep moving, and keep Bob moving. For the first time in my life I felt that faith was the only force of any worth: fate (or providence) was in control and there was nothing either of us could do but keep moving.

Every day we expected to see helicopters, but only in the morning as the afternoon rain would prevent flying. I dared not voice my fears as to why we hadn't seen anything – that maybe, through some blunder, Neill's emergency plans had been mislaid or just plain forgotten. Dave Powell had said the Park HQ weren't over reliable and I kicked myself for not having taken him up on his offer to act as our cut-off. Surely Neill was at least capable of getting that right. Wasn't he? The most negative of thoughts crept into my mind: *Maybe there is no cut-off date.* I tried to push the thought to the back of my mind but the insidious little voice kept up a litany of doubt: *What if? What if there is no date? No one will know, our units won't miss us for at least another three weeks and they're bound to give us ten days' grace after that. With every day that passes I fear the onset of blackouts, or worse. And what did happen to the rear group, anyway? Are they safe? Are they dead? The thought of them being safe angers me – if only Neill had listened to reason, listened to the experience within the group, or for that matter outside the group, then we wouldn't be in this situation.* My anger gave me new strength, temporarily.

CHAPTER 12

Two more days

I'm feeling stronger today and strangely enough, although I've had nothing to eat for the last week, I don't feel hungry – no hunger pains, no cravings, just every now and then a warm feeling inside my empty stomach. Our speed is slow, but we don't have to worry any longer about navigation: no more marching off guessed bearings, no more attempts to negotiate steep and vegetated escape routes. The river's easy. Just follow the river. Follow the water is all we can do. Stay by the river, at least we'll have water.

I stop at a puddle and drink, scooping up the water in my hands. All thoughts of trying to clean the water and make it safe to drink are gone with the last of the steritabs. I place my hands back in the stagnant water and drink again. The cold makes me shiver. I look round at Bob, who's lagging behind.

'Bob!' No reply, he just looks at me and staggers on. 'Want some water?' He shakes his head and stops for a rest, sinking to his knees. I know I'm walking slowly too; everything must be done in extra slow time so as to avoid collapse, but I still feel strong enough to keep going. I study Bob's exhausted and lifeless face, the mirror of my own. I realise I'm on a high, but highs don't last for ever; soon I'll feel weak and feeble again. The realisation weighs heavy on my mind – will Bob be strong when I'm down? I stare into the still water, depression and despair welling up inside me.

'Come on, let's get going.' I offer a hand and pull Bob to his feet.

Some days after losing the others – *how many? I don't know. Just shut up and stop asking stupid questions* – and Bob and I are still no closer to escape. My wet fleece offers little in the way of insulation against the cold morning air and hunger gnaws at me, but I put all thought of food from my mind and continue packing the sleeping bag into the rucksack.

'Bob, what else do you think we can ditch?' I grasp the bottom of the bag and, turning it upside down, empty the contents out. Slowly and methodically we go through everything – do we need this, do we need that? By far the heaviest item is the climbing gear. I separate it out and feel its weight.

'Should we throw it?'

'I don't know. Will we need it again?' Over the last few days we have had to negotiate several tricky sections; if we dump the gear and then come across another big drop – well, it doesn't bear thinking about.

'I don't know.' Indecision rules, but the thought of carrying all that weight makes my mind up: 'I'll sling it.'

'Rich, look at this.' He held up a small conker-like fruit, holding it close to his nose. 'Smells good, what do you think?' I walked the few yards back to him.

'Where did you find it?'

'On the ground.' Bob pointed down; next to the tiny stream, scores of them lay scattered around. He opened one using his fingers and looked inside: moist, light brown in colour, but the flesh looked distinctly off. I smelled it. Instant hunger pangs, it smelled so good. I tasted the warm brown flesh on my tongue.

'Tastes good.' I cast my mind back to the bushcraft book I used to read as a child, trying to remember the don'ts – don't eat anything that tastes like almonds, don't eat off the ground, don't eat anything with a milk-like sap, don't everyone eat at the same time. I couldn't remember the 'dos', but common sense told me to let Bob try it first; without any prompting he devoured one and went for another.

'Bob – don't eat any more, just in case.' We stared into each other's eyes. He was like a man possessed. 'Help me gather them all up. If you don't feel any ill effects by tomorrow, we'll have a feast.' We spent several minutes rummaging around on all fours, I placed the harvest into the top of my large rucksack and we continued. The thought of being able to eat tomorrow cheered us up; maybe soon our stomachs would be full, maybe we'd find more of the same fruit later, maybe we could live off the land.

Steep ground and thick vegetation, but a blessed absence of bastard trees makes the going bearable. We scramble on, pulling on the dead ground, fingers sinking into the rotting plant matter, trying to find a solid grip. I feel a wet sensation on my lower arm.

'Watch out for the pitcher plants.' I stare at the repulsive carnivorous flowers, the digestive juices cold on my forearm and hand. *Can I drink that?* Using the parang I empty one out. Dead flies and other insects I have no idea even existed on this planet come flooding out. Unappetising, but . . . I pick another one and smell it, look inside. The flower itself is like cardboard, stiff and pale yellow with a hint of red at the edges, and a good four or five inches in diameter. It feels heavy with the weight of fluid inside; the inside of the rim has thin tentacles, I suppose to prevent its prey from escaping. I contemplate it for a while, but it's no good – the idea disgusts me and I throw it to the ground – I'll have to be a damn sight hungrier before I'll drink dead fly soup. Bob speaks from behind me as he catches up.

'You alright?'

'Yes!' Stupid answer. Stupid question, for that matter. Neither of us are 'alright'; we're hungry and exhausted, our bodies are practically torn to shreds and, apart from knowing that we're next to a river in Kinabalu National Park, lost. Still, questions like that are all relative – I'm no worse than when Bob last asked me, which adds up to feeling 'alright'. I wonder how he is? It's a while since he ate that conker, but it doesn't seem to have had any ill effects. Yet.

I'm fed up with these fucking leeches. This repellent just doesn't seem to be working.

'Bob, are you using this stuff?' He admitted not using anything. I smeared the last of the cream we'd brought in and around the top of my socks and boots, placing a dollop of it next to a leech which was making all haste to feed off me. It just crawled through it. I spent a lot of time throughout the day checking my legs and managed to keep the numbers down, but there were loads on Bob's legs, sucking his energy away.

The evening routine now merely comprised laying out the bivvy, stripping off boots and T-shirts and going to sleep. As I peeled off my socks, I noticed that the cream I had smeared over them hadn't repelled the leeches – on the contrary, they seemed to like the smell, which enticed them to climb my boots, but once they came into contact with the cream I had my revenge as their soft bodies dissolved, leaving only their heads and jaws embedded in the woollen material of my socks. Painstakingly I removed them one by one, head by head and jaw by jaw, until my eyes closed and I fell asleep.

I'm sitting on a boulder, left hand supporting my head. Across the stream is an upright stripped branch, straight and strong. I stare at it, transfixed. *What is it?* I lift my head to get a better view, seeing several other substantial branches leaning against it and, over the top of them, smaller ones to fill in the gaps and form a shelter.

Shelter! transfixed, I wade through the cold, shallow stream and wordlessly, Bob joins me. We search the shelter and surrounding ground, rummaging for any scraps of food the builders of this makeshift shelter might have left behind or stashed for a later date, but to no avail, it looks like it hasn't been used for a long time. *We must be getting close to somewhere – this is the first sign of human existence other than ourselves. We must be close, please God let us be close.*

Shivering uncontrollably, freezing water gushing around my thighs and threatening to topple me, I call to Bob. Come on. *Come on.* Turning slowly, so as not to lose my footing, I take a breath, ready to shout, and stop. *What's that? That's writing, red writing.*

'Bob, look!' I'm unable to control my excitement. 'LOOK!'

Painted on the downstream side of a boulder in red letters a foot high is a message and a date. *Maybe it's the rescuers.* Wading back up stream, *I can't read it, what does it say?* I feel like a small child unable to recognise the words; the letters are no problem but the meaning of the words eludes me. A strange sense of *déjà vu* overcomes me – did we write that? *How long has it taken us to walk out from here? Two days? More? We didn't write that, did we?*

No; the date reads 12/3/93 – it was written two days short of a year ago. Probably just another expedition marking its high point, nothing to do with us at all.

'Two more days!' Those words. We've been repeating them for days. Or has it been weeks? No matter; they may have lost any real meaning, but they still hold a talismanic importance for us. I must speak those three words at least once a day, or we will cease to exist.

Moans waken me from an uneasy sleep. Bob has forced himself into a foetal position, causing the sleeping bag to become unbearably tight around my bloodied legs and back.

'What's wrong, Bob?' I'm still only half awake.

'I'm going to puke!' He pauses for a few seconds, then kicks, hard. Head over the edge of the bivvy, he vomits, gasps for air and vomits again. I crawl out of the bivvy and check to see if he's alright.

Daylight invades my sleep, warm and uncramped inside the sleeping bag. My consciousness wanders; old friends and climbing partners drift by – Pete, Mac. Places – the Alps, Gogarth. Someone will wake me soon, then we'll have breakfast and go climbing. *Bob, Bob's an old friend, do you remember that time in the jungle, shit that was close.* Jungle. Bob. The painful return to reality.

'Bob?' No memory of last night. 'Bob, where are you?'

I'm lying a few feet away from Rich amongst some boulders, puking. When we crawled into the sleeping bag last night, I was feeling a bit off colour, and about ten minutes after turning in, I knew I was going to be sick. I got out of the sleeping bag, my stomach heaving, and knelt for a few minutes before I eventually threw up – about half a pint of bright yellow bile. I thought I might feel better once I had been sick, but things just got worse. I was sick again and then the chest pains started; I called out to Rich, but he was too exhausted to wake properly and merely suggested I drink some water. I started to fill my water bottle and as I bent over the stream, I was hit by a vicious bout of stomach cramps which doubled me up even further. My bowels opened uncontrollably and a watery diarrhoea ran down my legs and into the water from which I was trying to fill my water bottle. Racked by violent chest pains and still retching, I crawled upstream for a few feet in search of clean water, knowing that I had to keep drinking, partly to avoid complete dehydration, but also to give me something to throw up. I lay by the water in a foetal position and filled my bottle. I drank it, at least two pints. Two minutes later I threw up again, the diarrhoea returned and my bladder emptied itself. I had lost control of all my bodily functions and the chest pains were getting worse. The process con-tinued all night: drink, vomit, diarrhoea; all the time, the chest pains got worse, to the point where I was afraid that I was going to die. When they became even worse, I was afraid I wasn't going to die. As dawn arrived the vomiting and diarrhoea subsided, but the chest pains remained and I resigned myself to the fact that I couldn't carry on. There was no emotion – it was a quite logical decision – Rich would have to carry on alone. I couldn't walk and there was no way he could carry me. The dragon had won. I waited for Rich to wake, wondering how I was going to tell him to go on without me, and if I was going to have to make it an order.

Rich came to: 'Where are you, Bob?'

I answered through gritted teeth as he got out of the sleeping bag: 'Over here. Rich, I can't breathe, I can't walk. You'll have to go on without me.'

'Oh yeah? Who the hell do you think you are? John Wayne? Up you get. You're not having the sleeping bag anyway, so you'll have to come with me.' He packed the gear away, shouldered the rucksack and walked over to me. He prodded me with his boot, dragged me to my feet, slung my arm around his shoulder and staggered off down the river. I blindly put one foot in front of the other and after a couple of hours the chest pains started to ease. At one of our rests I discovered that I could stand by myself; Rich moved off and I followed like a zombie. I had nothing left. I just stared at the floor and put one foot in front of the other.

As the chest pains decreased, however, so the pains in my arm and hand became worse. My hand was now very badly infected; if I fell and knocked it I would pass out for a few minutes, and when this happened I would drift off into my own little world, thinking not of food or safety but whether my wife and my son Robert would be financially secure. What if they didn't find my body? How long would it be before the insurance company pronounced me dead and what would she do until they paid her? Would she lose the house? Would she meet someone and remarry, and how would Robert react to a stepdad? Every time I dreamt of Sue and Robert with another man I would come round and the thought would spur me on, but I was fading fast and I knew it. I had one, maybe two days at most left in me but I was passing out more frequently and so was Rich.

We'd just fall over and lie there until we regained consciousness. If I collapsed Rich would be sitting next to me when I came round, concern written all over his face, and ask me if I was OK. *OK? No I'm not. I haven't had any food for over a week, my hand is giving me a shed load of pain, and I'm battered and bruised all over. I'm passing out every couple of hours, I've lost my two front teeth in a fall, I'm trapped in a jungle half-way across the world and on top of all that I ran out of fags ten days ago.*

'Yes, I'm alright.' The answer was always the same and when Rich passed out it would be my turn to ask the same stupid question.

I was finding it hard to concentrate and, unwilling to talk, started to turn in on myself. All I wanted to do was put one foot in front of the other, but even this simple task was draining my strength and I was concerned how Rich would cope on his own; he needed someone – anyone – just to talk to and reassure him that everything was going to be alright.

It was strange. Rich was the strong one during the day, always spurring me on: 'Not long now, Bob,' he would say, and I would look him listlessly in the eye: 'Yeah, not long.' During the long dark nights, however, as we lay in our sleeping bag hugging each other to keep warm, I felt that it was me who had to be the strong one. Before we fell asleep I was always saying that we would get out and what a story it would make in the mess over a few pints, but how many more nights could I spend, sitting in the dark with tears in my eyes and saying to this young lad, 'two more days, Rich. Just two more days?'

Dusk was falling, so we started to look for somewhere to sleep and soon found a hole in the river bank that led into a cave. It wasn't very inviting and smelt awful, but at least it would shelter us from the rain. Inside, Rich took the dirty, damp sleeping bag from his rucksack and started to clear the ground of stones; we always tried to make it as comfortable as we could, but the more body weight we lost the more uncomfortable it became as the ground dug into our bones, and the more the cold affected us. I got out my head torch to have a look around and near the back of the cave I thought I saw something moving above me; I shone the torch up to the cave roof and the hairs on the back of my neck crawled. Bats. Hundreds upon hundreds of the creepy black things, hanging from the roof of the cave. I thought it best to go back to Rich, who was lying in the entrance in the sleeping bag. He asked me if I'd found anything.

'No, not really.'

'I have,' he said, 'look.' With that, he held up an old polythene bag. 'I found it when I was moving that big stone over there. It's an old noodle packet. Been here a fair old time by the look of it, but we must be going the right way. What do you think?'

Thoughts were rushing through my head at high speed and I wasn't sure how to answer him. If someone had been cooking in this cave at some time in the past, then they must have been a good way from home – a day's march at least – but my biggest fear was that it might have been left by Neill's unsuccessful expedition in 1982. They had abandoned that expedition after moving up the river for four days and if this was their high point it meant another four days for us. However, Neill's party had been fit and had food; in our state it might well take us ten days.

Rich's discovery didn't spur me on or raise my hopes – it had exactly the opposite effect. I came to the conclusion that I was going to die. The only thing I could do was carry on as far as possible to help Rich, who was stronger and might make it. I turned my back so that he couldn't see my face and started to move some rocks.

'Yeah. Looking good, Rich. Just two more days and we'll be home.'

The cave was as black as pitch and Rich had a bad night. He kept on asking me to talk to him, and not really knowing what to talk about, I started to tell him my life story. It ended up more like a church confession, and every time I stopped to dwell on something from the past he would tell me to carry on. The sound of my voice was reassuring him that he wasn't alone and helping him to unwind, and although I didn't think he was actually taking in a word I said, it seemed to help him. It was a long night of mixed emotions: tears filled my eyes as I told him about my time in a home when I was six, how my mum took her own life when I was twelve and we laughed at some of the things I had got up to in my teens. Some of them I'd got away with, some I hadn't, and the latter had got me put away in some of Her Majesty's prisons for periods of time. I talked about Sue and Robert, and about things I hadn't spoken of for years, not to anyone. The long confession seemed to help Rich, and as I talked,

I realised that it was helping me too. It made me realise that I'd done a lot in my thirty-seven years, more than some people accomplish in a lifetime; I'd tasted all sides of life, good and not so good, and I reflected that losing this fight with the dragon might not be such a bad thing after all. At least I'd be remembered – not for my contribution to humanity, but for my dramatic exit.

We were both glad when dawn broke. I had a sore throat and Rich had earache. We packed the sleeping bag away. My turn to carry the big rucksack. One damn foot in front of the other.

Eyes won't focus; everything just looks green. Looking at the blue of the rucksack helps, something man-made. I study Bob's face as he tries to fill a water bottle and the corner of my mouth turns up slightly. I haven't seen him smile in days. Come to think of it, I haven't seen *any* expression on his face for days. In fact, both our faces have been expressionless for days; the effort is too much. Our descent from humanity has robbed us of the ability to show our emotions, though we still feel them.

Bob's fading and I'm not far behind him. I should be able to outlast him, but the thought of being left to fend for myself is terrifying, more frightening than the thought of dying. *Don't leave me alone, Bob. I don't want to die alone.* Each day it becomes harder to remain positive.

I rest on a rock half-way across the river with the water flowing smoothly by, charming me almost to the point of sleep. Upstream Bob's still slowing and I will him to move faster. On the horizon I see the silhouettes of birds floating on the breeze, oblivious to our desperate fight to survive.

A large earth scar on the river bank catches my attention. *There's something odd about that ...* I stare into the sodden mud and my mind starts to play tricks; a line appears, and then another. *Animal tracks?* In the middle of the scar a solitary stick stands upright, stripped of all its bark and looking just like the ones that marked the path in Easy Valley. *Look Rich, a path.*

'Path?' *Are we looking for paths?* 'Bob, look, is that a path?' I turn to see him standing up to his thighs in fast-flowing water. Has he heard me?

'Bob, a path!' He lifts his head and a listless face, a mirror of my own, stares back at me. He's having a bad day.

'This way, mate, follow me.' His face falls to stare into the water and he continues the slow, sluggish stumbling that is all we can muster.

Water tugs hard at my legs, threatening to topple me; if I fall I'll only have to walk back upstream. Over the last few days I've been letting the water take me, washing me away with its quiet power, allowing me to gain distance with no effort. Waterfalls are still common, and large ones too, but the risks are outweighed by the ease of movement. This time, however, I can't afford any drifting downstream as I don't have the strength to regain the distance lost to the current.

I gain the bank but the mud is too slippery to drag myself out, and the more I try the harder it becomes. Out of breath, but determined to climb to the white stick, I look around for another way up. Nothing obvious appears and downstream being easier than up, I move a few yards down and try again. This time I try to haul out on an overhanging branch, but my arms are too tired to pull all my body weight up. Despair starts to take over. *Just give up, for fuck's sake give in.* Arms at my side in the water. Thoughts of my wife and children. *Pull yourself together, get OUT!* The tears sting in the open wounds on my face as aggression takes over, and flinging my hands around the tree and swinging my legs onto the bank, I find my feet on dry land again. I look over to Bob who has managed to scramble up the bank and is now lying face down in the mud.

My sodden boots, clean and glistening black from the water, sink into the golden brown mud, changing their appearance within seconds of starting the climb. I wobble zigzag up the path until, what seems like an eternity later, I realise that the stick has gone. Have I passed it, have I kicked it over?

'Come on Bob, almost there.' He just stares at me. I repeat it, to no further response. *Keep going, Rich. He'll catch up. If need be, if I get out, I'll send someone back.* Our slow progress comes to a halt; we're near the top of the scar, but the ground is impossibly steep. The river seems a long way off but it can't be more than a hundred feet. *Long way down, Rich. Long fall. Never mind – maybe the mud will slow you down.* I climb on, two steps forward and two back, until, ten minutes later, Bob joins me, and I've made no progress. In silent despair we slip back down the mud to the river.

I sit on the bank, resting, waiting for Bob to join me. It seems to have been raining for weeks; blue skies and warmth are distant memories, and the cold is taking its toll.

I stare listlessly into the trees that line the bank as Bob drops on the ground next to me. While he regains his breath, he too stares into the trees.

'Orchard!' I look at him. Is he losing it? 'The trees, in line, look!' Moving a few yards to one side, I peer into the darkness; sure enough, the trees are in an almost perfect line, and the ground is flattened and completely cleared of all smaller shrubbery. My chest tightens with excitement and breathing becomes uneven. *If this is an orchard then there must be people. Food, maybe even roads, cars. Phones. If this is an orchard then there must be paths to some local settlements leading from it.*

'Bob, paths. There must be paths around here somewhere.' We hadn't given up hope, but the thought of actually getting out was becoming increasingly distant and we had both come to accept that we wouldn't be getting out today. Whether today meant now or in a week's time was irrelevant, it wouldn't be today! But now, today, we've found something man-made. The first sign that the nightmare might be ending. However, there's no path. We both search as fast as our malnourished bodies allow, but with no success.

We find ourselves sitting on a fallen log, *a square fallen log?* This is a very strange place. My eyes close and square banana trees, heavy with fruit, invade my dreams. A sharp jab in my arm.

'Rich. Wake up. Look, this log's been chain-sawed.' Returning to my senses, I touch the sodden wood between my legs. *Fucking square banana trees!* You prat, Rich.

'Chain-saws must be heavy, right?' Bob nods in agreement. 'There must be paths around here somewhere!' Part of my mind is struggling with another idea, something fundamental that I can't quite seem to grasp. *If we are in an orchard, then what fruit are on the trees? Food. We're sitting under food.* Flinging my head back to stare into the canopy, I see that the short stout trees are easily climbable and that blackened yellow fruit decorates their branches.

'Bob, food, look. Look. Wake up.' Panic-stricken, I start to shake him. 'Wake up!' There's little response. *Collect it, Rich. Get the fruit, climb the trees!* Reason quietly departs via a side exit; I'm hijacked by the dark side, a primeval urge that wells up from my subconscious. I would kill anybody who tries to stop me climbing these trees.

High in one of the trees, unsure how I got there. *Did I climb the tree? You must have. Pick the fruit. Pick the fucking fruit!* A man possessed, ripping at the blackened fruit and dropping them the short distance to the floor. Working my way higher, the branches become thinner. I lose all concept of who and where I am; to pick this fruit is the sole reason for my existence.

There's a deafening thunderclap. Air rushes past, greens and browns fill my vision. *This is good, relax, enjoy, sleep, it won't hurt* . . . The ground hits me violently from behind. All movement stops and, stunned, I drift off into an uneasy sleep.

Muesli, you like muesli. Right. Listen to me Rich. To stop all this nonsense, all you have to do is find one of those two-kilo bags of Alpen. And a black and white cow.

No muesli, no cow, but the rain has stopped. We gather up my harvest and both try biting into the fruits, but the time-hardened yellow peel threatens to break our teeth. Plan two: use the parang. Placing a fruit on the square log, I wield the two-foot-long blade high above my head and bring it down as hard as my weakened arms will permit. The fruit is incredibly tough; the heavy blade cuts only half-way through and we use the blade as a hammer until the fruit eventually splits into two equal parts. Eagerly we both grab a half and take a mouthful of the hard inner flesh. The saliva in my mouth dries out as the wooden flesh turns to an inedible, stringy pulp. We spit it out and, undeterred, take another mouthful, and then another. We sit on the ground, our backs on the log, surrounded by spat-out, semi-chewed lumps of flesh that look disturbingly like cat sick.

'We'll try to cook it.' I look at Bob but he doesn't respond. 'Help me gather some firewood.' Still no acknowledgement. I wobble to my feet and go off in search of wood. All the trees have fruit on them and there seem to be no paths leading anywhere; there aren't even any paths in between the trees, for that matter, and small bushes and long grass have started to take root. I realise that this place is abandoned and despair creeps back.

The bark of one tree seems to be different from the rest and the top branches seem to be almost palm-like. They would make a good shelter. As I lean against the soft bark of the tree it bends and gives; I try pushing it over, but to no avail. Frustrated, I kick and pound at the base. The soft bark gives in and my hands leave a mark on the trunk; I swing the parang, and to my surprise the blade sinks almost half-way through the soft tissue that lies just below the bark. One more swing and the fortyfoot tree falls.

Like a small boy after some act of great mischief, I feel pleased. The exposed wood seeps water, and using the knife again I slice a sliver off and examine it. Taste it. Almost sweet and very moist. I take a bite, chew and swallow, but the thought of Bob's illness puts me off further experimentation and I return to searching for firewood.

I return to Bob with what little semi-dry firewood I have been able to find and set about building a fire. The lack of any dry tinder makes it difficult, particularly as we only have three matches left, but eventually I manage to start a small fire. The light and warmth kindles a little optimism.

'Someone might see the light.' Still no response from Bob. I hang the soaked sleeping bag over the fire in an attempt to dry it and rest a few of the large branches from the fallen tree across the square log so that we can sleep in relative luxury tonight. The fruits present a problem in that I don't know how to cook them, and I settle for lobbing them at random into the fire.

Bob bursts into slow motion and pulls the sleeping bag from the improvised washing line. He crawls into it and into the treacherous subconscious cravings and ravings for food and comfort that we both periodically and involuntarily exchange for sleep. At intervals throughout the night I pull the fruit out of the fire in hope that the heat might have performed some sort of miracle and transformed it into an edible feast. All I get is burnt lips.

CHAPTER 13

The skin of our teeth

Awakening to the same old feelings of pain and despair, I view my dim world. The blurring of the boundaries between normality and abnor-mality, dream and nightmare, has reached the point where nothing seems to make sense any more. I need to speak.

'You awake, Bob?' A quick poke in the back brings him round. 'Today. Today we'll get out.' To be honest I can no longer see a way out. Today and tomorrow have no meaning any more; we exist in a timeless limbo of leeches and hunger. I'm unable to grasp the concept of safety as anything other than just that – an abstract, of no practical relevance to our situation. I can't make the connection.

Slowly, we break camp. Putting cold, wet socks and then boots on my feet takes an eternity, and every time I place something on the ground I lose it or forget what I was doing. Bob passed this stage a few days ago, just before he stopped talking. We're turning in on ourselves, gaining no support from each other, but eye contact communicates more than any words can. Pain and anguish, exagger-ated by our pale, emotionless, bearded faces.

Lying face down I see a leech making full steam ahead to feed off me. *I haven't seen any leeches for days or have I just stopped noticing them?* Before it has chance to sink its teeth into me I gain our strange log and continue the task of footwear.

'Bob, there's got to be a path around here somewhere.' Still no response. Everything packed. 'Right then, help me look for this path.'

I start walking uphill, looking for fresh parang cuts, or even old healed-up ones, just some indication there is a world outside this green confusion. Ten minutes later the small plantation perimeter is covered, I've found no path and Bob is still down by the log.

'Bob?' A face I hardly recognise stares back, the flicker of life in his eyes almost extinguished, even from fifty yards away. He's losing it. If he gives in, I won't be capable of continuing. He can't just give in, he mustn't give up, he can't let this beat him. 'Bob!' I stumble as fast as I can down the hill.

'BOB!' If he dies it will leave me alone, in here, with this green monster that bites, scratches, cuts, freezes, imprisons me. A green hand grabs at my feet sending me headlong; *get to Bob, get to Bob, now before it's too late.* I escape the clutches of my green tormentor and reach the log.

'Bob, you OK?' I smile. The lights are on but no one is home. 'Bob!'

'Bob, come on. Move!' Anger rises and I scream at him at the top of my voice: 'FUCKING MOVE!' *I'm not going to let you die on me, I can't make it by myself.*

'Move!' Spittle flies from my mouth, landing in his face only an inch away from mine. Nothing, not a fucking flicker. *Grab him Rich, shake him Rich, punch his fucking TA lights out but get him moving!*

My hands fly forward to grab at his fleece and hit him hard, very hard, in the centre of his chest. The blow sends him plummeting backwards out of control and he hits the floor violently, making no effort to break his fall, like a man shot in the head and dead before he hits the ground.

I stand in silence. I didn't meant to hit him, just grab and shake him. *I've just decked a senior rank. Shit. I'm in for it now, we're going to have a fight.* I drag him to his feet, so that we're face to face once more.

'Talk to me, Bob. Are you OK?' At last there's a response, a flicker of recognition in his eyes.

'Yeah I'm OK, you bastard.' His voice is so quiet I can barely hear it, and the lip movements aren't quite synchronised with the words, as if his character has been badly dubbed. He isn't the man I know.

With no path in evidence the only option left open to us is back to the river to take our chances there. *Should get out tomorrow.* It's always fucking tomorrow. Why can't it be today?

The river's being its usual self, although it does seem flatter and the spurs aren't quite so locked together. The exertion of the set-to I had with Bob has left me exhausted, but at least he's moving now.

Resting on a boulder, I watch as he tries to negotiate a small waterfall; he moves as though the water were treacle. In places, the banks of the river have deep, water-worn channels, scoured out by the river in flood, but dry now and sometimes offering an easy option for bypassing difficult sections. Bob disappears down one and I wait to see if it's another dead end.

'Rich!' I hear Bob's voice easily over the roar of the water. He sounds excited. *Excited?*

'Coming.'

'Bridge!' Bridge?

'Bridge!' He's lost it. He's finally cracked, his mind's broken.

'RICH, I found a bridge, a bridge!' This from a man who hasn't spoken for days. I can hear the emotion in his voice. Visions of a concrete motorway packed with cars travelling at speed. Feet pounding and thighs burning with the sudden exertion I wade into the river. The cold and depth slow me, my footing goes and I plunge headlong into the water. I submerge for a while, arms and legs still pushing to get me to the far bank, the safe side, the concern for breathing secondary to that of getting there. Clambering out I see Bob sitting, head in hands, and crying.

'Look, a bridge!' No motorway, no cars. Stuck in the jungle with a madman.

'Where, Bob? Show me where.' He points to his left.

'It's here, Rich, can't you see it?' I slump as the adrenalin runs out. There's no bridge. I walk towards Bob; the boulder he is sitting on is formed into an almost perfect step. It even looks like concrete. And behind him another.

'Look, Rich, a path.' My heart misses a beat and my stomach turns as my eyes fall on the well-made and defined path. 'Look!' To my left, stretching out over the river, is a wire bridge, with a few wooden planks as floorboards. Tears fill my eyes and I sink to my knees. We hug each other. Time passes. Something actually man-made, something that isn't connected with us or the expedition. Outsiders, people who can help us. And food.

Which way to go? If we go right we might be walking away from somewhere, and as for left, it might be miles that way but only a few hundred feet the other. A debate ensues, settled by the fact that we both only really want to walk over the bridge so the direction is irrelevant, and right, northish, wins. In our state, walking over the narrow planks isn't easy, and the wire supports on both sides do little to stabilise our passage, but we're not going to miss out on the treat of crossing it.

On the far side the path follows the river for a short way and then turns at a right angle up the hill. The excitement and energy soon wears off and the low feelings hit hard, along with a stitch, and the pain of our burnt-out, wasted legs. Maybe we should have gone the other way.

The sides of the path are lined with wood and the ground well trodden; litter is scattered about, some of it looking new, and we pick bits up hoping for a scrap of food. *Wait here, Rich. Someone will find you, you can give in now. It's OK. Relax, go to sleep.* My eyes close but my legs plod on regardless. The path becomes steeper and we're forced to rest more frequently. The freedom of being able to move with such little resistance through the jungle is exhilarating. My feelings roller-coaster back up; I can see the connection. There is an end to it, after all.

The path takes turn after turn and each time I half expect to see some form of savoury. I start to search the ground more carefully, in the hope that someone has dropped a packet of crisps, and the thought of finding food becomes all consuming. I'm convinced I'll find a packet of salt and vinegar crisps.

Hot, we strip down to just shorts and boots. We come across a small hut made of bamboo which reminds me of a bus shelter, barring the fact that we're on a path no more than a few feet wide. It has three walls, a roof and a floor three feet off the ground. We both sit in it. We must be getting close now. Suddenly the floor gives and we find ourselves sitting on the ground; this old rickety hut is obviously not used very often and in a poor condition. *Maybe this path isn't used any more, maybe it's like the other paths and doesn't actually go anywhere.* We stay where we've fallen for a while longer.

The path continues, closed in on both sides now and still steep. The oppressive greens crowd in again, resurrecting all the fears of the past days. We round a corner and a waist-high fence bars our way. Unaccustomed to distance, my eyes won't focus at first, but after a few seconds the ground over the fence snaps clearly into view: cleared of all trees, just their stumps visible, and right in the centre a large bamboo hut.

Without speaking, we make headlong for the hut, slowed briefly by a small stream with steep sides. Like the last, this one has its floor high above the ground. We stand in front of it, out of breath, and call up to any occupants; no reply comes, so we enter. Our prime concern is food and the search begins. Some medication is all we find. Depression sets in. I lie on the floor of the hut, staring up into the rafters. A small white plastic bag hangs from a nail; standing, I pull the bag down and peer inside.

'Fish heads!' Sitting back down with Bob to share the dried, shrivelled portion of fish, eyes still intact, I briefly question the wisdom of eating it, but hunger gets the better of me.

Bob rests and I go outside to try and find another path. *Maybe this hut is all that is here. Maybe we went the wrong way at the bridge.* I search the underside of the hut and find a similar fruit to that of the orchard last night. I return inside and use the parang to slice it to pieces, but the wooden flesh is no more edible than before. The thought occurs that maybe there's a map in here and standing, we resume the search. A warm, sticky liquid runs down my legs.

'Oh fucking hell, Bob!'

'What?' He stares at me, ready for the next disappointment.

'I've just shat myself. Look!'

Looking at my legs, a sly smile creeps over his face. 'Don't worry about that, Rich. I've been doing it for days.'

'You dirty bastard, and you haven't been washing.'

'Neither have you.' My embarrassment gone, the absurdity of it all makes us laugh for the first time in days. We stagger out of the hut to search for a path.

There has to be a path. This can't be a dead end. The vegetation at the top of the clearing seems less dense and easy progress brings us to what we think is a path. We stumble on, our rests more frequent and longer, and the pain of getting moving again after each one becoming almost unbearable.

The ground is covered with grass. Not knee-high shrubs, or bastard trees, but proper grass. Bob points with his left hand; the right is useless for anything.

'Rich, can you see anything over there?'

'Where?' The ground is opening up and there's too much to take in.

'Over there, look!'

'I can't see. What?'

'Power lines!' I strain my eyes and suddenly the sharp outlines of steel pylons and power lines come into focus against the blurred greens and browns of the jungle.

'There's got to be a road there, got to be.'

'It's got to go somewhere.' Excitement overwhelms us and the pace increases, although we can't hope to maintain it for long. A small abandoned hut – we ignore it. In front of me a massive concrete slab. A noise to my left. *That's the cow. I wonder where my muesli is.*

Other weird noises violate the silence. *Singing? Look Rich a hut, with washing hanging out to dry. People!*

Climbing the concrete slab turns my legs to jelly and, staggering to keep my balance, I rest on the fence, out of breath and unable to shout. *Where's Bob, Rich? There's food in there!* Incapable of climbing the fence, I fall forward and the momentum deposits me on the other side; I lie there for a few seconds regaining my breath and bearings. The thought of food drives me on towards the hut which, like all the others, is five feet off the ground. Great. More steps. At the top of them, several pairs of children's shoes. I enter the hut and a small child about the same age as my daughter stares at me. Foolishly, I stare back.

'Food?' Clearly alarmed and more than a bit scared, the child runs out of the hut. *I didn't mean to frighten her, but I've got to find the kitchen.* My sodden boots make hollow thuds which echo around me. At the end of the hall is the kitchen and on my right a giant rice boiler, full to the top and steaming hot. I plunge my hands into the hot rice, burning them, but I don't care, my mouth's full.

I hear a noise from behind me and look up, rice dripping from my mouth. A short, middle-aged woman stares back at me; our eyes, locked together, seem to betray a mutual fear of what the other might do. My mouth burns – I'm finding it hard to swallow the hot rice, but I stuff another handful of rice in anyway, the bland texture and taste almost overwhelming my senses.

The woman takes a deep breath, walks towards to me and, gently taking my arm, leads me to a small table in the centre of the room. Feeling increasingly unstable on my feet, and too weak to protest, I sit down. A large bowl of the same rice appears in front of me and instinct takes over; hunching my shoulders and lowering my head to protect my food, I shovel it into my mouth with my fingers.

Other plates of food appear from nowhere and the noise level in the wooden hut increases as Bob is led in to sit next to me, looking every bit as bewildered and confused as I feel. The realisation that we've made it to safety slowly dawns on us both and as we look at each other a hint of the old us emerges. We even smile.

'Fucking made it! Piece of cake. Do it again tomorrow.' It hasn't completely sunk in though, as we sit there holding hands. *We might get out, but not today.* The twelfth of March. Nearly three weeks since leaving Park HQ and we've made it on only ten days' food.

Directly in front of us, propped open by a wooden pole, is a glassless, shuttered window through which we can see Mount Kinabalu with a ring of cloud just below the summit. Swirls of mist cause the peaks to vanish momentarily, giving me the impression that the mountain is mocking me. I feel intimidated, feeble and very small; my chest tightens, and my breathing becomes laboured and uneven. Mesmerised by the light on the mountain, I feel the panic rising in my chest and stomach. The massive hole that forms Low's Gully is full of mist – I can't see it but I know it's there. All the colours of the hill seem too bright, the noise around me too loud and my overloaded senses switch off. My body involuntarily relaxes and my vision blurs.

Pain in my legs and someone holding my shoulders. I open my eyes and see nothing but green. I close my eyes and see nothing but green. Green.

My limbs are moving without my permission. I look at a young woman. Small children laugh and talk loudly, pointing and staring at our semi-naked bodies. Dark-haired, brown-eyed children, innocently staring me straight in the eye. Visions of my daughter's deep brown eyes.

Bob sits, clutching a bowl of something, and an old woman tends to our cuts. Our dirty, sodden bandages are removed and we are treated with some kind of antiseptic; my legs sting as it is applied to my festering cuts. Bob's hand comes in for particular attention.

Despite Richard's tender loving care I had become increasingly worried about my hand; it was black, the fingers were the size of fat pork sausages and it smelled of rotting meat, which is exactly what it was. The swelling had spread to my arm and pains were shooting right up to my shoulder. Initially, the old woman applied an antiseptic liquid from a jar to our lacerations, but when she saw the state of my hand she obviously decided that something stronger was called for and went to get an even older woman, who turned out to be her mother. She produced a jar which, I later found out, contained an antiseptic, a whole black and yellow snake, scorpion venom, and bits of centipede.

'I ain't fucking eating that!' She took my arm and before I could protest plunged it into the jar. I would have hit the roof had they not been holding me down – iodine was peanuts compared to this. Hearing the screams, the villagers decided to pack the children off and by the time my hand was removed from the jar, thirty seconds later, the room was almost empty. I looked at my hand, realising that it was looking and feeling better already, and that I could feel the warmth spreading up my arm.

'Did that hurt?' The usual stupid question. From that moment on, I had no problems with infection although it was obvious that I was going to need the attentions of a surgeon.

The background chatter of children disappears as they are ushered away to spare them the sight of our wounds and the sounds produced by Bob as he is being treated. I become stupidly self-conscious about how we look and smell.

After a short time the stinging pain in my legs eases and is replaced by the pain of a shrunken stomach overloaded with food. Closing my eyes and rocking backwards and forwards helps.

We're pulled to our feet and led back out to the hallway, where they've prepared two makeshift beds for us. Instinctively, still a little threatened by these kind people, we huddle up to each other on the floor. Belly hard and head spinning, I drift off again into the greens of my dreams.

Light green, dark green, and more greens, bitterly cold water, and granite, cramped, painful and restless sleep. Cold, wet clothes, and confusion. Doubled up in agony. *Did I eat some of the fruit Bob ate? I'm sure I didn't.* Hands tug at my body to roll me over, and like a drunken man I fling my arms out to stop me rolling off the floor. I lie on my back as my legs are forced out flat, and see elderly faces staring into my frightened eyes. A large jar of the pickled dead things is placed next to me and, rolling my head to one side I see, floating in the jar, a black and yellow snake. The old woman massages the potion onto my stomach and the pain recedes.

We are disturbed from our sleep again by the noise of the children's return, and I see for the first time some male faces in the crowd.

'Does anyone speak English?' No reply, just friendly, smiling faces. Bob tries to talk to them, but to no avail. The old woman is still rubbing my stomach. The pain has gone and I no longer feel threatened, just tired. I sleep some more.

We eventually woke to nudges from one of the women I recognised from earlier, who had brought some clothes for us. We dressed and I felt a little less embarrassed. The hall filled with even more children and from somewhere near the door a voice spoke in broken English.

'You go to Kota Kinabalu?'

A bit more with it now, I answered: 'Yes. Who are you?'

'I take you to Kota Kinabalu.' I still could not see who I was talking to. Sitting up, we peered into the crowd and a young man emerged. 'I drive you to Kota Kinabalu?'

'Yes, when? Today?' My questions seemed to cause some confusion as to what 'today' meant. I decided to try and find out if they had any news of the others, but my question was forestalled.

'You British soldiers?'

'Yes,' I replied.

'Three more British soldiers come to Melangkap Tamis.' I'd made the assumption that we would be the first out, but it appeared we were not; Britt, Steve and Pete had escaped to another village the previous day. Relief washed over me.

'That will be Steve, Britt and Pete.' Bob nodded and we grinned at each other. I was eager to hear that we were the last out.

'What about the others? What about the other five?'

But the young man just repeated: 'Three soldiers at Melangkap Tamis.'

We were unsure how long it would take to get back, and unwilling to leave without some food. We were told that there was a small shop and I rooted through the rucksack for some money, before heading for the shop with what appeared to be the whole population of a large school following me. First on the list was anything edible, followed by some canned drinks, a large plastic container of sweets for the children and two pairs of flip-flops. Feeling like a lightweight

Father Christmas, I trudged back to the hut, where Bob had by now explained to the young man when 'today' was and we had a lift. The whole village seemed to come out to say goodbye; several cameras materialised and a short enforced photo session took place.

Our transport took the form of a pick-up car. All three of us crammed into the front and we set off towards Kota Kinabalu, stopping periodically to either pick people up or throw up. The dirt track seemed to go on for ever and the jungle on either side of the road was still a threat. I retreated inward, frightened by the renewed proximity of the jungle, terrified of the car breaking down, of having a puncture, or, worst of all, a crash; thankfully, our view of the mountain was obscured by clouds, but I could feel its presence up there, glowering down on us, and I tried to concentrate on other things: brightly coloured cars passing us, multi-coloured washing hanging up on wooden huts and small stalls selling locally grown fruits at every other bend.

After two or three hours the huts started to become more substantial and wood was replaced by concrete. Garages, shops, cafés, petrol stations, but most importantly very few greens and no jungle. We stopped now and then to let passengers alight. The traffic was light and soon I recognised the main street of the city; we directed the driver further along but were unable to explain exactly where we wanted to go, so he dropped us off in a side street which turned out to be no more than a hundred yards away from the Travellers' Rest. My legs were weak and the heat intense after being so cold for so long; we began to overheat and the effort made our heads feel light.

We arrived at the Travellers' Rest and sat next to the resident street cobbler, who promptly offered, for a small fee, to help us in any way he could. We declined his kind offer and started the long climb to the third floor, taking long rests at each landing. I'd felt quite strong earlier, back at the kampong, but now, trying to walk up three flights of stairs, it really came home to me how ill we were. Entering the hostel, we encountered the usual mixed band of foreign visitors milling around: Australian, Chinese and someone from Dorset. Ditching the bags on the floor we collapsed into the bamboo settee and watched the activity continue around us. We received some strange looks which seemed to say 'what the hell happened to you two', but our aroma stopped anyone getting close enough to ask any questions.

'Fucking hell, where did you two get to?' The familiar accent of our one and only Geordie.

'Steve. Good to see you mate.' The bubbly, round Geordie was not quite so bubbly or round any more. 'Where are the others?'

'Britt's through there with Pete, sleeping.'

'What about the officers and the Chinese?' Steve's faced dropped.

'Nothing – they're still in there.' We all knew what that meant – they'd be going through what we had. I pitied them. Unsure of the date and how long we had spent in there, I glanced at my watch.

'It's the twelfth today. We should have come out almost two weeks ago.'

'No one knew we were there.' His face hardened. 'No one knew we were in there. I walked into Park HQ's office and they didn't believe me.' We had hit the crux of the whole thing.

'There was no cut-off date?' My voice rose. 'No one knows about this?'

'Park HQ do, now.'

'What about the UK, Hong Kong, our units, our families?'

'Britt's organised a helicopter, through the HQ, for tomorrow, but that's it.' I sat down again and Steve disappeared into one of the dorms.

Bob spoke: 'Rich, this is the fuck-up to end all fuck-ups!' I was finding it hard to comprehend why the basics hadn't been done. 'We've lost a half Colonel, a Major and three Hong Kong Chinese nationals.' He paused. 'The shit is going to hit the fan. I'm the senior NCO; and you're the climbing instructor.'

We sat in silence for a while, watching the quiet life of the hostel, while I tried to picture the faces of the men who would be sent in as a rescue. The whole place was going to be turned upside down. Finding thinking too much at this stage counter-productive, I left Bob sitting there and went to see Britt. He was lying on his bed, awake and clean-shaven.

'You've shaved?' A stupid question, but I couldn't get over how well he looked – almost as if nothing had happened.

'Glad to see you two could make it.' We both deliberately avoided the question of our split; now was not the time or the place to start an investigation that would no doubt turn into a heated argument. 'There's two spare beds over there.'

Bob and I slept for the rest of the afternoon. The food I had eaten at the kampong sat heavy in my stomach and I felt like I'd swallowed a brick.

I woke to a violent sound of rumbling and a severe pain in my abdomen. The room was dark but I could feel the walls moving, and the soft noises of people sleeping were of no comfort to me. I belched, felt the unturnable tide of vomit ascending; Canute-like, crawled out of bed with my hand over my mouth and stumbled towards the door, heading for the nearest toilet on the balcony. I made it just in time and a spectacular five-finger spread was diverted into a small sink.

Out of breath, I sank to my knees, all the pressure I had felt inside my stomach gone. I sat on the floor with my back against the wall, sweating intensely, and the nauseating stale taste of stomach acid burning my nose and throat. It was cooler out here; I curled up into a foetal position, happy despite my discomfort, and my mind drifted off to the fate of the others.

'I think I'll use the other sink.' The Australian accent brought me reluctantly back to reality – the comment had seemed to be aimed at me for some reason. I found my feet, but my bloated stomach stopped me from reaching full height and I peered at the porcelain.

'Oh. That sink.' The vomit was too solid to be washed down the plughole. I made an attempt to clear it, but it was too much in my delicate state. This time I managed to make it to the hole they call a toilet, which luckily doubled up as a shower. I spent the rest of the night on the balcony and the hostel staff spent most of the following day dismantling the U-bend.

Steve and Britt left early for the helicopter search organised by Park HQ, returning by mid morning with no positive news. I noticed that Pete seemed to be very isolated, both mentally and physically, from everybody else, and I found this strange – after the experiences Bob and I had had, we were inseparable, and I had a distinct feeling of insecurity if he wasn't around me. Pete was very quiet and withdrawn, which worried me, and in an attempt to reassure him we tried to get him to join in with us, but he remained distant.

By mid afternoon the longawaited monsoon darkened the skies, and the local traffic ground to a halt as the litter-filled gutters struggled to drain off the excess water. Bob and I alternated between milling around aimlessly and sitting in a stupor, until two people from Dorset befriended us and pointed out the obvious – that we should at least go to the hospital to get checked out. It was something I knew we should do, but I was unsure of the standard of the local hospital; Pete was even more reluctant but bent to peer pressure. Britt and Steve, who appeared to be none the worse for their experiences, went back to bed.

Bob and I telephoned our wives to let them know we were safe before, accompanied by the Dorset couple, we went by taxi to the Queen Elizabeth Hospital, where Pete was admitted to one ward with a severe leg infection and Bob was admitted to the AIDS ward – he had lost twenty-five per cent of his body weight and, at only seven stone, it appeared to them as if he were dying.

On my return to the hostel I was greeted by Robert New, veteran of the New and Pinfield attempt on the gully and now living in Sabah, and David Powell, who had, after our conversation at the Panar Laban hut, offered to act as a cut-off for the expedition, but been very bluntly turned down by Neill. When, a week ago, there was no sign of us, he had suspected something was wrong. However, in the absence of any firm evidence or plan of action, he felt, on the grounds of his last conversation with Neill, that he couldn't act.

However, unknown to us NCOs, David had carried some of Neill's and Foster's personal effects down off the mountain three weeks earlier, and although it seemed an unlikely place to find it – Park HQ or the British Consulate would have been more sensible places – we searched the officers' bag for any trace of an emergency plan or contact numbers. Our investigation revealed only pyjamas, a hardback book and other items which don't really belong on a mountain.

With no light shed on the whereabouts or fate of the others, we went to the bags we had all left at the hostel before leaving Kota Kinabalu and searched for any missed pieces of information. Steve and Britt had searched these the previous day in the hope of finding an emergency plan and contact numbers but, like us, found nothing. Robert New gave us the telephone number of the British Consulate and also informed us that everywhere (except Burger King) was closed due to Ramadan.

It was vital that we inform our units in order that a rescue operation could be organised and we decided, in the absence of anything official, to phone Britt's girlfriend Sadie, who worked at the Royal Logistic Corps Headquarters in Deepcut, probably the best place for the alarm to go. However, it was early Sunday morning back in the UK, and this meant that we wouldn't be able to phone until late on Monday afternoon KK time, when the working week would be starting at HQ. This delay was unavoidable but worrying: with the deterioration in the weather, and judging from our own condition, we felt that the rear group – who had all been less fit than us anyway – were almost certainly in a bad way and that any delay could have very serious consequences. Another source of worry was that the local press had started sniffing around; they were extremely polite by the standards of the average British newshound, and not at all pushy, but it could only be a matter of time before the story broke in a big way.

Robert and David left, promising to help in any way they could, and I retreated to the balcony, accompanied by severe wind and extremely painful heartburn, the result of an overloaded stomach. With Bob in hospital I felt very isolated and longed for his company. I remembered one of the things that had kept us going: 'two trips to Burger King and we'll be OK.' The truth was very different. Looking at myself in the mirror earlier, I had seen the body of a starving twelve-year-old – just skin and bone. At the hospital I'd weighed myself but thought the scales were out; they gave my weight as nine and a half stone. I had been twelve stone when I left the UK – surely I couldn't have lost two and a half stone in the last eight days? As I lay on the settee in the sweltering heat of the tropical night, I looked again at my puny body and muttered under my breath: 'maybe three trips to Burger King?' I slept, waking every few hours wanting to vomit but producing only a succession of earth-shattering belches.

The heat of the sun woke me and I took a cold shower; it cleared my head, but my stomach was no better and I felt very weak. I tried to walk down the stairs but the effort was too much, so I just went back to bed on the settee.

Several European couples came to talk to me – with the news breaking in the local press, everyone wanted to know what was happening and if the others had been found. These well-intentioned visits served only to increase my anxiety and despite my dreadful stomach pains I eventually made the short trip to a bakery two doors down to purchase some peanut butter waffles and take my mind off things.

Mid afternoon came and behind closed doors Britt made the call to his girlfriend, who passed the news via another officer to Britt's

OC. He informed Neill's HQ and the ball was rolling. After he'd finished I called my unit. Neill and Foster were both senior and prominent members of my Corps, and the senior NCO with whom I spoke knew both officers well. My news was received in stunned silence – something I would get used to over the next few hours.

From the moment the UK was informed a telephone duty was instigated; we were all unsure what was going to happen next and wanted, as far as possible, to keep on top of events. How high up the chain of command had the alarm gone? Had someone sat on it in order to keep it quiet? We knew that the relationship between the UK and Malaysia at the time was strained, and that diplomatic relations had almost come to a halt because of the Pergau Dam affair. Would the Malaysian authorities be prepared to allow in rescue teams that would almost certainly consist of specialist military units?

We didn't have much time to think about these questions, as several very senior officers called almost immediately – some more irate than others, some more familiar with the situation than others – and it became quite obvious that we were a major embarrassment, not only to the military but also to the British and Malaysian governments, who knew nothing of our little adventure training exercise. I got the distinct impression that there was a game of exploding 'pass the parcel' in progress, and that we were the parcel no one wanted in their lap.

Sitting by the phone later that evening I was surprised to get a message from a Malaysian girl that Bob was outside in a taxi. We went down and found him in a terrible state, but once we'd paid the cab driver and given Bob a cup of tea he calmed down enough to tell us his story.

Once I'd been admitted I spent an hour lying on a trolley in a corridor before being taken to a ward with about sixty beds, where I was put in a corner next to a glassless window and had a drip set up. I thought this was for dehydration, although it was in fact a glucose drip, but being a stupid Janner I thought I needed food, not fluid. Nobody seemed to speak English, I spoke no Malay, and every time somebody came I shouted in vain for food, not fluid. Whenever it rained I got soaked and I lay there, lonely, sick and afraid, until four in the morning, when I was overcome by a spasm of diarrhoea.

I lay there in my own excrement, aware that my wounds were likely to get infected, and decided that I needed a shower.

I got up, and screamed as all the wounds on my back and buttocks were stuck to the sheet; pulling it off was agonising and I felt as if I'd ripped acres of skin from my back. The sheet itself looked like an accident in a pizza factory. One of the nurses came over to see what the fuss was about, and all I could do was make the most basic of pleas: 'I need food.' She didn't understand.

I slumped onto the bed and sat there crying, swearing at everyone in general and no one in particular. I didn't have the strength to do anything for myself and my whole system felt as if it was collapsing; I reverted to childhood, screaming hysterically that nobody loved me and calling out for Rich to rescue me. A doctor came and took my drip out. I raged at him, but he couldn't understand me and left. A few minutes later, a female doctor appeared and was treated to the same stream of abuse, which she bore surprisingly well, waiting until I'd run out of steam before responding.

'What seems to be the problem?' I looked at her blankly – the last thing I had expected was someone who spoke English.

'I've been left here and my mate's fucked off.' She asked for more details and I told her my story. She explained about the glucose drip, but I insisted I needed food and she said she'd see what she could do. I felt more relaxed when she left and pondered the odd coincidence of meeting an English doctor (for that was what she was – she'd married a Malaysian colleague) in a place like this. An hour later, a big silver platter with a domed cover arrived, and thinking I'd miraculously been transported to the Ritz, I took the lid off.

'Where's the body?' On the platter was a fish head on a bed of what looked like seaweed, and for a moment I was transfixed by the glassy stare of the cod head, before gingerly lifting it in the hope that I'd find something edible.

'Where's the rest of you, then?' Nothing. It was too much; I felt like the victim of an elaborate practical joke, and the whole platter went flying across the ward to the accompaniment of more tears and swearing.

One of the long-suffering nurses called the English doctor, who promised to try again but warned me that the kitchens were closed due to Ramadan. She returned some time later with a packet of two-minute noodles. I must have seemed very ungrateful.

'How the fuck am I going to cook these?' An hour-long pantomime ensued as I tried to explain to the Japanese couple on my right that I needed some hot water, and eventually the wife boiled them using the wok and stove she had with her. I ate the noodles and ten minutes later my bowels opened uncontrollably. I started screaming, two male nurses arrived – I think by this time they had decided I was so deranged that a bit of muscle was called for – and I tried to explain my state and that I needed a shower. They lifted me from the bed and dragged me through the AIDS ward, which was occupied almost entirely with child prostitutes handcuffed to the beds. Even though I was completely self-absorbed, the sight shook me; I could feel my reason going and my disintegration became total when I saw the state of the bathroom. It was absolutely filthy – excrement all over the floor and walls, overflowing toilets, and an appalling smell – and I wedged myself across the doorway, screaming hysterically. I was terrified of going in there and my open wounds becoming infected. The nurses tried to push me in but I fought back with a strength that I thought had long since deserted me, and eventually they gave up, walking off to leave me collapsed on the floor crying for Richard. Once the tears had subsided I heaved myself to my feet, walked down the corridor and promptly shat myself again. I stood there with it running down my legs and saw an open door, which to led into a comparatively clean kitchen. On the worktop was a gallon of blue surgical scrub. Using a kidney bowl, I poured half the surgical scrub over me in an attempt to disinfect my wounds; it was even more excruciating than ripping the sheet off earlier had been, but it was worth it just to know that I was clean and infection free. I washed my shorts in the sink and poured surgical scrub over them, before tottering back through the ward to my bed.

I was surprised to find little buns, biscuits and sweets beside my bed: it transpired that the nurses had told the patients my story, and that they'd taken pity on me and given me these little presents. I ate them gratefully and shat myself again. I lay on the bed, wallowing in ex-crement and self-pity, but feeling rather humbled by the fact that these poor people had given me their food.

It was now mid afternoon, and the nurses had set up my drip again. I decided that if Rich hadn't turned up by eight that evening I would leave and spent the next few hours watching the door. Nothing happened, so at the allotted time I pulled the drip out and got up. Clad only in flip-flops and shorts, bearded, emaciated and slightly mad, I walked past the funny looks of the patients and reached reception. A nurse spoke to me in Malay.

'Sorry darling, I'm going home to England. I've had enough.' I had no money and no clear idea where I was, but knew that if I could find Burger King I would be able to find the Travellers' Rest.

'Burger King.' The driver didn't understand, so I adopted the usual English tactic of shouting and waving my arms around. He threw me out onto the pavement. I tried another cab.

'Burger King.' Eventually, I managed to make myself understood; the effort left me close to breakdown. From Burger King I was able to direct the driver to the front door of the Travellers' Rest where, upon discovering I had no money, an argument broke out. It was the last straw; I sat in the back seat, babbling semi-coherently, and tried to explain what he needed to do.

'Third floor. Rich. Pay you.' I rubbed my thumb across my fingertips in what I hoped was the universal sign for money and pointed up at the third-floor windows. He finally entered the hostel and returned a few minutes later with Rich. I'd never been so glad to see him.

We chatted on for a while after Bob finished his story, and when my phone watch ended we went back out to the balcony and bed. My anxiety over what was to come was as uncomfortable as my medical condition. I felt dreadful.

The following morning Bob decided that he needed proper medical attention for his hand, and it looked as if the only place he was going to get it was back in the UK. By far the easiest way would be to go via the British Military Hospital in Hong Kong – everything would be taken care of once we arrived back inside the military system. Bob certainly couldn't travel alone in his state, and as Steve and Pete had both lost their passports in their struggle to escape the gully, the only person able to travel with him was me. I talked to the Frenchwoman who ran the hostel and she suggested that I go to see Danny Chow, a local man who ran a travel agency nearby, which happened to be one of the only shops open.

Danny was more than a little surprised to see me; he'd heard the rumours but hadn't seen or heard anything official yet. Like everyone around us he bent over backwards to help us and after only an hour

I had acquired two plane tickets for the following day. David Powell offered to take us to the airport and it seemed that we were all set. I was glad to be leaving in a way, and although I knew the trip would take a few weeks, that we'd have to stay in BMH Hong Kong for a while, it would be good to get on a plane and at least start the journey. My mind turned to Neill and the rear group; none of us had voiced our fears, but we all feared the worst. Leaving without an organised rescue in place, or even knowing whether one would be possible, I felt I was letting them down. David Powell's words came back to me: 'There are only four men in the country capable of going in there – two divers, me and *you*.' It echoed in my ears. I was twenty-five per cent of the rescue team, but I couldn't even walk, what use could I be? I longed to be fit, to have the physical strength to go back in.

I returned to the hostel and sat next to Bob on his phone watch, keeping my fears and thoughts to myself. As time wore on, the situation was further complicated by the attentions of the British press who, after receiving several refusals to talk, started to adopt the tactics that have earned them their present exalted status in society. They posed as friends, acquaintances and even officers in their attempts to prise a story from us. During a lull in the action I took the opportunity to phone home, learning that the news was just starting to filter through and questions were being asked in Parliament.

The phone rang yet again and I beat Bob to it: 'Travellers' Rest, Corporal Mayfield, sir.'

A local accent. 'I am General Hussin bin Yussof.' Silence.

'Morning, sir.' I couldn't think of anything else to say.

'I am calling to ask how many regiments you require to search upstream for the five missing soldiers?' I'd never had a General or his army at my disposal before – it seemed a bit much for one lowly Lance Corporal. Bob was the senior NCO and it was definitely time to pass the buck.

'Hold the line please, sir.' I placed my hand over the mouthpiece. 'Bob, I've got some General on the phone who wants to know how many regiments we need to search upstream.'

'How many men in a regiment?'

'Oh. Er, between 600 and 800 men, but we'd only get half of that - the rest would be on rear party.' I couldn't help feeling this conversation was a wind-up or another press stunt.

'We'd better have two then!'

'Could we have two please, sir?' It was just like ordering a couple of take away-pizzas.

'Certainly.' And the phone went dead.

The next morning, while boiling up one of the 'compo' meals, I overheard an irate Bob on the phone to someone. From what I could gather, we'd been ordered to stay put, but Bob was having none of it; sticking to his guns, he explained that he needed urgent medical attention to his hand, Hong Kong had already been informed of our arrival and that we'd be of no use here. The conversation ended abruptly and I offered him a coffee.

'Problems?' I enquired.

'No, we're going to Hong Kong today.'

'Who was that?'

'Just some Lieutenant Commander.' He shrugged his shoulders. 'You packed?'

'Ready when you are.'

We gave the rest of our expedition cash and local currency to the remaining three. Until the men from the MOD came with their magic cheque-books they would have to pay their own way. In the afternoon, David Powell turned up to take us to the airport, in a four-wheel-drive pick-up. As we said goodbye to the others, the ill feeling between Britt and us surfaced; nothing was said, but the atmosphere was brittle and it was not a happy parting.

Kota Kinabalu's new airport was only a short drive from the city centre, giving us just enough time to feel the benefit of the vehicle's air-conditioning before stepping out again into the humid air.

The Air Malaysia plane was as modern as could be wished for, but travelling in the cramped seats of economy class is never the most comfortable of experiences, and in our condition – swollen-stomached, vomiting, farting and belching – it was a nightmare, especially for our fellow travellers. I stared out of the window as we taxied across the runway and wondered yet again what had happened to the rear group. *If they're still alive then they must be on their last legs, going through hell.* The sound of the plane's engines was unsettlingly like that of the rushing water in the gully and my mind drifted off into the jungle, into the cave we slept in and the time I honestly didn't think we'd make it. Whereas before I couldn't make the connection between the cave and safety, here on the plane I couldn't make the inverse connection, insulated as we were by twentieth-century technology. On one side of the runway was the sea and on my side was the mountain, looking small from here – there was no detail, just the outline. It could have been a cardboard cut-out.

CHAPTER 14

Glad to be alive

Leaving the ground seemed to hold some deep but unspecified significance for me. I felt rather shaky and was relieved when the seat-belt light went out and the hostesses came round with hot flannels. They helped a bit, but I felt very nervous of what was about to happen and had serious misgivings about the way in which the way the military might act. The hostesses reappeared with a new trolley offering alcohol. We knew it would hurt, but then everything hurt, so it made no difference. The temptation was too much and a double brandy later it hurt.

I assumed the best flying position and sorted through the several cheap tapes I'd bought from Centre Sport. The one that seemed to fit my mood best was 'Nevermind' by Nirvana, and after listening to it for well over an hour one song stuck in my mind: 'I'm on a plane, I can't complain.' Staring out of the window, the grey whites and white greys of the clouds started to change subtly; a hint of blue appeared, then purple, and the colours slowly degenerated through reds and oranges to browns and, finally, the hated greens. The faces of the lost five floated past my window, pictures and events from the past, accompanied by stabs of emotion. Pity and regret; if only I had had the balls to stand up more to Neill, they'd be alive now, even on the plane. I smiled, revelling for the first time in my safety. 'I can't complain.' *I'm in fucking agony but I can't complain.* A great wave of anguish and relief swept over me; I closed my eyes against the tears and slept, haunted by the green dreams.

I woke only once during the flight, to refuse an offer of food from the air hostess. Bob nudged me awake in time for me to fasten my seat-belt, and as we went through the nerve-racking experience of landing at Hong Kong's Kai Tak airport for the second time, I realised something had changed. Our short sojourn in Kota Kinabalu had been a transitional period, during which our focus had shifted from the immediate worries of our fight to survive to a growing concern about how things were going to resolve themselves: 'What happens next?' and 'When are the fingers of blame going to start pointing, and at whom?' Disembarking from the plane threw this change of priorities into sharper relief and as I walked through the humid night air my sense of foreboding deepened.

The cooler air, bright lights and blessed absence of green inside the terminal relaxed me a little. Still feeling very weak and ill we made our way to Immigration Control, sitting and resting every few yards; by the time we arrived, our plane load of people were long gone but there were still long queues waiting for visa stamps. Unable to stand for more than two or three minutes, we decided to wait for the queue to die down, but what appeared to be several flights later it became obvious that the queues were never really going to get any shorter. Eventually, after cutting through the red tape and armed with a two-week visa, we collected what little luggage we had and headed off into the crowds to face the music.

So far so good; we hadn't been dragged off the plane and apart from the odd look of revulsion no one was paying much attention to us, but I still had butterflies in my stomach and my sixth sense was working overtime. We followed the crowd and found ourselves standing out on the pavement, where several British army uniforms were hurrying around. Maybe they weren't expecting us. We sat there, lost and bewildered, until a tall Staff Sergeant approached us.

'I take it you're Sergeant Mann?' He looked clean to the point of being polished, and fit.

'No I'm Mayfield, this is Sergeant Mann.' Formalities over, he summoned a soldier to carry our bags and load them into a staff car, whose driver adopted the role of tour guide, pointing out various sights, but my mind was elsewhere. We had been informed by the Staff Sergeant that before we went to the hospital, we had to go and see Lt Col Kerr, OC of the Royal Logistics Corps battalion in Hong Kong.

We weren't stopped at the barracks entrance and a minute later the car pulled up at an impressive building that I assumed to be the Officers' Mess. After sitting for any period of time, standing was difficult, and this occasion was no exception, but we eventually managed to lever ourselves out of the back seat and were led through the main reception into a lounge, where two men in suits and a woman stood up to introduce themselves: Lt Col Kerr, Major Noble and his wife. They were all smiles, which heightened my sense of unease.

After an hour of map drawing and explanations I started to feel tired and very on edge; I yawned and asked for a break. We were fed steak and chips – not the best thing for someone suffering from malnutrition, but it did taste good – and while we ate they disappeared, no doubt to mull over what they'd just heard. Half an hour later they returned to tell us the car was waiting to take us to the hospital. All three gave us their cards, offered to help in any way they could and thanked us for talking to them when we were obviously so ill. Their attitude towards us seemed to have softened and I felt more at ease. Maybe I had been oversensitive and misjudged them.

The staff car sped out of the barracks and headed off into the night; tall buildings, busy night life and neon signs flashed by my window, and what seemed like seconds later we arrived at the British Military Hospital. After showing our ID cards at reception we were led away to a small treatment area, where we received a half-hour examination before being packed off to one of the wards.

BMH Hong Kong is a massive place, but as we were wheeled along corridors to the lifts it appeared to be a ghost town; one of the effects of the British pull-out from Hong Kong was that BMH was scheduled for closure and the winding down process was well advanced.

At the end of such a long day I was feeling completely exhausted. We were placed in separate rooms by the army nurses and given a cocktail of pain-killers and sleeping tablets to go with our drips, along with a tube of Eurax cream for our wounds. The control unit for the lights and the emergency buzzer were placed in my hand and I was left alone, tired out but unable to sleep. I wanted Bob with me; alone in this neat, sterile environment, my insecurities threatened to overwhelm me, and I scanned the room frantically for anything that would divert my mind. On the floor, strangely out of place against the scrubbed and polished precision of the tiles, was my rucksack – dirty, battered and torn, and a physical reminder of the jungle.

Dense and green, thorns pulling at my trousers, pain from the biting leeches and more pain from falling all the time. Cold water and night, dark and sleepless nights, wet and cold. Green.

The sandpaper sleeping bag is gone but the burning pains in my legs remain as I regain consciousness in the cold of the night. Remembering where I put the control, I press the alarm and wait. *She should be here by now. Press it again. Open your eyes, all you need is some Eurax to relieve the burning. Where the hell is she?* My patience is fast running out – my legs are burning up and it's excruciatingly painful. *Turn your head, shout, scream, get some attention.* My mouth opens silently, but the scream inside my head is deafening. *NURSE! Why can't they hear me? Where are they? Press the alarm again, press it. Wait, dickhead! You're pressing the light button. In that case, why is it still dark? I'm so doped up I can't even open my eyes. Find the alarm press the alarm if only I could see.* I fumble with the plastic control, but again nothing happens; I lie still, hoping for the pain to stop, but it just throbs away unceasingly. *Keep your cool Rich, think. Where's the Eurax? On the side next to your washing things.* Anything to make the pain stop. Guided by memory rather than sight, my hand flies out to the right. *Open your fucking eyes!* I can hear the despair in my mind's voice. Knocking things off the cupboard, my fingers clasp around a plastic tube; I empty the contents over my legs and rub. A strange smell fills my nostrils, and the burning sensation lingers on. Black changes to green.

'Bob, Bob don't get too far ahead.' On top of a ridge. We hoped to be able to see something useful from here. Everything is dead, and these fucking leeches. I slice them off my legs with the parang.

There was a sick, dizzy feeling as my eyes opened but, to my relief, a hospital ward surrounded me. A strong smell of peppermint filled the room and the bedclothes were scattered about the floor after my struggle last night. Lying naked on the bed, I felt a stinging sensation returning to my legs.

I looked down at my puny body; my thighs were white, smeared with – toothpaste? The memory of last night's panic flooded back. *You wanker! Couldn't open your eyes!* Toothpaste. I didn't know what drugs they had given me but it must have been bloody good stuff.

Bob had had a bad night too, so we insisted on being together and were moved into a two-man room. The monotonous routine of hospital life was frequently broken by the gorgeous army nurses who, with a half-empty ward, had nothing too demanding to fill their time.

Major Noble came to see us accompanied by his wife, who happened to be a Senior Nurse and somewhat more experienced in the nutritional field than ourselves. Finding us lying in bed with severe stomach pains, she pointed out that, as well as the obvious hot and spicy foods, we should stay away from anything rich, anything made from dairy produce and especially anything fizzy. Bob and I looked at each other, and at the litre bottle of Coke on the bedside cabinet next to the extremely large and now empty box of mints. We didn't care, we were happy.

We were told that a major search and rescue operation was about to swing into action, under the command of Major Schumacher, commander of the jungle warfare training team in Brunei, who would be flying into Hong Kong to talk to us that evening. I asked Major Noble for advice on what would happen next; he answered my questions as best he could and offered the help of a friend in the Army Legal Corps.

That evening Major Schumacher arrived as planned; he had been well briefed and seemed very efficient and knowledgeable, although I couldn't help but feel that he was just confirming what he already thought. He stayed for only forty-five minutes before departing for his flight to Kota Kinabalu, where he was made up to Lieutenant Colonel. After he went, the nurses offered me the same concoction of drugs that I'd had the night before, but I declined their kind offer and made do with two new tubes of Eurax.

The following afternoon a Colonel from the Army Legal Corps came to see us; despite having no clear brief as to what (or in this case what not) to tell us, he was very open with us about what he thought would happen next. He gave us two pieces of advice which proved to be invaluable. Firstly, he said, we shouldn't talk to the press, because we would have absolutely no control over what was written and the chances were that in doing so we could perjure ourselves. The other point was that the MOD would take a very dim view of anyone making money from an event such as this. He expressed a personal view that anyone doing this was of the lowest calibre.

I was concerned about Pete's fall as, being the senior climbing instructor in the front group, I should have enforced the wearing of helmets during any time we were on steep ground; in reality, this would have meant wearing them permanently for well over a week, which was obviously impractical. The Colonel informed me that because Pete was TR&A qualified, no blame should be attached to me. I remained unconvinced but was slightly reassured.

Bob's main concern was that he was the most senior person in the front group and as such he felt that he should have been able to do more, but as one of the less experienced members he was told that no such blame should be apportioned in his direction either.

The Colonel did a great deal to reassure us that, from what he already knew, we would be absolved from any blame. However, he went on to say that characteristically the MOD would probably say too little and too late, and that just because we'd been vindicated didn't necessarily mean that we'd still have a career at the end of all this. I had the distinct impression that because he hadn't been briefed on what to tell us he felt slightly uncomfortable about being so truthful and open about the way in which the Ministry operates in these circumstances. He left his card in case we needed any more advice and departed. I suddenly felt very vulnerable and couldn't wait to get back to my unit.

There were two things that happened every evening: we would watch the television news in the hope that the other five had been found, but see only speculation and various inaccurate maps and diagrams; and the duty senior NCO would come to visit to see if he could be of assistance.

One of these visits brought home to me the potential tragedy of the situation. The duty senior on this particular evening turned out to be an old boss of mine from the Squadron. We reminisced for a good half-hour before he left in search of his driver, who then promptly appeared, shook both our hands and introduced himself as one of Kevin's friends.

He asked the usual questions – how, what and why – before saying, in a rather accusatory tone: 'You know that Kevin has only just been married?'

'Yes.' I thought of when we first met, on the plane over to Brunei, and Kevin proudly announcing that he'd been married just two weeks earlier – we had all joked that he should be on honeymoon and not swanning around with us.

'His wife would like to know if *you* think he is still alive.' He looked me straight in the eye, demanding a truthful answer. I couldn't lie and say yes. I couldn't raise her hopes because I honestly thought they'd all perished. I stared back at him, trying desperately to be strong.

'No. I think they're all dead.' My voice sounded shaky and a mass of emotions welled up inside me. He shook our hands again, thanked us and left.

They shouldn't have been on the expedition. They knew that. I knew that. I tried to convince myself that I had done my best to influence Neill. *But they're dead now, I didn't do enough.* Guilt and grief engulfed me and I left the ward to be by myself.

We repeatedly asked Major Noble to authorise us to leave Hong Kong; we had already given all the information we could that might be of use to the rescue operation and were just kicking our heels. Bob and I were waiting one day in the tiny nurses' office for him to return our call, when a very attractive young female doctor walked in sporting long blonde hair and a supermodel's face, wearing a white coat and with a stethoscope hanging around her neck. She asked if we'd seen another doctor whose name nobody seemed to be able to pronounce, and of whom we'd never heard. We told her that no doctor of that name worked here, but that we could go and get a nurse, who might know. She left the small room quickly in search of her elusive doctor. I smelt a rat; we looked at each other and in unison said: 'Press!' We carried on talking for another five minutes until the phone rang, and I answered.

'Ward ten, Lance Corporal Mayfield, sir.' Out of the corner of my eye I caught a flash of white and blonde as the suspicious female doctor charged into the room.

'You're Corporal Mayfield!' Her little eyes were beaming, having found her quarry.

'No.' I stared her straight in the eyes, trying to make her believe that someone else had answered the phone.

'You're Sergeant Mann!' She turned to face Bob and gleefully offered a hand to shake.

'No.' He wasn't even tempted to hold her hand.

From the other entrance, the Senior Staff Nurse charged through the office, grabbed the bogus doctor by the shoulders of her white coat, picked her up off her feet and carried on walking out of the office and through the corridor to deposit the white-coated imposter in the lift, muttering obscenities about the press in general. I was just glad that the lift door was open.

'Hello?' I recognised the voice on the other end of the phone as that of Major Noble and realised that he'd been waiting while our little scene with the reporter was played out. 'I've got some news; you should be able to fly back to the UK in a few days, but you won't be able to leave the hospital because of all the press interest.' He reaffirmed that we were not under any circumstances to talk to the press and that they might even try to pose as doctors to get in and talk to us. A phrase involving the words 'stable doors', 'horses' and 'bolted' sprang to mind but I bit my lip and listened to the rest of his advice. He suggested that we start making statements, as they might well help in the search for the others. Bob thought this very unusual and correctly suspected that anything we wrote or said would be used later.

Various English and local papers where brought to us by the nurses, along with chocolate and goodies. The story of the search for the others occupied a lot of column inches ranging in importance from the front to the middle pages and strangely, contained odd pieces of information that we felt could only have come from someone on the expedition. We knew it wasn't us, which left the other three as suspects. We made an educated guess that it was Britt.

Several bunches of flowers arrived from 'local friends', which we both thought a little strange as we knew no one in Hong Kong, but later guessed it was the press trying to identify us by following the flowers to their target.

I called my unit several times but gained no further information as to what was happening in the UK or on the mountain. Bob was in daily contact with a senior from his TA unit, and an officer that I knew from earlier service who was privy to the odd situation report coming out of Kota Kinabalu; these were our only sources of information. We felt the onset of the Mushroom Syndrome – being kept in the dark and fed on nothing in particular.

My dreams still had a frightening realism about them and occurred every night whether I took drugs or not, and I decided to stay off the drugs as doing this made me feel better the morning after. Our physical health improved, and as our wounds healed faster and the constant pain of eating started to subside, we upped the pressure to be sent back home. There had been talk of an inquest or Board of Enquiry in Hong Kong, but this proved to be impractical, and on the evening of 18th March, Major Noble phoned to tell us that flights had been booked for the following morning. He also informed us that we were not to call anyone in the UK about our impending journey. The prospect of flying home economy class – eighteen hours in the cheap seats – really didn't appeal to us, and after a return call he promised to try and upgrade us.

When Major Noble came to take us to the airport the following morning he confirmed that we'd be travelling back club class. On arrival at the airport, just thirty minutes before our flight, our passports were taken to be stamped, we were whisked through customs and left in the executive lounge to wait for our flight. I watched the news on the lounge TV and felt very uncomfortable when, for the first time, all the expedition members were named. The call came for our flight and we boarded the plane, but I still found it hard to believe that we were finally going home. We'd been told to make ourselves known to the cabin crew in case of any press trouble, but this seemed to be the least of our problems; vomiting and diarrhoea were still more of an issue for me.

Eighteen hours later, and feeling more refreshed after the flight than before, we landed at Gatwick, clutching our free bottles of champagne, and were met by five bigwigs standing at the door of the aircraft. I recognised one as the CO of the Joint Services School of Adventure Training and another as Colonel Hall, Neill's boss back in York; the other three I didn't know but guessed that they were very senior officers. They took us by the arm and led us away, telling us to keep our eyes front and not to talk to anyone. As we passed a dozen reporters, I couldn't help feeling like a Russian spy defecting from the East.

Our passports were taken and other officials joined us as we were purposefully propelled down the passageway until, without warning, an official opened a door that appeared at first sight to be no more that a section of wall and led us through to a dimly lit corridor with boxes, cleaning materials and other paraphernalia littering the dark sides. We took turn after turn, and in this shadowy world that passengers never see, I completely lost my bearings. My apprehension was increased by the solemn, silent manner of our party.

'Er, where are we going?' I aimed my question at the person holding my arm.

'To the Special Branch office.' *I'm sure he said that without moving his lips, or was it just too dark to see? Shit, we're going to get interrogated. Make conversation, find things out.*

'I was told our wives are here to meet us.'

'Yes.' *His lips didn't move that time either, I was watching. Maybe he's a ventriloquist and this is some sort of subtle softening-up process before the interrogation starts in earnest.*

The noise of other passengers was everywhere and I formed the impression that the walls were in fact only partition walls; on the other side was normality and no defecting Russian spies. Somehow, the fragility of the barrier dividing us from the mundane served only to reinforce my fears when I realised how easy it was for the secret world to reach through that barrier and touch ordinary folk like us.

We emerged from the secret passageways of the unknown into a large empty hall. There was not a civilian in sight, but the noise of the airport was all around us. Bob was led off into one office and I was led to another with the two officers I had recognised.

'Corporal Mayfield. We're going to tape this, hope you don't mind.' I just smiled – I was not in a position to say no. The two officers introduced themselves, confirming their identities, and knowing who I was talking to set me slightly at ease.

'This is a very serious situation.' I hate it when people state the obvious. 'This interview is only to help us piece together what happened, so that we can mount a more effective search.' I just smiled again. I had confidence in the military syste
m, but why were these senior officers trying to gain my confidence? If what they were saying was true then they could just come out and ask their questions. Having a Major and a full Colonel explain themselves to me made me feel very uneasy.

They asked their questions and I answered as truthfully as I could remember. And then they asked more and I answered those. It was naïve of me to think that all the people in Hong Kong had not been talking to people over here, but the extent of their knowledge was vast. I had nothing to hide and so I just answered and answered, expanding where they asked me to. As I talked their expressions changed – sometimes a disbelieving stare, sometimes hostile as if what I was saying might have some personal effect on them. Never mind; what more could I say than what happened?

I looked at my watch. Two hours had passed. 'Just another few questions.' We continued, tape after tape in the machine, until they ran out of them. And then they continued some more, with questions that had an edge to them: leading questions, questions with implications for the front group. Why did we leave the rear group? Did we leave them on purpose? Did we think they were dead? Did we take any of their food? Questions that were of absolutely no benefit to the rescue teams, and questions I was not prepared to answer without legal support.

'I feel sick.' I took a more blatant look at my watch; I had been here for well over four hours.

'Just a few more questions.'

'I'm going to vomit!' I wasn't, but I wasn't going to answer any more questions either.

'Just a few more minutes.' A forced smile crept across his face.

'Is my wife here? I want to see my wife!' I didn't return his smile and I no longer trusted them. *This isn't for the rescue teams! This is an interview for the courts. They're being underhand.*

I repeated the question. 'Is my wife here?' My tone and posture took on a more aggressive edge.

'Yes, Corporal Mayfield. Would you like to see her now?' I returned the forced smiles they both sported and was led into the room Bob had been taken to just as he was being led out to be interviewed. I thought of warning him what he might face but my reactions were too slow and he was gone.

I recognised several faces in the room, one of which was my wife Sandy, but before I could go to her a man approached me and introduced himself as Major Proud, TA and head of some army press office. Major Bristow (my new OC, who had taken over from Major Ruff shortly before we left the UK) came over and shook my hand, but all I wanted to do was see Sandy.

The door opened and Bob walked in looking very pleased with himself. He'd only been gone for a few minutes; I wasn't quite sure how he'd got out of the questioning but I wished I had done the same.

Formalities over, Major Bristow took my bag and led me out of the room, closely followed by everyone else. An airport official handed over our passports and within seconds we found ourselves standing out on the pavement; my four-hour chat apart, I'd never cleared Customs so fast!

A senior rank from Bob's unit came into view driving a white hire van with the words 'Bullock's Hire' written in large black letters on the side. Bob and I laughed out loud, thinking it was probably a joke on the part of the man driving, but it turned out merely to be the highly appropriate name of the hire firm.

The journey from London to Plymouth would take several hours in the van and I was expecting to have to explain myself again for the benefit of my OC, Major Bristow; after all I was now his responsibility, and he would no doubt have to report first hand to my CO, Lt Col McNinch. He would also have to see me through the obviously impending post-mortem (whatever that entailed) and represent me.

Bob, although TA, was technically also one of Major Bristow's soldiers, yet during the journey he asked only one question: 'Was it poorly organised?' We both replied with a yes; what else could we say? That was the only time my OC asked for our opinion of the events.

We arrived back in Plymouth and Sandy told me that my unit, the Commando Ordnance Squadron, had been openly hostile and insensitive towards her. This was manifested most pointedly when she was asked if she would like to accompany the OC to the airport: on picking them up, Major Bristow had told Sandy and Bob's wife, Sue, in no uncertain terms that they were there only because it would be beneficial for the MOD to appear to be 'doing the right thing' in the presence of any press. After this event I decided that the only officer I could trust and who appeared impartial was Captain Gordon, the second in command of the unit, but shortly afterwards he was posted and a more junior officer took his place who seemed keen to impress his superiors.

Three days after arriving in the UK I became seriously ill, with classic malarial symptoms, and within an hour of each other, Bob and I were taken to separate hospitals.

I wasn't sure whether I was well enough to be at home during those three days; on top of my general debility, the jet-lag had taken its toll and I was finding it hard to walk up the stairs or do anything remotely physical. The children had boundless energy that I couldn't possibly hope to match and on this particular evening had gone to bed early. Curled up on the settee, I drifted in and out of a disturbed and disturbing sleep.

The temperature seemed to be fluctuating wildly. The air around me was freezing, but when I curled up tightly in an effort to keep warm it became too hot. There was no happy medium and the discomfort bordered on pain; I was hot and cold at the same time, my legs felt like I'd just run a marathon and cramp gripped my muscles. A strange yet familiar dreamlike feeling overtook me and, detached, I drifted off into a safe, warm, secure subconscious. It didn't last long and soon my green incubus returned with a vengeance. *How did I get here anyway? Sleep, you'll be OK.*

Voices from far off pierced the cold. 'Can you walk?' *Stupid fucking questions again – of course I can.* People were all around me and I moved like a drunk until the real cold of March air hit me and the sudden shock brought me back to something approaching reality.

'Can you walk?' Two men in naval working dress. *Where the hell did they come from?* Led by a man on each arm, I felt as if I was under arrest until they helped me into an ambulance and I was allowed to sleep again.

Helped out again into the cold night air I stumbled, with the support of the sailors on each arm, back into the warm. As I was probed and poked, my obsessive subconscious had me back in the mountains.

'Drive carefully, blue-light him straight to Derriford Hospital. I'll put a Medical Assistant in the back in case he stops breathing.' The voice wafted through my mind and I realised vaguely that I must be in a hospital – presumably the Royal Naval in view of the uniforms. Whoever they were talking about sounded in a bad way. I didn't realise it was me. I slept, until the sudden wail of a siren and a ghastly feeling of travel sickness woke me briefly.

My next feeling was of cold again but this time there was a reason – someone was taking my clothes off. I curled up into a foetal position and a woman's voice chided me.

'Wake UP! The least you can do is help me!' *Who the hell is that, who rattled her cage?*

'They tell me you've just come from the Far East?' She paused for an answer but all I could muster was a nod of my head.

'Was it nice?' *Nice?* I opened my eyes and an NHS nurse smiled sweetly. I shook my head. 'You were taking the malaria prophylactics?' She nodded her head to indicate the right answer and in reply I shook mine.

'But you were treating the drinking water in your hotel room, weren't you?' She nodded her head again, and again I shook mine.

'Well it's no wonder you're feeling a bit poorly then, is it? And, you know, you really should try to put on a little more weight.' I wanted to scream at her, but all I could muster was a nod of my head. I'd have given anything to be back in BMH with all those lovely army nurses.

Freezing cold, I grabbed the bedclothes and wrapped them around me, but the sheets were brutally taken away by the wolf in nurse's clothing. *If I'd gone private I'd have bedclothes.* All I could do was shiver myself into a sleep.

I woke periodically as people in white coats and face masks stuck sharp things into my various soft bits. Eventually I escaped from my dreams and woke fully to what I thought must be the next day, but my watch told me it was three days later. The buzzing in my ears seemed to indicate I must have been a guest at a loud rock concert, and the taste in my mouth suggested that for an encore I had eaten half a dozen plastic bags. I felt like shit but at least I was back with it. I surveyed my surroundings: a small room with one window through which there was no sky, just a tower block. Painted walls and green NHS curtains, a drip in my arm and the lights on low. Noise from the corridor and shadowy figures passing by my door. I tried to get up but my body was too weak even to reach the call button and summon a nurse. I went back to sleep.

A soft voice interrupted my dreams and I opened my eyes to see a nurse staring at me from behind her mask.

'Glad to see you awake, Richard.'

'Why are you wearing a mask?' A hint of fear coloured my voice.

'It's only a precaution, we're not entirely sure what you've got. It may be infectious.' I could tell from her eyes that she was smiling, trying to set my mind at ease, but I didn't trust her, or her mask.

Over the next few days my temperature dropped from 41 degrees to the more usual 37 and I started to feel something like normal, although I was still very weak. I was moved to a conventional ward, consisting of three beds lined up on each side of the room and an open corridor with other rooms leading off it. Nurses and doctors bustled around, visiting me occasionally to take blood samples: judging by the amount of blood they were taking, I began to wonder if they were reverting to medieval methods and kept a sharp eye open for leeches. My nightmares continued every time I closed my eyes, but I was feeling stronger by the day and even took the odd walk down to the TV room to help relieve the boredom.

I was sitting up in bed reading the latest edition of *High*, the climbing magazine, and waiting for the next set of test tubes to be filled with my blood. The curtains around me were drawn, and as people brushed past on the other side they moved gently, giving them a disturbing 3-D effect. I carried on reading the article.

Out of the corner of my eye I see the greens and browns of the curtains swaying gently from side to side, and slowly the dirty colours creep out across the floor to touch the edge of my bed. I move closer to the middle of the bed, not daring to look up. A trolley goes past; *it sounds like rain and the vegetated floor takes on a wet look, with water dripping from the leaves and hanging vines. Thick branches and bastard trees bar any real progress. My map is wet, but even if it was dry and readable it would be of no use to us – it was just guesswork, information taken from aerial photographs. I stare, trying to penetrate the foliage, but I can't see Bob. A voice, not Bob's though:* 'This is Richard . . .' *Maybe it's the others, the rear group, or even Britt. I turn my head towards the sound. Greens and browns moving violently: I'm falling! But without movement. Out-of-focus jungle colours fill my sight. GET OUT. MOVE! RUN! Go, now, before it's too late! I roll to the right, pushing the bushes and rotten debris out of the way to force a hole through the jungle.*

I found myself back in the corridor, sweating, shaking and shocked at the realisation I had been awake throughout the nightmare. My arm was still behind the curtain attached to the drip, the needle pulling my skin tight under the bandages. A disembodied voice came from behind the curtains.

'Where's he gone?' A friendly face appeared. 'Are you alright?'

'Open the curtains.'

'We only want a chat.'

'I don't care – open the curtains.' She opened the curtain and I returned shakily to the bed to be informed that all the blood tests had come up negative – nobody had any idea what I was suffering from – but they were continuing to send samples to the Tropical Disease Centres in London and Liverpool for further analysis.

As time wore on and the rescue operation turned up nothing apart from the odd food wrapper and sardine can, I became more and more convinced that the rear party had perished in the gully, but on the 26th of March two of the nurses walked in and announced that they had been found. I was still half asleep and it didn't really sink in.

'Who?' I asked.

'The others, look!' She shoved a handful of newspapers under my nose. I was flabbergasted – I had honestly come to believe they were dead. Watching the TV coverage of their rescue by helicopter later that day, I realised they had been rescued from a point just above New's Pools – a mere thirty-six hours from where we had last seen them at the top of the abseils. I couldn't work out what had gone wrong, but it later transpired that the ropes had twice jammed around a tree, and that each time they had had to bivvy before attempting to free the ropes the following day. It must have been on one of these attempts to free the ropes that we saw the lone abseiler; the result of this was that the section between the bottom of Easy Valley and New's Pools had taken them four or five days in comparison to our thirty-six hours. (The jamming of the ropes was discussed at the Board of Enquiry, but the cause of the jamming did not come to light until the publication in 1995 of the officers' account of the expedition. Neill had apparently dismantled the belays I had left in place, which were designed to allow free running of the rope, and replaced them with belays that did not allow the ropes to run freely.) Once they arrived at New's Pools they were unable to go on or retreat and were forced to wait for a rescue that could only be instigated if the front group survived. On this day in hospital I knew none of this, of course, and had to wait several tense months before the details were known.

A week after leaving hospital I was back at work and received a phone call from Paul Edwards. Having observed the normal pleasantries, Paul got right down to business: 'On the grounds you were lost in some jungle abseiling.' He paused at the word 'abseiling' as if to imply it was a particularly naff expedition pursuit. 'I've entered you into the Army climbing competition at Bristol on Saturday.' I thanked him for his consideration but had to decline his offer to compete, as I was completely unfit. However, I said I would attend – it was the first Army Open Championship and would be a great opportunity to see old friends.

We discussed the events of the last two months. Paul repeated the advice we'd already had about not talking to the press and offered to help in any way he could. He'd been hearing various rumours – some good, some bad – but having known and climbed with me on and off for two years, he felt sure that I had done nothing wrong and reassured me that any investigations would prove that.

In my condition I was not really capable of driving from Plymouth to Bristol, but I managed to cadge a lift from a climbing partner and spent the journey in my usual travelling position. The climbing wall in Bristol is in an old church – St Werburgh's – and is a state-of-the-art climbing training facility, with well over a thousand square metres of climbing surface. On our arrival it was packed and it took several minutes to find Paul, who was organising the competition. As we talked we headed off towards the rear area of the wall and he told me that after our phone conversation he had asked a few questions in the right places.

'You have nothing to worry about; I've spoken to several people in the know. Neill's come out and stated that it was always safety first in the rear group, but they had more injuries than the front group. You advised the right thing – not to do it in the first place. It's not your fault he didn't listen to you.' We stopped walking. 'And besides it's not particularly safe to starve to death.' I laughed, but he did have a point. 'Oh by the way – you're in the isolation zone now. You'll have to compete.' Once in isolation, competitors must stay there until it's their turn to climb; they are not allowed a prior view of the competition climbs. I protested that I was too ill, and that if my OC found out, I'd be in trouble, but Paul wouldn't take no for an answer. I finished third overall, having fallen off everything at two-thirds height; the expedition had not impaired my technical ability, but I was desperately short of stamina and fell off regularly at forty feet regardless of the difficulty of the climb in question.

I had five more short stays in hospital, and with each stay my unit seemed more distant and unco-operative, to the point where on one occasion I was taken straight to hospital from an extra duty and, by design or accident, my wife was not informed. This was the final straw for her and she made a statement to the press condemning the way in which we were being treated.

I was unsure how I had come to be in such an uncomfortable position but got an inkling when I was summoned to see my CO. He said that there was a Colonel Connaughton trying to contact me. I was told not to talk to him under any circumstances and informed that he represented a danger to my career in the army, so I agreed not to have any contact with him.

(Some time after the Board of Enquiry I was surprised to receive a call from Connaughton, and even more surprised to hear that Bob, who had given him my number, had agreed to see him. I declined to comment over the phone and hung up. Very confused I phoned Bob, who said that Connaughton was completely trustworthy and had arranged to have an interview with him that weekend. Bob told me all he knew about Connaughton; he was a retired officer of great integrity whose main interests were writing articles for various MOD publications on topical subjects, and who had also written several historical books. Bob also told me that Connaughton was going to speak to all the expedition members which I found very disturbing. Why had I been warned against speaking to him? I phoned Connaughton and agreed to a lengthy telephone interview.)

Prior to the Board of Enquiry I was feeling very isolated and felt I could no longer trust my unit. I turned to friends in other units, such as Paul Hughes, for support, and decided that where necessary I would pay for legal advice.

From the moment when the story first broke while we were still in Kota Kinabalu, there had been an enormous amount of press interest, but Bob and I followed the advice we had been given and said nothing before the board convened; although we later spoke to Connaughton, who at the time of writing has not published any material from our interviews. Keeping a low profile was not easy as the media became increasingly energetic in their efforts to track us down and gain our comments. This is well demonstrated by one incident in particular: a daily paper sent a reporter to Bob's son's school in an attempt to interview young Robert. Unluckily for the reporter, the school had been warned of the probability of such an event and informed Bob; the offending reporter left, red-faced and slightly bruised.

Other expedition members, it seems, were not so cautious, as headlines and comments from a small selection of the many articles the story generated show. The cuttings also demonstrate how the story evolved in the media:

> 'Five missing in Borneo jungle.' (*Guardian*, 17th March)
>
> 'Rescuers find traces of soldiers missing in Borneo.' (Jonathan Mirsky and Andrew Pierce, *The Times*, 21st March)
>
> 'Storms hamper rescue.' (*Guardian*, 21st March)

And then, on 23rd March, in *The Times*, an article based on a telephone interview from a hotel in Kota Kinabalu; the interviewee was Britt, and on the same day the *Daily Telegraph* ran a similar story, telling of some of the tensions in the team.

More cuttings:

'ESCAPE FROM DEATH VALLEY – SOS in pebbles leads rescuers to jungle Brits.' (*Evening Standard*, 25th March)

'HOW I BEAT DEATH VALLEY . . . we had food for ten days but we realised on day six that we might be in a survival situation.' *Daily Mail*, 26th March) [This comment from Neill is quite revealing; day six was the day that I went back up from our bivvy below the first two abseils to speak to Neill at the rear group's bivvy site at Alphabet Rock. Surely, if at that point Neill realised we were in a potential survival situation, the prudent decision would have been to call the whole thing off while it was still possible to do so.]

'Hell and hunger all on home video.' (*Independent on Sunday*, 27th March) [Ron flirts with Hollywood!]

'Lost laundryman of Borneo faces enquiry.' (*Evening Standard*, 31st March) [A reference to Ron's unit: 714 Laundry Platoon, TA.]

On 6th March I was at home on sick leave when I received a phone call from Bob.

'Turn the TV on for the evening news – Neill's giving a press conference.' I settled down to watch and sure enough, there it was. Neill, Foster and Britt all looked very chummy at first, but as Neill spoke I saw the colour drain from Britt's cheeks; he obviously hadn't been expecting what Neill said. He accused the front group of 'disobedience' and said that 'they proceeded down the gully without his authorisation'.

'Jungle expedition leader tells of anger at being left behind.' (Ray Wilkinson, *The Times*, 7th April)

I could hear the sound of my career disintegrating around me but was unsure what to do about it. I decided to maintain a low profile, and later that month received a boost to my flagging spirits when the BBC screened a feature about the expedition on their *Here and Now* news programme. It contained an interview with Neill and also had comment from Lord Hunt. A highly respected figure in the mountaineering world and the establishment, Lord Hunt led the expedition that resulted in the conquest of Everest in 1953. He was very critical of the concept, planning and leadership of the expedition.

Neill, in reply to Lord Hunt's comments, said: 'Until he has all the facts, which I don't have at the moment, I would think it was a slightly premature decision. In hindsight I consider it to be, and at the time I considered it to be, a justifiable objective.'

This last comment of Neill's seemed rather contradictory; after all he had, at the press conference, already made a public judgement about the front group, prejudicial to any enquiry and at a time when he was not in possession of all the facts.

I waited anxiously for the Board of Enquiry to start.

CHAPTER 15

Out of the frying pan . . .

When the official letter came ordering that I attend the Board of Enquiry, I tried through my unit to find out what it would entail but no help was forthcoming. Bearing in mind Neill's premature comments on television, I thought it wise to seek further legal advice, which I did through my solicitor. Armed with the relevant information, I informed my CO that I would attend the Board of Enquiry because he had the power to order me to attend, and that because it was to be conducted under oath I had the right to maintain silence and would do so unless I had legal representation. I knew that by pushing so hard for legal help I would further alienate my CO, but I already felt so isolated that it made little difference to me. He decided that an officer from my unit should attend the Board of Enquiry to act as my adviser. For the first week Major Bristow himself (an old friend of Neill's) would attend, but I was relieved when he was replaced by a Royal Marine officer who had no connection with Neill.

When the time came I signed for a hire car, and with Bob driving and the OC sat in the front we set off towards Imphal Barracks in York. I felt more than a little nervous – an official Board of Enquiry is a serious business, and the fact that it was all to take place on the site where Neill's unit was based made me very uneasy.

About two hours into the journey, and for no apparent reason, I felt the urge to look out of the back window. Behind us, blue lights flashing, was a police car. The driver mouthed the words 'pull over' at me.

I smiled sweetly, turned, and leaning over Bob's shoulder, said: 'Bob, are you using your mirrors?'

'Yes.' The speedo was not quite into three figures.

'There's a police car behind us.'

He glanced in the mirror. 'Does he want to pass us?'

'No, I think he wants us to pull over.' Bob pulled over, got out of the car, and spent several minutes talking to the policeman. He returned to the car with a speeding ticket and a long face.

'I'm not worried about what my unit is going to say, but Sue's going to give me hell when she realises I've got to pay a forty-pound fine!'

With the constabulary satisfied we set off again, and a slight misunderstanding about junctions saw us heading in the wrong direction to jibes of 'no wonder you two got lost', and 'were there no sign posts in the bloody jungle?' from Bristow, who had now taken a back seat. The events of the journey served to lighten our moods, but they did cause us to arrive late at Imphal Barracks, much to the annoyance of Bristow who missed tea and biscuits with Major General Cordingley.

A member of the guard escorted us to Headquarters Eastern District, where the enquiry was to take place and, issued with passes to enter the building, we were ushered through a door marked 'Quiet Please, Board of Enquiry in Progress'. I felt like a schoolboy who hadn't studied for his exams and was about to enter the examination hall. A second door, marked 'No Entry' was opened for us and we walked in.

To my left, against the wall, was a long table from which four officers stared at the late arrivals, and ahead of us were rows of tables; sober-faced, Neill and Foster stared at us from the front row, while in descending order of rank the rest of the expedition sat behind them, revelling in our late arrival. The only member missing was Chow, who was in hospital in Hong Kong recovering from a back injury sustained during the rear group's wait for rescue. The usher showed us to our seats in the penultimate row, and Bristow sat behind with two senior officers, one of whom I recognised as Neill's direct superior.

The Colonel who was Head of the Board introduced the other members: a Lieutenant Colonel, Major Noble and a Captain who was an army lawyer. The Captain then took over and explained that this type of hearing operated under oath and that if at any time we felt it necessary not to answer a question we had the right to silence. If at any time a question was asked that would incriminate the person answering, he would inform us of the fact by saying: 'You do not have to answer that question unless you wish to do so.' To my astonishment he added that we had the right to cross-examine any member of the expedition. With the formalities over first Bob and then I took the stand which consisted of a chair in front of the Board, to take the oath.

We were told that the Board had convened on 25th April, two weeks earlier, to discuss the planning and aims of the expedition along with the personal background details of all expedition members. No sooner had I returned to my seat than I was asked to take the stand, and explain in as much detail as I could remember the training at Plymouth and Ripon.

I explained that in effect we only had one day's training, which consisted of two abseils, and that as safety on abseils seemed to be the biggest issue, I had introduced more advanced abseil protection techniques using shunts and prussik loops. I said that I had been led to believe there would only be two separate abseils of no more than 150 feet, and that we would be able to leave in place two ropes to cover an escape if the need arose. I added that although I had been told by various people and Colonel Neill himself that he was an ML, I had some doubts about his ability because of his apparent lack of knowledge of the equipment or techniques I was using. At the time it did raise some doubts about the whole expedition, but I thought that maybe he hadn't done any climbing for a very considerable time and was perhaps a bit rusty.

The Board sat in silence for a few moments and then Major Noble addressed me: 'Corporal Mayfield, you appear to be under the impression that Colonel Neill is an ML?'

'Yes sir.' More silence. I felt very uncomfortable.

'Corporal Mayfield, are you telling us that Colonel Neill told you he was an ML?'

'Yes sir.' I felt extremely exposed sat out in front faced with such senior officers who not only appeared to be very knowledgeable about climbing, but had also probably been privy to information I would never have.

'Colonel Neill, tell Corporal Mayfield what qualifications you have.'

'I hold the Mountain Leadership Training Board's MLC, and the Top Roping and Abseiling Supervisor's award. Anything to do with rock climbing or multipitch work was down to my expedition adviser, Corporal Mayfield.' I turned to face him and stared him straight in the eyes. He smiled at me; I felt the blood start to leave my face and my mouth went dry. 'If Corporal Mayfield thought that when I said ML, I meant Royal Marine ML, he is quite clearly wrong.' I left the stand. The Board accepted that there had been a misunderstanding, which was probably fair on this point, but the exchange was fairly typical of what was to ensue during the four weeks the enquiry ran. It was extremely intimidating having to answer to such a large group of senior officers and we NCOs all felt we were on the spot. The pressures on Neill and Foster were different, as senior officers are not often called upon to explain themselves and when they are, it perhaps takes place behind closed doors on a one-to-one basis with another senior officer; having to do so in front of other ranks must have been an uncomfortable experience for them, especially when the other ranks in question had, on occasion, completely different recollections of what had happened from that of the officers. We NCOs had, prior to the enquiry, only limited contact with each other and hence little chance to discuss matters, yet our evidence was nevertheless consistent.

The anatomy of the expedition was dissected in every detail, which meant there were occasionally long periods of boredom such as the whole afternoon spent discussing sardines in an attempt to ascertain just how much food the Chinese had with them! In contrast, other sessions held the attention with a vengeance, dealing as they did with crucial issues, the finer details of which were often in dispute.

Command and control of the front group was one of the major issues and one that was complicated by the fact that Neill had at no time formally placed anyone in command of the front group; normally, the senior would have had the responsibility, but Bob, although a Sergeant, was one of the novices and therefore unable to lead. Pete was qualified to lead mountain walking but the majority of his experience was in the UK, Britt and Steve held no mountaineering qualifications and I, although a JSRCI, was the second most junior person in the group. In his evidence, Neill at first referred to the front group as 'Corporal Mayfield's', implying that I had responsibility for what had happened, but the Board soon concluded that as no one person had been placed in command, decisions were taken on a group basis.

David Powell testified that Neill had ignored his advice, but the crucial issue was Neill's insistence that had the front group waited for the rear group to catch up, the expedition would have been completed safely and successfully. To this end, he asserted that I had disobeyed orders on three separate occasions and establishing the truth or otherwise about this was a pivotal point in the enquiry.

The first instance of my supposed disobedience concerned Neill's alleged order to me to find out if the café at the lower hut on the tourist route was still serving food; this might seem a minor point, but it was the first time in the enquiry that Neill accused me of disobeying orders, an offence which would usually carry a severe penalty. The Board concluded there had been no disobedience because there had been no direct order. The second instance, concerning my failure to make the RV at Easy Valley Col, has more relevance; the Board concluded that as arranging an RV does not constitute a direct order there had been no disobedience and that the contingency plan in the event of my missing the RV had been observed. The Board accepted that it would have been inappropriate for me to leave the front group at that time.

The third instance was probably the most serious and concerned the front group's decision to carry on; Neill alleged that he had given me an order to wait indefinitely at the bottom of the abseils but, crucially, could not recall the last part of our conversation at Alphabet Rock, when I had said that we could wait only until the following morning. It was established, and confirmed by Ron himself, that Ron was not a party to this conversation but later, in what appeared to be an attempt to reinforce Neill's position, Ron asserted that he *had* been a party to the conversation. The Board were openly hostile to this change of story and the officer representing me said to me, in a quiet aside, 'don't worry – the Board aren't stupid.' The Board dismissed this allegation and accepted that the front group had not abandoned the rear group.

The Colonel in charge of the Board said to Neill: 'Did you honestly expect the front group to wait indefinitely, running out of food and with no possibility of escape, after all that Corporal Mayfield had told you?'

Neill's reply was blunt and surprising: 'Yes.'

The Colonel's reply to this seemed to have a hint of sarcasm about it:

'What were you going to do, turn up at the bottom of the abseils with five loaves and two fishes?' I could sense Neill's discomfort from two rows back.

In hindsight, from this moment on it became apparent that the finger of blame was no longer pointing at the front group, although

I still felt very apprehensive. The enquiry continued, and once the Board had finished hearing evidence (on 24th May) they retired to consider their conclusions and also to visit Kinabalu and Hong Kong.

Its findings not were released until September 1994 and the intervening months were worrying for everyone.

I had several more stays in hospital; the cause of my illness was never established, but worse than this were the psychological problems I was undergoing for which I received no counselling until the end of the year. I must have sorely tried the patience of those around me in my unit and at home, for my behaviour was unpredictable, to say the least. I realised that, whatever the findings of the Board of Enquiry, my career was finished – I would always be thought of as the Corporal who abandoned the officer commanding the expedition. The Board's findings (see appendix), which vindicated the front group and me, were published in September, but I had already applied for Premature Voluntary Release. This came about on 6th January 1995, but because the release process had been accelerated I was not entitled to the usual resettlement programmes and found myself propelled into civilian life unprepared, unsupported and unwell.

Kevin has left the army, and Lam and Chow are to do so shortly. Britt is still serving, as are Steve (now a full Corporal) and Pete. Bob remains in the TA; he has had three operations on his hand and is due to have a fourth which he hopes will restore its full use. Ron has pressed his last pillow case and is no longer serving with the TA. Neill is still a serving Lieutenant Colonel.

Bob and I are older and wiser and because of our shared experience now have an unbreakable bond between us – the one positive outcome of an expedition which nearly cost us everything.

Glossary

Abseiling Descending a rope in a controlled manner, usually by utilising a descendeur such as a figure of eight.

Ascendeur Any device for climbing fixed ropes.

Belay Anchor point for a climber or rope; (verb) to safeguard a climber's passage by holding the rope.

Bivvy Abbreviated form of 'bivouac' – overnight stop without tents, usually made more comfortable by using a bivvy sack – a waterproof outer shell that covers the sleeping bag.

Col A marked depression in the summit line of a mountain.

Croll Mechanical ascendeur.

Descendeur Any device used as a friction brake in abseiling.

Figure of eight Aluminium descendeur.

Hat Derogatory Commando or Para term for non-specialist personnel. Also used as a general term of abuse in cases of incompetence.

JSMEL (Joint Services Mountain Expedition Leader) A mountain-walking qualification run over a two-week period.

JSRCI (Joint Services Rock Climbing Instructor) Multi-pitch rock-climbing qualification, with emphasis on teaching and rescue techniques. Twenty-day course, with at least two years' previous climbing experience needed.

Kampong Malaysian village.

Karabiner Oval aluminium snaplink, used for attaching climber to rope, rope to belay and a multitude of other uses such as fixing washing lines.

ML	(Mountain Leader) A Royal Marine qualification, normally available only to marines, but a small number of extremely motivated army personnel are permitted to attempt the course every year. The course is eight months long and very comprehensive. The main job of an ML is to provide a safe passage through mountainous areas by finding routes and fixing ropes, all done on a massive scale: 600 men with all their equipment.
MLC	(Mountain Leadership Certificate) Civilian mountain-walking qualification.
Proff	The nearest civilian translation of this piece of army slang is 'perk', or 'freebie.'
Prussiking	Ascending fixed ropes by means of a prussik loop, a thin cord loop which can slide up the rope but locks in place when a downward force is applied. Mechanical equivalents include Crolls and Jumars.
Shunt	Mechanical device used for protecting abseils – if the abseiler lets go of the rope, the Shunt locks automatically and stops the descent. Can also be used as a descendeur.
Sling	Nylon tape loop used for setting up belays, e.g. by fixing round a tree or rock spike.
Top Roping	A method of safeguarding a climber by an anchorman belaying a rope from above.
TR&A	Top Roping and Abseiling: a week-long course for single-pitch work under fifty feet.

Appendix One

OPENING STATEMENT TO THE PRESS FOLLOWING THE BOARD OF ENQUIRY BY MAJOR GENERAL PATRICK CORDINGLEY DSO GENERAL OFFICER COMMANDING EASTERN DISTRICT

Exercise Gully Heights was a British Army adventurous training expedition which took place in Sabah, East Malaysia between 16 February and 25 March. The aim of the expedition was to descend the north side of Mount Kinabalu by way of a deep ravine, known as Low's Gully, exiting the mountain area along the Penataran river.

The expedition was conceived, planned and led by Lieutenant Colonel Robert Neill, a member of the staff of my headquarters here in York. Members included Major Ron Foster, a Territorial Army officer, five British Army non-commissioned officers and one NCO and two soldiers from a British Army unit in Hong Kong.

During the course of the expedition, the party became split, initially into two and eventually three groups. Two of the groups, consisting, in total, of five British NCOs, eventually reached safety on 12 March. The remaining group, consisting of two British officers and three Hong Kong Chinese soldiers, became trapped and were rescued from Low's Gully on 25 March after a major search involving elements of both the British and Malaysian armed forces.

As the General Officer commanding Lt Col Neill, the leader of the expedition, I ordered a Board of Enquiry to be convened to investigate the planning of, preparations for and conduct of the exercise. The president of this Board was a senior army officer currently serving in Hong Kong and the members were chosen for their knowledge of adventurous training and of the jungle environment. One of the staff from my legal branch was also a member of the Board.

The Board sat, here in York, from 25 April until 24 May. The president and members of the Board subsequently visited both Hong Kong and Mount Kinabalu. All members of the expedition were in attendance throughout the Board proceedings in York with the exception of one of the Hong Kong Chinese soldiers, Pte Chow who was in hospital and unable to attend.

The aim of this press conference today is to brief you on the findings of the Board of Enquiry and the actions which have been taken as a result of it.

However, before doing this, I wish to make a few general comments about adventurous training. Such training has, for many years, been an important and integral part of the process of development of our soldiers, non-commissioned officers and officers. It provides an invaluable method of developing many highly desirable skills and attributes. Self-discipline, self-reliance, the willingness to take the initiative and the ability to overcome fear are all qualities which are essential in combat and which we therefore prize in our soldiers and officers. They are characteristics which can be developed and honed by involvement in adventurous training.

Hence, the importance which the army attaches to adventurous activities which, over the past two years, have involved some sixty thousand soldiers on two thousand expeditions of which some one thousand two hundred have been undertaken overseas. Nothing which has come out during this Board of Enquiry has cast any doubt on the continuing value of adventurous training as a method of development of soldiers for the army and therefore our commitment to it remains as strong as ever.

Turning now to the findings of the Board of Enquiry and the actions which have been taken as a result of it. I will divide these into two parts. First I will cover the recommendations concerning procedures, equipment and qualifications and, second, I will cover the findings of the Board which relate to those who took part.

First, procedures, equipment and qualifications. The Board of Enquiry concluded that the regulations and procedures were fully followed during the planning of the expedition and that there was nothing absent from those regulations or procedures which could have prevented the expedition from going wrong. I would stress that the qualifications required for this expedition were met in full.

However, we learn by experience and we are continually refining our procedures for the planning and approval of adventurous training exercises. The Army Adventurous Training Compendium will be amended to include the recommendations made by the Board of Enquiry.

These amendments are relatively minor and are designed to ensure that those responsible for approving expeditions can be sure that the degree of difficulty and element of risk in any adventurous training activity has been fully assessed during the planning stage and, further, that it is reflected in the qualifications, training and experience of those taking part and the safety equipment which is available to them.

Finally in this section, the Board recommend that a review of the qualifications required by those conducting abseiling should be carried out. This has been done and it has been decided to introduce a two – stage system to ensure that those supervising abseiling are correctly qualified. This will involve attendance on two courses – the rock climbing proficiency course and the rock leader training course. The details of the more stringent qualifications will also be included in the amendments to the Adventurous Training Compendium.

I would now like to cover the findings of the Board which concern the individuals who took part in the expedition.

The Board formed the opinion that the planning for the expedition was conducted thoroughly and professionally, the qualifications of the leader and team members met the safety requirements and that the correct authorisation procedures were followed. The Board commended Lt Col Neill for his plan to assemble a mixed group including regular, territorial and Chinese soldiers. However, the Board considered that Lt Col Neill's judgement and leadership during parts of the expedition were flawed and that the decision to take the less experienced members of the group into Low's Gully was over-ambitious.

Lt Col Neill has been interviewed by myself and by the Deputy Commander in Chief of the United Kingdom Land Forces and these findings have been pointed out to him and discussed with him.

At one stage during the expedition, Lt Col Neill became ill and, for a short period, Major Foster assumed command. The Board formed the opinion that certain of the decisions taken by Major Foster during this period, whilst completely in line with the overall plan, subsequently contributed to the situation of jeopardy which developed. I have interviewed Major Foster and pointed this out to him.

Finally, the Board recommend that the conduct and performance of Cpl Brittan, LCpl Mayfield and LCpl Cheung was such as to deserve formal recognition. I am pleased therefore to announce that these three NCOs have been awarded commendations for their actions during the expedition.

Appendix Two

BRITISH MOUNTAINEERING COUNCIL ADVICE TO CLIMBERS

The BMC Participation Statement:

The BMC recognises that climbing and mountaineering are activities with a danger of personal injury or death. Participants in these activities should be aware of and accept these risks and be responsible for their own actions and involvement.

Advice for Climbers and Mountaineers:

Serious climbing and mountaineering accidents are thankfully rare, but when they do occur it can be difficult for the authorities in the host country to know what action should be taken without some basic information. It is good practice to leave details of your itinerary and insurance with a responsible friend or relative at home and also in the host country. Even travelling in Europe it is wise to have photocopies of passports, insurance certificates, travel documents and next of kin telephone numbers and contact addresses in case of genuine emergencies. On excursions to remote mountains where no formal mountain rescue service exists, all the above information should be sent to the British High Commission or Embassy who will need these details if authorisation is required for a military helicopter evacuation or similar rescue operation. If you feel for your particular trip it would be helpful you are welcome to attach to your insurance application form an outline itinerary and a next of kin telephone number and contact address for use by the BMC in a serious emergency.

Reproduced with kind permission from the BMC Insurance Guide 1995.

FOOTBALL AND THE ENGLISH